pick of punch

1992

pick of punch

Edited by
David Thomas

A PUNCH BOOK

Published in Association with
HarperCollins*Publishers*

*'Couldn't you at least wait until half-time so
we could discuss our communication problem?'*

HarperCollins*Publishers*
77-85 Fulham Palace Road,
Hammersmith, London W6 8JB

Published by HarperCollins*Publishers* 1992

9 8 7 6 5 4 3 2 1

Copyright © Punch Publications Limited 1992

A catalogue record for this book
is available from the British Library

ISBN 0 00 224060 2

Designed by Matthew Le Maistre Smith
Compiled and produced by Amanda-Jane Doran
& Emma Shortt

Printed in Great Britain by
HarperCollinsManufacturing Glasgow

contents

the words:

The World According To
MR PUNCH

If you sit in the editor's chair at the head of the Punch Table, you see on the wall at the far end of the room, directly opposite, a portrait of the magazine's first editor, Mark Lemon. He is a huge, imposing, bearded figure. He could be the prophet Isaiah, disguised in Victorian tailoring. Or he could be Karl Marx, after six months on the Mama Cass diet. Either way, he does not look like a man whom one would wish to offend unnecessarily.

Here, after all, is the great patriarch who founded and for many years ran a magazine that has become a national institution, perhaps even an international one.

For one of the most intriguing things about Punch is the degree to which its global reputation dwarfs its modest circumstances. Go where you will, from California to Kashmir, and you will find that the name of Mr Punch has gone before you.

Elsewhere in this book, Stephen Pile discusses what it is about Punch that attracts such attention, but for now let us accept that the aura around the magazine is as massive and imposing as the figure of Mark Lemon himself.

It calls up images of...yes, yes, dentists' waiting rooms, I know...but, apart from the tooth-wrangler's ante-chamber, Punch is all bound volumes; old cartoons with extraordinarily long captions; portly gentlemen in overstuffed armchairs – and

'It's just his way of saying he's 150 years young'

that's just the magazine's staff. So if I said that the conversation at a Punch Lunch included the appalling joke, 'Which planet do you see if you put your head between your legs?...Uranus!' one might be forgiven for thinking that this was just typical of the declining standards of a once great pillar of British literacy.

Except that one would be wrong: the joke was made by Shirley Brooks, later to become an editor of Punch himself, at a lunch held in the late 1850s.

It was recorded by a young Punch contributor called Henry Silver, whose careful notes of table talk include much smut that is unrepeatable here – most of it concerned with female genitalia; announcements by Thackeray that the completion of his next book will be followed by a quick trip to Paris in search of continental sex; jibes about the celebrated impotence of the great art critic Ruskin; complaints about income tax, and attacks on Mark Lemon, who held the outrageous view that working men should be allowed to form unions.

The point of all this being that however august Mark Lemon may have become, when he and his partners started Punch, they were young, boisterous, drunken, rowdy and randy. Their intentions were radical as well as comic. Their comedy was often schoolboyish in the extreme. Meander through the early volumes of Punch and you will find attacks on the royal family which even the present editorial staff would scarcely dare to print. And you will find gags that make Shirley Brooks's planetary pun look positively sophisticated.

Over the years, both the radicalism and the juvenilia disappeared. Punch, ensconced in its magnificent premises in Bouverie Street, with marbled halls, deferential porters and plaster busts of former editors, became a weekly dose of light relief for the middle-brow middle class. Its editors, as H F Ellis has described to us would drift from cricket pavilion to

Pall Mall club, correcting proofs at home after a substantial and well-watered dinner.

Such minor matters as layout and typography were left to the printers' tender care. There was no need to decide on a cover: it was always the same one. And the idea of design as we know it today cannot have impinged upon *Punch* until the last 30-odd years of its existence.

How different things are today. We live in a glass-partitioned, air-conditioned box, on the seventh floor of a brand-new office block, overlooking the Thames at Blackfriars Bridge. The furniture is slick, modern, corporate and grey. The carpet is a lurid shade of mulberry fool.

On our desks are the Apple computers which are used for all the sub-editing, design and typesetting of the magazine. As recently as 18 months ago, we still worked on typewriters, sent great bundles of paper off to typesetters to be turned into galley proofs; stuck down words and pictures onto layout sheets, amid great clouds of spray mount glue. Now this magazine is brought to you via a series of digital impulses, an accumulation of software, stored on little discs.

Those clubbable old gentlemen of days gone by turned out a magazine whose pages first brought the world such comic wonders as *The Diary of a Nobody*, *1066 And All That*, *Now We Are Six*, Nigel 'Down With Skool' Molesworth, Franglais and 'Father's Day'. In these pages Steve Punt pays his tribute to *1066*, whilst Miles Kington and Hunter Davies, respectively, play havoc with French and pay tribute to family life.

Will we, with our micro-chipped gadgets and gizmos be able to create a similar gallery of wonders? It would certainly be nice to think so. My hope is that the magazine can recapture the energy, adventure and *joie-de-vivre* that inspired its founding fathers. *Punch* should never be a slave to fashion, but it should be well aware of the world outside. That, after all, is by far the best way of making the outside world – and particularly those parts of it in search of sharp, literate, weekly entertainment – aware of it.

Punch was not created in order that men might write whimsical essays about lawnmowers. It was set up as a vehicle for poking fun at the pompous and the powerful, and as a means of using satire to point out injustice and wrongdoing. That is why Mr Punch carries his stick. Long may he continue to wield it. 🎭

David Thomas is the editor of Punch. He does not look at all like Karl Marx.

'Hello, where's the mobile phone off to?'

'Funny that. You're not the first one who thought Cheetah would be a chimp'

'Oops!'

'Oi! Can't you read?'

'What are you wagging your tail at you cheerful bastard?'

'I know it's what you want to do, Desmond, but there's not much call for a lifeguard in Hemel Hempstead'

'That's the one officer, he did it!'

'Earrings... I won them at the funfair'

'Part of me says yes but the other part says neigh'

'You're not my normal doctor'

'No, don't tell me. I never forget a face'

'He's got fleas'

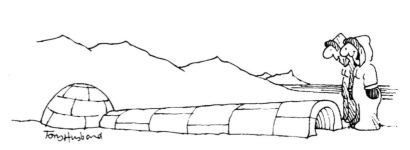

'Mmm. Like the hallway'

Join the greed movement

The conscience-free world of unethical investments

I'm fed up to the back teeth of the caring Nineties. What a veritable pain in the backside all this Green, environmentally-conscious, politically-correct, caring crap is. The 'carers' no doubt think of themselves as liberals, but they are, of course, fascists trying to stamp out the few pleasures left to the rest of the population. It's impossible to eat without finding oneself lectured by some jerk on the evil of salt, meat, fat, sugar or monosodium glutamate. Places to light up a calming cigar are thinner on the ground than signs of upturn in the economy. People regularly bang on the window of the Roller to complain about its fuel consumption while one takes one's life in one's hands when one ventures out in the winter wrapped up, as nature intended, in a comfortable fur coat.

It is becoming impossible to enjoy oneself.

My Christmas was considerably cheered by those Danish researchers who discovered that the greenhouse effect doesn't exist and that we'll be lucky to get an increase in temperature of 1.5°C which, in any case, is due not to man using aerosols to eradicate manly smells emanating from his armpits, but to the sun burping.

It isn't hard to find other Green chimeras. As that sage of the radio and printed page, Mr Victor Lewis-Smith revealed in the *Mail on Sunday* the other day, those who send paper off for recycling

'Timothy Hamilton! Don't let emotion creep into business!'

'I'm just here to make up the numbers'

or who use recycled paper are doing more harm to the environment than good, for the de-inking process pollutes much more than the manufacture of paper from scratch.

Those sanctimonious twits who drive to bottle banks are not only wasting fuel but also pumping carbon monoxide into the air, all to recycle an odd bit of glass. They no doubt use lead-free petrol but, unless the report is suppressed by embarrassed governments, we may soon hear more of research showing that lead-free petrol is more damaging to the ozone layer than the nasty old stuff.

Goodness knows how much of their dwindling resources manufacturers have to waste in complying with the legislation these people manage to pass: getting rid of CFCs in aerosols and fridges, ordering factories to clean up waste rather than letting nature do it for them and coercing people to shun good, old-fashioned, honest products such as booze, tobacco, meat and the like.

This alarming trend has even spilled over into investment. Over the past few years, insurance companies and unit trust groups that give no more than an organic fig for 'caring' but which can spot a bandwagon worth jumping on within moments of it rolling have set up umpteen Green funds, conscience funds and ethical funds.

I feel the time has come for the commonsensical amongst us to hit back. I propose setting up a black fund, a portfolio comprising the sort of companies that would make any self-respecting Greenie faint with shock.

I am totally serious about this and you will ignore it at your peril. Surely you can't have forgotten Oofy's much-vaunted 'Portfolio of Dogs', set up in 1986 when hi-tech stocks were all the rage? Shares got into this portfolio only if their names were calculated to send you to sleep. There were no acronyms, just good wholesome names like Baggeridge Brick, Foseco Minsep, Hicking Pentacost, Newman-Tonks, Thurgar Bardex, Volex and their ilk.

While the market as a whole rose by 15 per cent in 1986, the 'Portfolio of Dogs' soared 61 per cent. Over three-and-a-half years, the market rose 65 per cent while the dogs continued to shower the market with dust from their heels, making a startling gain of 182 per cent!

Of course, not one of the City's big financial groups is level-headed enough to establish up my proposed black fund for real. So we shall have to content ourselves with a paper portfolio until the concept is proven.

After consultation with a few ethical investment groups about the companies least likely to be allowed into their funds, those groups jostling at the starting gate (restricted, for the moment, to UK-quoted companies) are BAT (tobacco), Ladbrokes

'Yes?'

'Bloody Joneses'

— PILBROW —

(gambling), National Power, Shell, (chosen with a pin – any oil company would do), Barclays, GEC (25 per cent of profits come from defence), De Beers, Highland Distillers, English China Clays (which wins a special award for littering the Cornish landscape with breast-shaped heaps), Lonrho, NSM (Northern Strip Mining), Astra (defence and fireworks), ICI, Tomkins (owners of Smith & Wesson), Vickers (not only tanks, but also fuel-guzzling Rollers), Huntingdon International (contract animal testing), Hanson (Imperial Tobacco, Consgold, Titanium Dioxide production), British Airways (the world's favourite consumer of kerosene) and BTR (for its South African connections).

There you have it. The 19 constituents of Oofy's black fund. If you know of any really black companies missing, do let me know.

I am struggling to keep my hands apart. Whenever they come in close proximity, they want to rub together with glee. For the first time, the forces of evil – the drinkers, gamblers, armourers, polluters and exploiters have a way of judging their progress against the do-gooders, the environmentally-conscious, the Greenies and the ethically-aware.

May the worst man win.

Money Box

HAS ANYBODY TRIED using the *Financial Times* trendy new prices pages? You might think the new font for the *Times* is bad, but wait till you turn to the back of the *FT*.

I've lost literally hours over the past couple of weeks trying to find familiar companies that have been reclassified and then attempting to make some sense of the ludicrously over-designed modernist layout.

Could somebody tell me whether there's a word for people who feel compelled to tinker with things, particularly those things that work perfectly well to start with?

The lady's not for returning

Thatcherism is dead in the water – whoever wins

Whatever their own political persuasions, journalists tend to look for the most interesting outcome of any given set of circumstances. Thus, at the time of the last Tory leadership election, a victory for Michael Heseltine would have been by far the most professionally exciting result. It would have guaranteed a complete change in the way things were run at Westminster. But it was not to be.

The chances are, however, that whichever way the cookie is crumbled on April 9 we are in for the shake-up we were denied with the departure of Mrs Thatcher. Some results will be more interesting than others; none, alas, will be revolutionary. All the same, whatever happens promises well for my trade.

There was a time when it looked as if Mrs Thatcher would never go. It was simply impossible to imagine how she would depart. No one ever thought she would go voluntarily.

A Minister of the Crown told me once of being present at a Cabinet committee meeting when she disagreed with her then Chancellor, Nigel Lawson, and sensed that the rest of those present were also against her. 'All right then,' my friend claimed she said, 'If that's how you feel, I'll go. I'll resign. That's it.' At which point, according to my informant, everyone looked absolutely horrified and said: 'Oh no, Prime Minister! Please don't, Prime Minister! We didn't mean it.'

I never reported this story because I didn't believe it. Does it sound like Mrs Thatcher? No? Well, exactly. What my

'It's that crackpot Mark Lemon with his idea for a comic magazine. I'd give it a week...'

source was up to, I have no idea; all I do know is that while the world was waiting to discover how Mrs Thatcher was ever going to be toppled, the most unlikely possibility was that she might admit she had been wrong about something and ask for her P45 without more ado. The reality of her departure has, I think, proved this thinking right.

If Michael Heseltine had won the leadership in November 1990, he would have wanted to call an immediate general election. His friends and colleagues were trying to persuade him that this would not be wise – what on earth would happen to the British election campaign if the country had

to go to war in the Gulf half-way through? The wise old heads believe that they would have prevailed and that he would have been forced to wait until the spring. By that time, of course, he would already have effected a great many ministerial and policy changes, but there would still have been sufficient sense of novelty about everything he touched to have ensured his eventual victory at the polls. Then the country would truly have known that the years of Thatcherism were over.

John Major's rejection of the policies and principles held by his political predecessor has been much more gradual. The process will, of course, be greatly expedited if the Tories form the next Government and the Prime Minister can claim to be his own man with his own mandate. Oh, but how much more interesting it will be if the other lot are given a go for the first time in 13 years. It is a source of some regret to me that this column will not be here to report the changes. A lot of fun is promised.

At the time of writing the anxiety in Tory Central Office has shifted to sheer bloody panic. A Tory friend of mine who has been trying to write nice things about the Conservative campaign has been tearing his hair out in desperation, not just because

Dispatch box

NOTHING will keep Paddy Ashdown from the fray. There was *nearly* a chance when he got locked in a lift at the Horseguards Hotel the other day, but the prospect of being out of the front line for a few hours was more than he could bear. The Liberal Democrats' leader and their campaign chief, Des Wilson, got into the lift high in the hotel. The doors shut and

stuck. 'We could be here for hours,' said Wilson, into whose tired brain had crept the thought that they could just sit down and have a little sleep until they were found.

The idea clearly horrified Ashdown. Not for nought did he train in the jungles of Borneo. With his bare hands he forced the lift doors apart, freeing the duo in an instant.

they are doing so badly – but because they deserve to. Mrs Thatcher departed for the United States because the Conservative Party wanted her out of the way for the last week of the campaign. I'm told, though, that she went with some relief – because she wouldn't be around to witness what promised to be the ghastly ignominy of election day.

It is with some pride that I am able to bring you a useful etiquette tip from the Denis Thatcher Handbook Of Handy Hints For Husbands.

One of the greatest difficulties Denis has faced over the years – and it has increased as the world has turned to harassing the smoker – has been how to keep awake through the after-dinner speeches without the benefit of a cigarette. Denis, of course, likes to light up whenever possible, but he does recognise the propriety of waiting until after the Queen's health has been drunk. Alas for him, the speech proposing the loyal toast can sometimes take a very long time. Indeed, I recall being present at a formal state banquet in Malawi when the Life President, His Excellency the very elderly Dr Hastings Banda, had been speaking for 45 minutes proposing the toast and had still only reached 1947.

'It doesn't seem the same since the sponsorship deal'

Anyway, news reaches me of how the most loyal of husbands handles this kind of situation without falling unconscious at the table. You sit with one elbow on the table and rest your head on one hand. You place your index finger against your chin and rest the upper jaw on the top of it. That way, says Denis, you can achieve the sometimes difficult feat of appearing interested in what is being said. If, however, you should fall asleep the finger immediately goes into your mouth and down your throat and wakes you before the cameramen have had a chance to snap their shutters. 🐍

'Good, life is passing the Smith-Watsons by as well'

'Here, I don't like the look of this'

The pack of Punch

Whose life is a sexual Gobi desert? Who's trapped in the body of a mad Irish woman? STEPHEN PILE meets Mr P's staff and finds out

Anthony Powell, the novelist, once wrote an account of *Punch* in the Fifties. Entering the office, he wrote, one had 'the impression of arriving in a convalescent ward; no one seriously ill or crippled, indeed, all likely to be out and about fairly soon, but still none of them quite A1 at the moment.'

The problem, he said, was 'the peculiarly muted atmosphere, the apparent physical enervation, the inward-looking personal exchanges, a surrounding despondency.'

Today our most venerable humour magazine lives in an open plan room on the seventh floor of the alarmingly sleek *Daily Express* building overlooking the Thames. Word processors wink and glare from every desk. There is a television permanently on at one end of the office, competing with a rock radio station at the other.

In one corner is the desk of the 13th editor, David Thomas, who is invariably described as an Old Etonian. More surprisingly, he has been known to wear a pink linen jacket to work, was deputy editor of *YOU Magazine* and once did an unforgettable impersonation of a fried breakfast along with a member of the advertising department. He was a particularly impressive sausage. Everyone thought so.

At 30 he was the youngest *Punch* editor ever appointed. He is also the first to have written a definitive reference work on Sergeant Bilko. According to the staff, he is a keen dancer ('a triumph of commitment over co-ordination') and once cleared the ☞

ILLUSTRATION: WILLIAM HEWISON

That's the way to do it! — That's the way to do it!

DAVID THOMAS — Editor

entire audience of a charity evening at the Groucho Club in Soho by singing Muddy Waters's hit, 'Mannish Boy'.

Ever since Mitchell Symons, who writes Guttersnipe, made a large fortune selling his idea for a quiz game – *Everyone's Equal* – all round the world, the editor has been full of similar jackpot schemes. His latest wheeze is a film script based upon one of his own actual nightmares in which he was chased by his word processor. Amazingly, it is now in the hands of a Hollywood agent.

The deputy editor, Roland White, is the only person on the *Punch* staff who looks as if he should actually be there. Roland is an Englishman and a gentleman who travels in from suburban Barnes. 'He doesn't get angry. He gets cross,' according to the editor.

In theory you can see Roland behind a lawn-mower, but in practice he is not a gardener. He once had to review some gardening books and decided that he should prune a few roses just to get the feel of it. He had pruned three or four when he found a five pound note in the rose bush and quit while he was winning.

Roland deals with the 70 to 100 unsolicited manuscripts that arrive each week at *Punch*. He takes this seriously and says that the most common opening sentence is, 'I have never got the hang of the video.'

Sitting opposite him is Sean Macaulay, the features editor and TV critic, whose desk was covered in floral underpants that were about to be road tested. 'Tied to a Skoda and drenched in boiling coffee,' according to Roland.

An elegant, gallingly handsome man-about-town, Sean is always smartly dressed and never misses an Arsenal match. He goes to midweek games wearing a pin-striped suit and Doc Martens, partly to keep his feet warm and partly to give himself a demotic flavour. Women are always going abroad to forget Sean.

i before e except after c, f'Chrissake!

ROGER PERKINS
— Sub-Editor

"Sorry, this has been done already. More than once. In fact, many times. No, we are not over-keen on visual puns... or are we? No, we don't steal your crummy ideas for our regular cartoonists to draw.... and so on.... and so on...."

STEVE WAY
— Cartoon Editor

How much this swells the population of places like Provence in any one year is difficult to tell.

One day Sean raced into the office shouting 'Go to the gents! Go to the gents!' At that time *Punch* shared a corridor with *Kerrang!* magazine, the bible of heavy metal rock music. (According to the *Punch* editor, *Kerrang!* staff all had fashionably thin legs. 'They made pipe cleaners look like Arnold Schwarzenegger. Their jeans were spot-welded on.')

It transpired that some lords of destruction belonging to a band called Anthrax were in the gents preparing for a photo session. 'Who's got my hairspray then?' went the petulant dialogue. 'Well, you've got my mascara.' The entire *Punch* staff trooped in one by one to observe the phenomenon.

And so (no connection whatever) to the cartoon editor. Steve Way wears permanent stubble, a Walkman for cricket commentaries and fairly way-out shirts. He still sends the traditional *Punch* rejection slip ('The editor presents his compliments and regrets that he is unable to accept the enclosed contribution') because there is no better way of putting it. To counter this formality he writes a brief note to the disappointed in violently purple ink.

The most encouraging thing he can say is that it took him eight years to get established as a cartoonist. His work got into *Private Eye* long before *Punch*. When he finally had his first one accepted by *Punch*, there was a three-year gap before the second. (The first was two skulls on the floor saying 'I've never liked his interpretation of Yorick.' The second was the same skulls saying 'I miss standing for the national anthem.')

He has a dozen regular cartoonists and a further 40 established people competing for a place. But he always hopes the mail will bring a new discovery. To this end he opens 15 to 20 envelopes full of cartoons a day and has used seven from first-time senders in two years. ('That is quite good.') Of these his three main discoveries have been Jonathan Pugh, Robert Thompson and Martin Ross, now regular contributors.

Surprisingly for a magazine with a 75 per cent male readership, modern *Punch* has a tradition of employing extremely clever women. Jan Abrams, for example, the previous features editor, was a Harkness scholar with a PhD from Princeton. She now runs a design institute in Chicago.

The chief sub-editor, Caroline Proud, has a double first from Oxford. Years ago she applied for a job in the *Punch* library but was turned down on the grounds that she was 'too quiet', which is pretty hard to imagine. The library is almost completely silent and has the faintly blue-stockinged atmosphere of the junior common room in an Oxford ladies' college circa 1950.

The subs table includes the oldest member of staff, Pete Silverton, who is now late thirtysomething and has just ghost-written *I Was A Teenage Sex Pistol*, the memoirs of Glen Matlock.

He is a committed prankster and had the idea of sending to publishers sections from *Mein Kampf*, P H Newby (the first Booker prize winner) and a short story by his eight-year-old son to see if they would publish it. One wanted to buy the rights to *Mein Kampf* ('an original turn of thought') but P H Newby's own publishers turned their man's work down flat. He also thought up the idea of pretending to be an emissary from Saddam Hussein to see if leading advertising agencies would take on the account to improve his image during the Gulf War.

Also on the subs desk at the centre of the office is Roger Perkins, a former English language teacher. He lives in Hastings. Indeed, his whole life revolves around trying to move out of that blameless town. Every now and then he comes into the office with a jaunty step and says, 'I've sold the house.' Weeks later he arrives with a long face.

Before coming to *Punch* he worked on the *Birmingham Post* but he could not sell his house in Hastings then either. One week he wrote a food piece in *Punch* entitled 'A Night Out in Hastings.' (One restaurant was French. One was a

chippie.) A man dogged by ill luck, he did shifts on the *Correspondent*.

The art editor, Fiona Hayes, was responsible for the redesign of the magazine. She always wears green because she is Irish ('An incredibly disciplined designer trapped in the body of a mad Irish woman'). Although proud of her Irish credentials and always nipping off to Dublin, she was, in fact, born in Scotland, brought up in the Bahamas and sounds Canadian.

She has three assistants. Of these Peregrine Haydn-Taylor and Matthew Le Maistre Smith also freelance as two thirds of the The Groovy Love Foundation, which appears, m'lud, to be a design studio. The former is generally broke and his day is punctuated by calls to and, indeed, from the bank manager. The latter is a quiet, competent, sensibly-haired human being who occasionally surprises the office with poetic statements like 'my life is a sexual Gobi desert.'

The contributors, who actually write the stuff are, by and large, read but not seen in the office. As a rule of thumb the names that sound like pseudonyms are real and vice versa. Oofy Prosser, a pseudonym, frequently gets lunch invitations from other Prossers wondering if they might be related. Hugh Fearnley-Whittingstall, by contrast, is the food critic's real name. (Unlike many food critics, he has actually worked as a junior chef in a fashionable London restaurant.)

Out of the sea of unsolicited manuscripts three writers have become regular contributors in two years. Recently the front desk rang up to say that one of them was asleep in reception and would somebody come down and collect him?

There is a strict no smoking rule in the editorial half of the office, because the air was getting unbreathable. Not so in the advertising half, where they resolutely smoke on. The boss over there is Barbara Patterson. She comes from Belfast and was once introduced by the editor as 'the Proddy with the body'. This has rather stuck.

Across the corridor is the marketing director, Steve Carter, who arrives with a motorcycle helmet under his arm in a style faintly reminiscent of the ghost of Hamlet's father. He spends a lot of time finding out who the readers are. In his office he has astonishing volumes of research, one of which contains the remarkable statistic that 214,000 housewives in the United Kingdom claim never to buy toilet paper. Of these 12,000 read the *Sunday Times* colour supplement.

He knows that 45 per cent of *Punch* readers are aged 15 to 34 and 25 per cent are 35 to 44. 'Elderly readers are very few indeed and this is not a recent phenomenon. *Punch* has always had a young male readership.'

He knows that 61 per cent of *Punch* readers live in

Go! Bike it!

Jangle jangle

FIONA HAYES — Art Editor

London and the south east, 42 per cent are single and 71 per cent have no children. He knows that they drink two and three quarter times more wine than ordinary mortals. He also knows that 33 per cent of *Punch* readers do not read the *Sunday Times* colour supplement, deterred perhaps by the regrettable standards of personal hygiene among so many of its housewife readers.

The person in charge of this entire circus is Mike Sharman, the silver-haired publisher, who is known either as 'Glider' because of the way he wafts down corridors or 'Miles' because of the astonishing resemblance he bears to Miles Drentell in *thirtysomething* (the grey-haired boss of the advertising agency who holds his head to one side and makes delphic, Zen statements).

Both of them say things like 'there are no problems only opportunities for solutions' and 'there is no yesterday or tomorrow only today.' Members of staff who have just seen *thirtysomething* for the first time come into the office gibbering: 'That's...it's...incredible...he's...just like...'

But if some things change others stay the same. People have, for example, been saying *Punch* is not as funny as it was for almost all of its 150 years. Even the supreme *Punch* contributor this century, P G Wodehouse, wrote to the editor saying he should ignore such comments and carry on regardless.

And so it remains. To mark the 150th anniversary Fleet Street has written its traditional long, prickly articles. The *Guardian*, for example, ran one that covered an entire half page. In the same newspaper a Cabinet split, the end of com-

munism in Albania, an erupting volcano in Japan and a story claiming that Beethoven was black could not match that length combined.

Why is *Punch* so important to them? The rivers are polluted. Kuwait is in ruins. Ministers of state are planning to kill dogs. And our free press devotes acres of shirty reportage to a small-circulation magazine that has the sole, laudable and difficult aim of trying to make people laugh. Quite frankly, I would not blame *Punch* if it got on the same banana boat as Dr Jonathan Miller to find a more encouraging atmosphere away from the rancid Brits. Florence? Fine. Suits me. In part, of course, you are not a proper journalist in this country until you have mugged *Punch*. Good lord, I have done it myself countless times and so has everybody else.

Three years ago *Loose Ends* on Radio 4 sent a reporter to some *Punch* occasion. The eventual broadcast was a wholly mocking report concerned with trying to find someone at the gathering who was actually under the age of 50. 'I know this,' says the present editor of *Punch*, 'because I was that *Loose Ends* reporter.'

But why are we quite so aggressive towards this magazine? (I can ask this question now in such a lofty way because like certain types of Himalayan puff adder I find that once I have bitten, all venom is gone.) Another constant is that *Punch* has always been subject to the same cycle of reform, consolidation and complacency. According to the *Punch* librarian, Amanda-Jane Doran, there have been three actual golden ages on which everyone agrees. (Other eras are more a matter of

All right, let's go for it —

MIKE SHARMAN
—Publisher

taste.) 'Traditionally the golden ages have coincided with the arrival of youth,' she says. The first was from 1841 to 1850 when the young Thackeray was limbering up his comic powers. In those days *Punch* was the only amusing item in the United Kingdom and such was its writers' celebrity that the public stood outside the weekly lunches to watch them go in.

But Thackeray gave up comic journalism and went on to waste his time writing novels. He left a school of *Punch* imitators who copied his characteristic style of masculine, much-quaffing, all-dining bonhomie. But they missed the sharp social observations that this relaxed chumminess disguised.

They carried on doing rather leaden Thackeray imitations for five years until the second golden age (1885 – 1890) when the young F C Burnand was editor. *Punch* grew raffish, wildly theatrical, distinctly modern and far less ponderous. In this period it published the Grossmiths' *Diary of a Nobody* in serial form and cartoons took off.

But young F C Burnand became old F C Burnand and things went quiet until the third golden age, the longest and most influential. It ran from the late Thirties to the early Fifties. *Punch* had revamped itself as a family magazine and went through a troubling period when it published 'There are fairies at the bottom of my garden', in all seriousness. But under the editorship of E V Knox the best *Punch* writing became surreal. In this period it published *Molesworth*, *1066 and All That*, A P Herbert's *Misleading Cases* and the unjustly ignored *Memoirs of Mipsy* (the memoirs of a minor aristocrat, as recalled by her adoring sister who can see no fault in her).

Gentle persuasion – – of course it's gentle persuasion.

BARBARA PATTERSON – Advertisement Manager

AMANDA-JANE DORAN – Librarian

T his was one of the few periods in *Punch*'s history when the writers and cartoonists were both on top form and equally dominant. In the Forties we can see the emergence of a particular type of light, English, lawn-mower-related comic essay on which *Punch* based its whole contemporary character and reputation. The great exponents of these polite, ironic musings were civilised humorists like H F Ellis and Basil Boothroyd.

But this type of essay is dead. (No, don't cry, darling. They have been dead for 50 years, but we have only just noticed.) I blame a) Flymos and b) the fact that we no longer have the same sort of society to sustain it. Britons have returned to type. When the first Brits got off the boat they were a sweating, grunting, non-Barbara-Cartland mob waving mutton legs in the air. And so it is today. Inexplicably, during the late 19th and early 20th centuries Britons started wearing linen jackets and panama hats and being polite and saying 'morning, old chap' at cricket matches. It was an aberration, now past: Gazza not Gielgud has been the typical Briton throughout the ages. *Viz* has got the full measure of our times and sells a million inimitable copies as a result.

Under the present *Punch* regime (as in humorous newspaper columns) there has been a shift away from the essay towards squibs, parodies, jests, japes and mock reports. Ironically, of course, this is a return to exactly the sort of approach they had in the very first issue of *Punch* in July 1841 that we are celebrating today.

Anyway, on with the party. One hundred and fifty, eh? Not bad for a man with a big nose and string of sausages. 🎐

Stephen Pile was named 1991 Consumer Magazine Writer Of The Year by the PPA for his features in Punch.

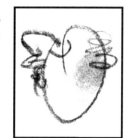

'I can't seem to remember what used to be there'

LAST MALE BASTION FOR 50 MILES

'I always say no pain, no gain'

DEATH VALLEY TOURS

'His name is George.
He'll be your personal vulture on this leg of the tour'

UNEMPLOYMENT B

'Sorry. We only whistle while we work'

'Fortunately we got the whole accident on video
so Jeremy Beadle's covering the funeral costs'

'...Look...I...mean...well, it's not really necessary...
well, not every time...especially the toilet'

'As I see it, Brenton, we're both men clinging to a cold, wet rock face.
Only I've found a nice dry ledge and
you're wearing rubber-soled slip-ons'

'Jeremy Paxman here. Look, I haven't got all night...'

'...had a sheep dip last night and I can't do a thing with it'

'Bloody Indians'

Memories

Frank Muir
Contributor

It always seemed an impossible boyhood ambition to work for *Punch* – and I had to wait until I was about 50 when Bill Davis asked me to do it. What I always loved about *Punch* was the sheer Englishness of its humour. I can still remember that dreaded moment at the end of a Punch Lunch when the editor got his briefcase out and it was time to sing for your supper. We used to tease Bill Davis something rotten at such moments. But not Alan Coren; Alan was always far too quick-witted to send up and you only retired hurt for your pains. Sadly, I think there's been a rapid decline in the amount of people who appreciate good humorous writing now. When people want witty domestic observation these days they're more likely to switch on a sit-com.

Joan Bakewell
Writer and broadcaster

In 1972, Bill Davis thought it would be a good idea to invite women to the Punch Lunch and I can still recall what a great divide there was between the feminists among us who thought it would be a good idea to go – to reform from within – and those who thought the whole thing should be boycotted. I suppose Bill thought we were all going to do quaint little columns on knickers and knitting for him. But instead we just completely took over and put together a special edition which Barbara Castle edited. I never got to carve my name in the Punch Table. I think that was always looked upon as a little boy's treat – which is a shame really, as the housewife in me was quite looking forward to mutilating a lovely piece of furniture.

150 facts about
150 years of
Punch
(Numbers 1 – 59)

1. *Punch* **first appeared on Saturday, 17 July, 1841.**

2. It was the same year that David Livingstone went to Africa, that Britain took over Hong Kong, that Joseph Whitforth invented the street cleaning machine and Thomas Cook invented the holiday.

3. The first issue cost 3d and sold 10,000 copies.

5. *Punch* was founded by author Henry Mayhew and engraver Ebenezer Landells.

6. It was inspired by *Paris Charivari*, a satirical daily.

7. There were three launch editors – Mark Lemon, Stirling Coyne and Henry Mayhew.

8. Lemon became sole editor in an early boardroom coup. He was 31 years old.

9. He was paid 20/- a week, and held the post until 1870.

14. The name *Punch* was chosen after a joke that it was 'nothing without Lemon'.

15. It escaped being called The *Funny Dog* – 'With Comic Tales'.

ALEXANDER SELKIRK SENT THE FIRST DESERT ISLAND CARTOON TO PUNCH.

4. The *Somerset County Gazette* called it 'the first comic we ever saw which was not vulgar. It will provoke many a hearty laugh, but never call a blush to the most delicate cheek.'

10. Mark Lemon was not always a popular editor but Charles Dickens called him a 'most affectionate and true-hearted fellow'.

11. This didn't stop Lemon rejecting every contribution from Dickens.

12. MP Joseph Chamberlain's work was also rejected by *Punch*.

13. But a book review by former Wolverhampton Wanderers striker Derek Dougan (The Doog) was printed in 1975.

CARTOONS: DAVID AUSTIN

16. Lemon set the style for the next four editors. They all wore beards, all wrote plays and none were skinny.

17. Lemon helped launch *The Field* and the *Illustrated London News*.

18. He also told Thomas Hardy not to write plays.

26. Theatre critics were originally paid seven shillings for 1,000 words. But they were expected to sharpen their own quills.

34. Injunctions were taken out in 1845 to stop *Punch* being sold at street corners to the sound of trumpets.

35. The trumpets were to announce another instalment of Mrs Caudle's Curtain Lectures, the advice of a nagging wife.

36. *Punch* was first to use the word cartoon for a comic drawing.

40. Kaiser Wilhelm II was so annoyed by *Punch* that he put a price on the editor's head.

41. *Punch* backed the losing Confederate Army in the US Civil War.

44. *Punch*'s price went up for the first time on 21 March 1917, from 3d to 6d.

45. During the 1974 oil crisis, Alan Coren dressed as an Arab to test reaction. He was booed by the Stock Exchange but welcomed at 10 Downing Street.

46. On 21 July 1860 *Punch* published an ode on the departure of the Prince of Wales to Canada saying: 'If the laureate won't do his work, *Punch* must.'

47. In 1897 *Punch* attacked men for not giving up seats to women in third class North London Line carriages.

48. In 1920 an editorial suggested that Ireland should become part of Denmark as both produced butter.

49. In 1925 *Punch* launched an appeal to raise £9,000 for the children's hospital, Shadwell.

52. A *Punch* cricket XI went to Holland to play The Hague in 1959.

53. *Punch*'s 100th anniversary was not celebrated as it fell during World War II.

54. There was a special edition ten years later for the Festival of Britain.

55. The 130th anniversary was celebrated with a Thames boat trip.

56. Tom Taylor, the third editor, wrote *Our American Cousin*, the play during which Abraham Lincoln was shot.

57. *Punch* cartoons were used for costume research on the TV series *Upstairs, Downstairs*.

58. *Punch* is the only magazine quoted in the *Oxford Dictionary of Quotations*.

59. During World War II *Punch* started a hospital comforts fund for wounded servicemen. ☞

19. A magazine called *Punch in London* was started in 1832 by the wit Douglas Jerrold. It closed after 17 weeks.

20. *Punch* struggled until 1842 when the first Almanack sold 90,000 copies.

21. Harry Grattan wrote the Almanack while in a debtors prison with Henry Mayhew.

22. The future was secured in 1842 when publishers Bradbury & Evans bought *Punch*.

23. In 1843 Lemon published a tragic poem – Thomas Hood's 'Song Of The Shirt', about the plight of low-paid shirtmakers – against the wishes of his staff. Circulation trebled.

24. The cartoonist Charles Keene (1823 – 1891) was a practical joker. He painted pieces of bread to look like plum cake and placed them on walls to trick passing children.

25. Art critic M H Spielmann was John Ruskin's favourite conjurer.

27. When Gielgud first played *Hamlet*, the *Punch* critic devoted his entire review to the actor's tights.

28. Another critic found Ellen Terry 'unpromising'.

29. In the 1850s, *Punch* campaigned against crinoline.

A FORMER EDITOR OF PUNCH HAD A PRICE ON HIS HEAD.

30. The novelist William Thackeray said he wrote for *Punch* 'only because of its good pay and great opportunity for laughing, sneering, kicking and gambadoing'.

31. Thackeray told his mother in 1842 that *Punch* 'was a very low paper.' He twice resigned.

32. He also wrote a song about the Punch Table, 'The Mahogany Tree'.

33. The Table isn't made of mahogany – it's deal.

37. The first colour drawings were published in 1906.

38. In 1980, a quarter of the staff belonged to Equity or the Musicians' Union.

39. *Punch* was often banned in France and Germany.

42. On a *Punch* outing, Jonathan Routh wrote 'A Present From Margate' on a pebble and sold it to a holidaymaker.

43. In 1848, *Punch* found there were 40 single ladies for every single man in Weston-super-Mare.

50. Editor Evoe Knox's waste bin was confiscated after he started a series of fires by flicking cigarette ends in it.

51. Margaret Thatcher was the first woman to attend a Punch Lunch, in 1975.

150 facts about
150 years of
Punch
(Numbers 60 – 85)

60. In 1942, *Punch* reported: 'Women are now being advised that vegetables help to make the hair more attractive. Only very small carrots, however, should be worn on the fringe.' Was this the worst joke ever printed?

61. *Punch*'s launch prospectus announced that, like the Prime Minister of the time, Lord Melbourne, the magazine would be OUT SOON.

62. Months later, *Punch* was able to string a banner across its office which asked: 'Why is *Punch* like the late Government? Because it's JUST OUT!'

63. The current editor, David Thomas, is the youngest ever. He was 30 when appointed.

64. The oldest was cartoonist and former art editor Kenneth Bird (1949 – 1952) who was 61 when he got the top job.

65. Editor William Davis (1969 – 1977) attempted to increase *Punch*'s popularity with the young. He also introduced the Caption Competition and Country Life.

66. F C Burnand, editor 1880 – 1906, was asked why *Punch* wasn't as funny as it used to be. 'It never was,' he said.

67. Burnand wrote a comic musical with Sir Arthur Sullivan called *Cox and Box*.

68. Bernard Hollowood, editor from 1958 – 1968, emphasised more serious articles, sharing Malcolm Muggeridge's belief that *Punch* should make its voice heard on public questions.

69. Hollowood was a Staffordshire county cricketer.

70. During World War II, editor Evoe Knox walked the streets of London during the Blitz with a bottle of whisky in his pocket, looking for people who might need cheering up.

71. Members of the Punch Table carved their initials in the table from a very early date. Mark Lemon was first to carve.

72. All editors carve their names at one end. Malcolm Muggeridge (1953 – 1957) made such a botch of carving his initials that it had to be redone on a piece of wood, which was then inlaid into the Table.

73. Prince Charles, Princess Anne, the Duke of Edinburgh, Princess Margaret, and the Duchess of York are all Table members.

74. When Prince Charles's private detective came to survey the Table room before a Royal visit he was shocked: 'My God,' he said, 'You've certainly had trouble with vandals.'

75. The Pears soap advertisement showing a tramp writing a letter starting 'Two years ago I used your soap, since then I have used no other', was published in *Punch* on 26 April 1884. The copyright was sold to Pears.

76. The cartoonist George du Maurier (1834 – 1896) began life as an analytical chemist but gave up when his father refused to allow a piano in the laboratory.

77. The cartoonist Leech (1817 – 1864) was a special constable.

78. This didn't stop him being twice sent to debtors prison – after backing friends' debts.

79. *Punch* writers used pseudonyms or initials until the rule was relaxed by Kenneth Bird.

80. Bird was the cartoonist 'Fougasse', who drew the wartime posters 'Careless Talk Costs Lives'.

81. Fougasse means 'mine' in French, a name Bird got during wartime service with the Royal Engineers.

82. Fougasse also means 'hearth-cake'.

83. Whatever one of those is.

84. Many readers cancelled their subscriptions after a cartoon published in 1954 urged Churchill to retire.

85. Anthony Powell, author of *A Dance To The Music Of Time*, was literary editor of *Punch* under Muggeridge. ☞

ALADDIN
TROUBLE

86. Powell scrapped short book reviews. If a book was to be noticed at all, he said, it should be done at length.

87. The *New Yorker* produced a parody of *Punch* on 13 January, 1934, called *Paunch*.

88. *Punch* returned the compliment on 7 April, 1954.

89. The cartoonist Richard Doyle, a Roman Catholic, resigned in 1850 when *Punch* become brutally anti-Papist. He had been appointed in 1843, aged 19.

90. Cartoonists Tenniel and du Maurier were both one-eyed.

91. Du Maurier's full name was George Louis Palmella Busson du Maurier.

92. According to tradition, Table members can demand to attend any Punch Lunch.

93. There are 43 living Table members.

94. The Punch Table seats 20.

95. *Diary of A Nobody* first appeared in *Punch* in 1888.

96. So did Geoffrey Willans's inky schoolboy Nigel Molesworth, in 1939.

97. Prince Charles carved his initials into the Punch Table and decorated them with a full set of Prince of Wales feathers.

98. The cartoonist Phil May is frequently said to have carved his initials under the Table after a particularly enjoyable lunch.

99. But he didn't.

100. During a contributors' outing to Cognac, Alan Brien finished off the carafes of brandy in all the bedrooms of their overnight chateau.

101. He didn't want to leave a bad impression.

102. Sir Francis Burnand, the fourth editor, caused a scandal by marrying his dead wife's sister.

103. Marrying your in-laws was illegal at the time, so the couple married in Switzerland.

104. The Charivari section was first introduced in 1902 as a series of one-paragraph jokes.

105. A Charivari is a procession of rough music made with kettles, pans and tea-trays used in France to make fun of unsuitable weddings.

106. Garibaldi once attended a Punch Lunch.

107. George Brown, the Labour Cabinet Minister, walked out of a Punch Lunch in fury at being called 'not a proper socialist'.

108. Conservative Cabinet Minister Norman Tebbit attended the same lunch as the 1990 Miss World.

109. He didn't walk out.

WAITER, THERE IS A FLY IN MY BISCUIT.

GARIBALDI NEARLY INVENTED A JOKE.

110. *Punch* invented the name 'Crystal Palace' to describe the site of the 1851 Great Exhibition.

111. And the phrase 'a curate's egg'.

112. The phrase grew out of a cartoon in which a bishop apologises to a young curate for giving him a bad egg. 'No, my Lord,' the curate replies, 'parts of it are excellent.'

113. Guinness advertised in the first issue.

114. So did the Theatre Royal, Drury Lane, Webster's Manganese Ink, Dinneford's Imperial Electrical Horse Hair Remover, the Royal Surrey Zoological Gardens, the Hungerford market steam packet and Thorn's Potted Yarmouth Bloaters (with Thorn's Tally-Ho sauce).

115. *Punch* hit its highest circulation in 1948.

116. It then sold 175,000 copies.

117. An American student wrote in 1990 asking to be Malcolm Muggeridge's assistant – 33 years after Muggeridge had retired.

118. No drinks advertisements appeared in *Punch* between December 1927 and August 1938 because of a dispute in the drinks trade.

119. The BBC produced a half-hour programme in 1975 taken from *Punch*.

120. Cartoonist Phil May (1864 – 1903) disappeared in Margate when he was supposed to do illustrations for a big December number.

121. So the editor hired a man to parade the streets bearing a sandwich board with the message 'Remember The Christmas Issue'.

122. Malcolm Muggeridge also edited Issue 69 of *Private Eye*.

123. This was despite the fact that *Private Eye* had attacked Muggeridge as 'a cynical little man without any real views or beliefs who affects a worldly wisdom fashionable among ageing pundits.'

124. *Punch* cartoonist Linley Sambourne was Lord Snowdon's great-grandfather.

125. Bernard Hollowood stood unsuccessfully for Parliament as a Liberal.

126. *Punch* did not appear for a fortnight in February 1947 because of a national fuel shortage.

127. So its cartoons appeared in the *Times*.

GENERAL GORDON SAW THE FUNNY SIDE.

128. Film critic Dilys Powell wrote of Woody Allen's *Manhattan* that the 'Rhapsody in Blue' score made her want to 'rush out into the aisles and dance.' She was 79 at the time.

129. *Punch* was launched on capital of £25.

130. The early staff of *Punch* set up the Punch Club. This became The Savage Club.

131. One of the first jokes in *Punch* was entitled 'A Conversation Between Two Hackney Coach Horses'.

134. Colonel Blount, from Evelyn Waugh's novel *Vile Bodies*, insists on silence at all mealtimes so that he can read his volumes of *Punch*.

135. *Punch* produced a West End theatrical revue in 1955.

136. 74 per cent of *Punch* readers are men.

132. One of *Punch*'s most famous cartoons was Dropping The Pilot, marking the end of Bismarck's rule.

133. Thousands of copies had to be scrapped when it was noticed that the Kaiser's crown was misdrawn.

137. 45 per cent of *Punch* readers are aged under 35.

138. On 26 September 1846, *Punch* predicted the arrival of the Underground train. The first Underground line opened in 1863.

139. Miles Kington, inventor of Franglais, lists 'eating parsley' as one of his interests in *Who's Who*.

140. Among editor Bill Davis's *Who's Who* interests is 'thinking about retirement'.

141. Barbara Castle edited a women's issue in 1972, braving feminist pickets as she arrived at the office.

142. On 7 February 1885,

Punch patriotically printed a cartoon celebrating the rescue of Gordon of Khartoum. Unfortunately, General Gordon had been hacked to death 12 days earlier.

143. Basil Boothroyd, former assistant editor of *Punch,* was the Duke of Edinburgh's official biographer.

144. One issue in 1971 was a parody of *Playboy*. The cover featured a naked woman protected by barbed wire.

145. Stephen Pile was voted the 1991 Consumer Magazine Writer Of The Year for his work on *Punch*.

146. In 1991, *Punch* fooled the *Sun* into running a story that eating custard and porridge enlarges penis size.

147. A *Punch* article was at the centre of a libel action in May this year, when former Tory minister Edwina Currie sued the *Observer,* winning £5,000.

148. It was a *Punch* cartoon from the First World War that gave ITMA its phrase 'It's being so cheerful as keeps us going' during the Second World War.

149. In October 1990 *Punch* ran a cover showing John Major dressed as Mrs Thatcher, in a blue suit and blonde wig. In November 1990, Major replaced Mrs Thatcher as Prime Minister.

150. This year marks the first time in 150 years of its existence that *Punch* is officially funnier than it used to be (proved by readers poll, Spring 91).

I DO NOT UNDERSTAND.

PUNCH WAS USED TO UNMASK GERMAN SPIES IN WORLD WAR I.

'Get lost! I want
to be worshipped
from afar'

'Raymond has never fully embraced adulthood'

'We can't invite
Isabel without
inviting Ian.
They're joined
at the pelvis'

'Yes, it has been a long time.
I'm just calling to see if I
should tear you out of my
address book'

*'Of course I had a good time at the film.
I always enjoy sitting adjacent to you for two hours in silence'*

'Tonight, please, no verbal nose-tweaking'

'I fancy myself to be a writer. What do you fancy yourself to be?'

WHO GIVES A MONKEY'S?

A CRITICAL LOOK AT MODERN LIFE
by Richard Littlejohn

No. 10 Birthday Parties

Yes, yes, I know it's not every day you're 150 but I hope Mr Punch is aware of what he is letting himself in for next week.

Birthdays are no longer the discreet celebration of the passing years they were when matron first cut his umbilical cord. If he has any sense at all he will lock himself in his oak-panelled study with a crate of 1841 claret and refuse to come out until it is all over.

Someone should have had a quiet word in his shell-like. Nobody in their right mind admits it is his birthday, let alone advertises the fact.

It will all end in tears, mark my words. Don't think the party that's to be held in the imposing surroundings of the Victoria and Albert Museum will make the slightest difference. No chance. They will find a way of getting in. Not just the old bores the Great Man has been trying to avoid since his by-pass, the ones who keep telling him how poorly he is looking, either.

One minute he will be quietly standing there sipping a flute of the widow's finest, the next he will be confronted by a moonlighting veterinary assistant from Penge dressed up as Juliet Bravo singing 'Happy Birthday' with all the tonal accomplishment of a castrated Rottweiler.

Before he knows what is happening, this ghastly creature will have stripped down to her cellulite and, pausing only to wipe a rivulet of sweat from her varicose embonpoint, she will roll a novelty mango-flavoured condom over his magnificent nose, pull down his trousers, bend him over the nearest exhibit and thrash him to within an inch of his life with her plastic truncheon.

The old fellow will be expected to smile throughout this ritual humiliation while his bucolic guests, none of whom are known to him intimately, but all of whom are crammed to the gullet with free champagne and taramasalata *vol-au-vents*, laugh themselves nauseous. Ha, bloody, ha.

Be warned. It's not too late to cancel. Birthdays? Who gives a monkey's?

*Richard Littlejohn is a Sun columnist.
He'll be 38ish next January.*

Liberté, egalité, hilarité

MILES KINGTON présente un petit lesson Franglais sur l'histoire de Monsieur Punch

1841 Naissance de *Punch*, la revue humoristique. Dans son foreword, l'éditeur explique les intentions de *Punch*. 'Bonjour. Nous sommes maintenant dans la quatrième année du glorieux reign de Queen Victoria. Et elle est sur schedule à continuer le glorieux reign jusqu'a 1901! C'est un long haul et no mistake. Nous avons encore...tenez, donnez–moi un morceau de papier et un crayon...1901, take away 1841...nous avons encore 60 annees à passer. Encore 60 années du Victorian era. Jésus pleura.

'Anyway, ce n'est pas un joke, ce Victorian era. Nous avons le Crimean War, et Gladstone, et Bismarck, etc, etc. Heavy going, n'est-ce pas? Oui. Donc, nous avons besoin de light relief. Et light relief est sur l'horizon. Il est ici. Il est nommé *Punch*! Oui, chaque semaine vous avez les meilleurs gags, les plus brillants humoristes, et un free offer d'un sachet de shampoo.'

'Pas mal, eh? Welcome au club!'

1842 Après un flying start, *Punch* glisse dans les doldrums. La circulation est sur le downward trend. Lord Melbourne note dans son diary: 'Aujourd'hui, j'ai parlé avec Queen Victoria. Elle m'a demandé mon opinion sur *Punch*. J'ai dit: "Pas aussi funny que dans les old days."'

Introduction de la Caption Competition. Succès fou. C'est un formula très simple. Vous prenez un ancien cartoon...Ah ha! Voilà le grand drawback. Les anciens cartoons n'existent pas. La Cartoon Competition avec les nouveaux cartoons? Unthinkable!

Solution: reproduire les classiques paintings de Leonardo, Turner, Gainsborough, etc! Winner du premier Cartoon Contest: C Thomson de Glasgow, avec une caption pur la Mona Lisa: 'I keep thinking it's Tuesday.'

1843 Après la surge de circulation avec la Cartoon Comp, nouveau downward turn. Depression éditoriale. Fluttering de nerfs partout. Et puis un stroke de genius! Un marketing survey! Avec readership profile, etc, etc! Formidable!

1847 Delivery du marketing survey. Beaucoup de statistics ('L'average *Punch* reader est un bishop dans Limpopoland, etc etc'), beaucoup d'analysis ('L'average *Punch* reader prit 14.8 stage-coach trips en 1846...') et beaucoup de flannel ('L'average *Punch* reader est très actif dans le water-skiing, missionary work, hypnotisme, hypocrisie, white slave trade, etc'), mais les recommendations essentielles sont claires:
1. Un movement immediate dans une down–market direction.

Queen Victoria en drag, pissé

2. Le changement du nom *Punch* au nouveau nom *Viz*.
3. Beaucoup de features comme Jean Fartpants; Guillaume le Poisson; Roger Bulpit, l'Homme dans le Pulpit, etc, etc.

1848 Le marketing survey reçoit le thumbs down. C'est le commencement d'un recurrent cycle qui marque le chequered story de *Punch*...
1. Readership downturn. 2. Marketing survey. 3. Rejection du marketing survey. 4. Readership upturn.

Winner du Grand Christmas Cartoon Caption Contest: C Thomson de Glasgow avec une caption pour la Mona Lisa: 'Gee, I don't know much about aviation, Mr da Vinci, but if you put the wings on top, rotating, and called it a "helicopter", maybe then it would fly all right...'

1855 1ère cricket match de *Punch*. Day trip à Boulogne pour la fixture de Gentlemen de *Punch* v Gentlemen de France. *Punch* XI: Hope, Keene, Leech, Oil, Lemon, Salt, Taylor, Tinker, Hon Seb Agnew, Mrs Burnand, Thackeray. 12ème homme: Wm Tidy. Résultat: Absinthe stopped play.

1861 30ème anniversaire de *Punch*: Spéciale édition, avec extra publicité, ie un petit poster dans les premises de Monsieur W H Smith à Paddington.

Inauguration du Punch Lunch. Thackeray écrit dans son diary: 'Aujourd'hui, inauguration du Punch Lunch. J'étais pissé comme un newt. Le food était terrible.'

1867 Commencement du légendaire 'Bargepole'. Il est jeune, optimiste et forward-looking, mais ce sont des early days yet. Beaucoup, beaucoup de lettres du readership: 'Qui est Bargepole? Son anonymité est maddening. Own up!'

Première visite de Queen Victoria (incognita) au Punch Lunch. Elle écrit: 'Visite au Punch Lunch en drag, pour raisons de sécurité. Pissée comme un newt. Le food était horrible.'

1873 Cricket match contre Prussia. Le *Punch* XI est: du Maurier, Sullivan, Powell, Gilbert, Filbert, Bargepole, Dickens, Crippen, Jack, Ripper et Tenniel. 12ème homme: Wm Tidy. Résultat: Match abandonné après fisticuffs, et shellfire.

Winner de la grande Spring Bank Holiday Caption Competition: C Thomson de Glasgow avec une caption pour la Mona Lisa: 'We are not amused.'

nous allons aux dogs!

Rigide upper lèvre, old bean! C'est bally prés de teatime!

Bargepole been in?

1880 Crisis de readership. Seulement 8,000,000 lecteurs every week. Mais comment effectuer une augmentation? Inspiration – invention du Scottish joke! *

   * Explanation du Scottish joke. Dans le Scottish joke cartoon, il y a deux Highlanders, knee-deep dans le heather. Le premier Highlander tourne au second Highlander et dit: 'I keep thinking it's the Sabbath.' Collapse de stout Highlander.

1901 Désastre. *Punch* est sur le point de faire le launching des célébrations – 60 YEARS DE *PUNCH* – quand Queen Victoria poppe ses clogs. Oui, la vieille Queen fait le kicking du bucket, turning–up des toes, le passing-away, etc. Les célébrations sont cancelés.

1904 Nouveau marketing survey. Le report dit: 'Le readership de *Punch* fait toujours un up-turn dans le war-time. Dans le war-time, il y a un grand market demand pour l'entertainment et les gags, etc. Donc, organiser un grand outbreak de hostility. Un world war, si possible.'

   Ah, mais c'est difficile, ça. Un world war? Organisé par un petit humorous weekly? C'est un long-term project, ça. Dix years pour être sur le safe side.

   Bargepole écrit son premier article suicidal, sous le title: 'Call this a century? I'm off back to

le Mad dog d'Iraq

the 1800s.' Massif protest par les lecteurs. Retour triomphal de Bargepole.

1909 Première visite de Edward VII au Punch Lunch, en strict incognito. Après, il écrit dans son diary: 'Ma première visite au fameux Punch Lunch. Très impressif. Hélas, je fus pissé comme un newt. Mais je n'étais pas le seul. Il y avait un type avec un dirty raincoat qui était encore plus intoxiqué que moi, mais très amusant. Il avait le nom Bargepole. Je lui ai demandé: "Bargepole? C'est un nom curieux. Vous êtes le Duke de Bargepole, ou quoi?" Il m'a dit: "Votre majesté, c'était mon nickname dans Wormwood Scrubs, quand j'étais en prison pour attempting to start un world war."

   "Attempting to start un world war?" j'ai dit, un peu startled. "C'est intéressant. Racontez-moi ça."

   "Ah, non," dit Bargepole. "C'est très hush-hush."'

1911 Premier nervous breakdown de Bargepole. Il est absent du *Punch* pendant trois ou quatre mois. 'Bargepole est unwell,' dit *Punch*. George Grossmith écrit a Bargepole:

   'Cher Bargepole, J'ai une petite idée pour un smash hit West End show, nommé *Bargepole Est Unwell*. Nous ☞

150 Years d'Europe

faisons un mish-mash de vos articles pour *Punch*, nous obtenons les services d'un fameux actor, comme du Maurier ou Beerbohm Tree, et pouf! Bob est votre oncle! Que pensez–vous?' Bargepole ne repond jamais, et le stage show *Bargepole Est Unwell* est still-born.

1914 Outbreak de World War I. Le readership de *Punch* fait un zooming upwards. Brill! *Punch* forme une expeditionary force pour contribuer au war effort. A préciser, c'est un cricket XI, qui va à Flanders. Le line-up est as follows: A P Herbert, Haig, Foch, Phil May, Lloyd George, Maugham, Wells, Wodehouse, Bargepole, Morrow, Belcher et 1st Lieutenant C Thomson de Glasgow. 12eme Man: Wm Tidy Esq. Le résultat est un hopeless draw dans no man's land.

1916 Bargepole est lost en action. Massif protest du readership. Bring back le vieux curmudgeon! Ou est le master de bile et despair? etc, etc. Bargepole revient en triomphe!

1917 Révolution en Russia. Le circulation manager de *Punch* reçoit une lettre du Kremlin: 'Cher circulation manager, je regrette à dire que le Royal Family de Russia a été assassiné par accident, donc je veux terminer leur subscription. Yours, etc, Lenin.'

Le circulation manager répond: 'Cher Lenin, vous êtes un red-hot revolutionary, je sais, mais même pour un revolutionary il y a le feet-up time. Pourquoi pas essayer *Punch*? Avec *Punch*, même les pogroms et les purges ont le bright side!'

Lenin ne répond jamais.

1918 Winner du grand Armistice Caption Contest: Lt Col C Thomson de Glasgow avec une caption pour la Mona Lisa: 'If you know of a better 'ole, go to it!'

1926 General Strike. Cricket Match contre un Strikers' XI. Le *Punch* team est Bateman, E V Knox-Johnston, Groucho Knox, Boothroyd, Bargepole, Larry Sr, Pont, Ronald Searle et trois plainclothes policemen. 12ème Man: Wm Tidy. Résultat: Match abandonné après dispute concernant non-union manufacture de bails et stumps.

1936 Edward VIII fait sa première visite au Punch Lunch. Dans son diary il écrit: 'Aujourd'hui j'ai abdiqué, donc j'avais un free afternoon. J'ai sauté dans un taxi et j'ai dit: "Punch Lunch, et drive like hell." Le taxi-driver dit: "Je connais votre face, vous êtes Max Miller, non, vous êtes le bloke qui a abdiqué, vous etes le mari de Wallis Eaton, no, Wallace Stevens, anyway, vous êtes Edward le V, non le VI..." C'était horrible. J'ai dit: "Je vais vous mettre dans le Tower de London pour treason et lèse-majesté!" Il dit: "Too late, mate. Vous avez fait l'Abdication. C'est votre frère qui est King maintenant, George VIII, non, George IX, anyway, le Duke de Gloucester, anyway..."'

1941 Planning session pour le 100ème anniversaire de *Punch* est terminé en turmoil après la disclosure de World War II etc, etc. Il yest postponé a 1951.

1951 100ème anniversaire de *Punch* postponé, à cause du Festival de Britain.

1953 Ascent de Mount Everest par Tensing et Hillary. Ascent de *Punch* par Muggeridge. Il dit: 'J'ai un grand masterplan pour *Punch*. C'est un system de benign neglect.'

1956 Après années de benign neglect, il y a un crisis de readership. Même Muggeridge n'est pas un reader de *Punch*. Mutiny et back-stabbing. Le nouveau editor est B Hollowood, qui dit: 'J'ai un master plan pour *Punch*. Le survival.'

Le management dit: 'C'est tout?'

Il dit: 'Non. Vous connaissez le traditional cover?'

Le management dit: "Ah, oui! Le grand cover de Doyle, avec Mister *Punch* et Toby! Le glory de *Punch*! Pourquoi?'

Hollowood dit: 'Parce que je vais le mette dans la waste paper basket.'

1968 Arrivée de William Davis comme editor. 'J'ai un master plan pour *Punch*!' dit-il.

'Oui?' dit le management, avec un peu de suspicion.

'Je vais inaugurer une magazine pour British Airways nommée *High Life* et puis je vais partir.'

1977 Arrivée de Alan Coren, le nouveau editor. 'Oui, moi aussi, j'ai un master plan pour *Punch*,' dit-il.

'Dîtes-nous,' dit le management, un peu fatigué.

'Ah non, jamais,' dit Coren. 'C'est le grand mistake des autres editors. Il ne faut jamais annoncer le master-plan.'

1991 At last, le 150ème birthday de *Punch*! Grande publicité! Cricket matches! Temporary sanity de Bargepole. Mais mon Dieu – qu'avons-nous ici? Le Gulf War? Ah non – pas un bloody war pour ruiner encore un milestone de *Punch*! Mais le nouveau editor, l'Etonian vieux et yuppie, David Thomas, a un master-plan. Il écrit à Monsieur John Major.

'Cher M Major, c'est notre 150ème birthday en 1991, et votre sacré Gulf War va ruiner nos celebrations. La mort de Queen Victoria en 1901, le World War II en 1941, maintenant le Gulf War – ah c'est pas fair. Mais si vous terminez le Gulf War très rapidement, très vite, je donne mon word comme un gentleman que le staff de *Punch* vote Tory à la next election. Fair enough?' Le rest est history.

It's the Clarence Thomas guide to
sexual harassment

Hang on to your robes people, here comes the Judge!

Just follow our simple grope-by-grope steps...

GROPE 1: Wrong, all wrong. The first rule for the successful sex pest is: grab the initiative. Do it to your frisky assistant before they do it to you. Don't let them get the upper hand.

GROPE 2: Now that's a bit more like it! See how our geriatric gropemeister demonstrates the blindside fondle assault. Remember: being old doesn't mean you can't be bold.

GROPE 3: Here we see one of my legendary Capitol Hill legal workshops where we learn how to manipulate a well-hung jury. But you know, people often say to me, 'Hey, Judge, where's the pest potential in jury service?' And I say, 'You should see the service I get.'

GROPE 4: See what I mean, citizens?

NO GROPE 5: A quick warning to all those wanting hands-on goosing experience. Remember there is one drawback for the modern groper – self-defence classes. People, we're adjourned.

'Look on the brightside chuck, at least you've discovered a cure for baldness'

'Same every bloody year! Waste of time asking us to turn up'

Father on up the road

HUNTER DAVIES wrote the Father's Day column for _Punch_ for ten years. Now he takes up the story from where he left off in 1989

I made a mistake when I started writing Father's Day, back in 1979 when the world was still in short trousers, the bedrooms full and we had a little face at almost every window. I decided to call my children by their real names. I hate all those soppy euphemisms, such as Child Number One, the Son and Heir, or Our last Little Treasure, as I always suspect that once people make up names, they make up all the incidents. So from the beginning, I wrote about Caitlin, Jake and Flora, real members of the planet, who were aged 14, 12 and six when the articles first appeared.

It was going to be a six-week series, a dad answers back, giving his thoughts on family life, in reply to all those _Guardian_ women who had come out of the kitchen and were insisting on sharing their domestic lives and heroic struggles. I wrote it for ten years, producing 428 columns, how did I spin it out, during which time it became a TV series, with John Alderton as _moi_.

In my mind, they were Letters To My Mum, the sort of weekly chit chat we all pass on to our parents, picking on the nice things, flamming up the little incidents, avoiding anything too nasty or unpleasant. I was economical when it came to anything unhappy, and like all families over a ten-year spell, we had our share.

I retired the column in 1989, by which time I'd not just run out of copy, but out of children. Two had become students and left home and Little Flora, our baby, was about to enter the sixth form. If I had never revealed their real ages and names, I could have kept them at the same stage for ever and then started recycling, which would have been ecologically very sound for my bank balance.

I also made a minor mistake when I finished. There was naturally weeping and wailing from trillions of Father's Day fans, so I said I would do a round robin letter, every Christmas, giving the latest family progress, to all who sent me a stamped addressed envelope. I never thought about the photostating bill, nor the fact that the rotten Post Office keeps on putting up the postage rate. People sent envelopes in January, for me to return the following December. Cost me a bleedin' fortune, adding on the missing stamps.

So I'm vee pleased about this 150 thingy, giving me a chance to do this year's update. I can now go and steam off the stamps and

use them myself, no of course I won't, what a suggestion, am I not a man of honour, the father of integrity? Les enfants were never quite sure of this. They were not always best pleased to see their names in print.

It wasn't their school friends mocking, as that was not done. At inner London comprehensives, they do not pass comments about parents, homes, family background. Caitlin was at Camden School for Girls (I can mention it now, as she's long left) where there were girls with Really Famous Parents, such as Cabinet ministers and weather forecasters. Jake's school, William Ellis, also had its share of passing famous. It was the occasional teacher, reading an out of date column, making some elliptical remark in the corridor, which upset them. Jake for a while insisted his name had to be changed, so he became Jimmy for a few months, till he forgot.

When Jake went on to University, I was not allowed to mention it by name, though there were enough internal clues, but Caitlin didn't mind. None of them ever read the column, load a rubbish, how do you get away with it? Caitlin used to get fan letters; dopey lads in provincial public schools such as Eton fell in love with her, wanting to be her pen pal, but she never replied. I always did, being well brung up.

So where are they now? At this moment, what are they doing, Hunt? Let me see, 9.30 in the morning, Caitlin will have walked in her bare feet across the sands of Maun, back to her concrete hut, morning school over for another day, before the heat makes going out unbearable. She's teaching in Botswana, out in the country, part of some British Council scheme. We plan to go and see her this Xmas. She appears to love it, and the people. She writes huge long letters every week, what a good daughter, and we feel totally in touch. I file them in the family archives, carefully numbered, just because I like filling up the family archives.

When she finished at Sussex, she went off to the USA for two years to do research at Clark University, where she met a bloke from Botswana. This teaching job will last two years. Then what? Dunno. We don't ask. We know our place.

Dear Jake will probably just be coming home to his shared flat in downtown Madrid, knackered after another all night on the town. You have to stay up all night, see, 'cos the clubs in Spain don't really get going till four in the morning. Or it could be the football that's knackered him. He plays in an indoor league and is always being injured. Anyway, he's achieved his life's ambition, which was to live in a hot country and play a lot of football.

He doesn't write but he rings fairly regularly, one-second bursts, saying quick, ring me back, this is the number, so me and the Old Trout push and shove to return his call, hoping for some good gen, and it's always who scored for Spurs, Hunt, fanks, I've gotta go now. See ya.

He's teaching as well, English as a foreign language. After Cambridge, there I've mentioned it, he did a short TEFL course, then went to Turin for a year, picked up Italian, met a lot of Italian girls, and now he is in Madrid for a year, picking up a lot of Spanish, etc. He was always useless at languages, so we're surprised, and pleased, by his getting these extra skills.

Naturally, we don't ask what's next, though his dear mama cuts out job adverts from the *Guardian* and posts them to him, which he then loses, and I say yes, Gazza done well, and by the way, I'm told the BBC training schemes are very good, and I hear the Foreign Office is a real fun place to work.

I keep on thinking that at their age I was married, with a proper job, and was saving for a house, then I think what's wrong with teaching, what's wrong with going round the world and enjoying life while you can? I envy them in a way. No one is married these days, under the age of 50, and what's so great about a 'proper job' when anyone can get paid off and nothing is secure.

Little Flora is now 18, good gracious, still at school, so I won't mention it, with excellent GCSEs behind her, now doing her A levels, but she is not going to university. She's heard nothing but university talk over every meal for most of her life and found it really boring. She visited them at both Cambridge and Brighton, two of the country's nicest towns, and thought they were draggy. She much prefers the views and architecture of Oxford Street.

She has seen the other two, still not decided about what to do in life, and wants something more vocational, so she's going to art college in September. Then she'd like to travel. Oh Gawd, not another one. What have we done to make them all want to leave not just home, but the country?

Over the cocoa, me and the OT wonder what will become of them. I thought at 18, that would be it, end of days for fathering and mothering, but as long as we are here, and they are here, we'll still be chuntering away as parents. I can't see my ambition ever being reached. I thought by now I would be writing a column called Grandfather's Day. Fat chance.

The Best of Father's Day by Hunter Davies is available from Coronet Books, price £3.50.

ILLUSTRATION: ROWAN BARNES-MURPHY

'*I now allow her to stay for the port
and cigars, but...*'

'*She's building herself up. Soon she'll be ready to throw
herself under a racehorse*'

'*I know you're the doctor, but aren't you supposed
to force feed them with liquids?*'

'*I don't mind her flying
as long as she doesn't
neglect her household
duties*'

'Them land girls from London reckoned it would look better with curls'

'She's learnt all the new dances but she hasn't quite got the hang of smoking yet'

'Giles and I have an arrangement. I've told him he can be assertive on Sundays'

Memories

Mike Williams
Cartoonist

I've only been into the *Punch* offices about ten times in 15 years. On all occasions a lot of alcohol was consumed, so my memory is quite dim. I do remember being told once that the Archbishop of Canterbury had just been put into a taxi stiff as a board. Which Archbishop I do not recall. But then again, that was some years ago, and in the days when every visitor to a Punch Lunch seemed to go home the same way.

Roy Hattersley
Columnist 1979-88

Alan Coren thought it would be a great idea if I went out and about interviewing 'quirky' people; the Duke and Duchess of Devonshire, for instance, or the Bishop of Liverpool. The only trouble was, to everyone's distress, I liked them all too much – so we had to scrap it.

Alan's schemes and ideas have always been legendary. He once had a plan to take over a pub for the day and wanted me to play a retired major. Every so often, I would be required to rush in saying, 'has old Buffy Tufton come in yet?' and then rush out again, only to reappear later with the same query. It never actually happened.

I've never been like Alan; able to sit down and write a screamingly funny peice in the space of about an hour. Maybe, however, one of the main reasons I got to write books is that I couldn't face another Punch Lunch where yet again someone like Melvyn Bragg would say, 'well of course you're not a real writer until you've written a novel.' Oh bugger it, I thought – I will then.

1841

From *The Origin of Specious* to *Mine Camp*, STEVE PUNT presents the definitive chronicle of the last 150 years

At the time the Memorable Magazine, *Punch*, was founded, the Monarch was Queen Victoria (named after the famous Pub in Albert Square). Britain was indubitably Top Nation on account of the Empire and the Industrial Revelation, which was a Good Thing since it created Wealth but a Bad Thing since it created Poor Workers who had to send their children down Mines. This was also the time of the Coming of the Railways, which had been invented in 1825 (but had been delayed due to signal failure at Crewe).

In 1851 Britain made a Great Exhibition of itself. The Exhibition was held at Crystal Palace, which meant cancelling their home games for a month and much disgruntlement for their supporters, a group of whom later burnt the venue down in protest. But no one noticed because by this time everyone was involved in a War, which had broken out despite all the efforts of the Crimea Prevention Officer. The Crimea was memorable because of the Lady with the Lamp, otherwise known as Annie Nightingale, who played the wounded soldiers their favourite record requests. It was also the setting for the Memorable disaster, the Charge of the Fire Brigade.

1859 saw the publication of the Memorable book, *The Origin of Specious*, which propounded that Man was related to Apes. The author, Charles Darwin, faced much criticism, but made a lot of money from selling the TV rights to PG Tips. In 1861 Queen Victoria's husband, Albert Hall, died, and they named a building after him.

There was also a *Pax Britannica*, whereby the Empire brought peace to much of the World by selling them encyclopaedias, and the Populations were so busy trying to Read them that they could not Fight. Thus the Victorians were free to carry on being Victorian, being Not Amused and reading a lot of trollope. It was the age of the Novel and there were many great Victorian Novelists, like Dickens (who died leaving an unfinished work, *The Mystery of Edwin Dro*) and Hardy (who later went to America and met Stan Laurel). There were no good Playwrights as the Victorian taste was for Mellow-drama. They shied away from Emotion and were Sexual Hypocrites, although in 1889 they were Pruriently Interested in the case of the notorious 'Jack the Rapper', (who stalked the streets of East London shouting 'Yo! Bass!')

Alexander Graham Bell invented the Telephone, and three months later overcharged himself, refused to pay and cut himself off. No one noticed, however, as in 1887 Mr Benz invented the Car. His model was one Horsepower, which meant it could do the Work of one Horse, but attempts to make it jump a round at Hickstead failed dismally (although Sanyo Music Centre managed OK). However, Memorable Invention though the Car was, it did not sell very well, as no one had yet invented icky adverts with people rushing to see their kid being born.

In 1889 Gustave Eiffel designed the Memorable Edifice which bears his name. The Eiffel Tower was in fact a Mistake; Gustave had really designed it to be six inches tall and sold as a cheap souvenir by dodgy hawkers around Paris. By an Administrative Error it was built 800 feet high, and all the dodgy hawkers could do was stand around underneath to keep out of the rain.

Paris was, of course, Top City around this time because it was Gay and because of the famous Moulin Rouge dance, 'Can the Can' by Suzi Quatro (co-written with her brother Audi). This was also the time of the greatest Impressionists, led by Monet, Renoir, and Yarwood.

In 1890, Van Gogh committed suicide on being told that Don Maclean was writing a song about him. (He had very possibly confused Don Maclean with the other Don Maclean, who presented *Crackerjack*, and became very depressed at the thought of Peter Glaze trying to join in.) Van Gogh was, of

And All That

course, a very Memorable Painter, since he cut his ear off and painted the Sunflowers, although they were quite a nice colour already.

There were great medical Advances made around this time, notably with the invention of Inoculations, which were invented in 1893 – handy if you'd booked a foreign holiday for 1894. Another Memorable Invention, in 1895, was the X-Ray, which meant you could see Inside People, although not as far inside as Keith Freud, who was developing his Theories around this time, including Annual Retention, and the Super-eggo, and later on he developed the Oedipus Complex (shops, bars and restaurants, and parking for 600 cars).

The Wright brothers invented the aeroplane in 1903. Their first flight only went 120 feet before they had to land (due to a baggage handlers' dispute). Another form of air transport was the Zeppelin, which became Germany's terrible, much-feared secret weapon during World War I. The Kaiser hoped that the Zeppelin could bring London to its knees, by flying overhead all day playing 'Stairway to Heaven'. (The Government claimed that the guitar solo would be over by Christmas.)

After Germany lost World War I they demanded a replay and got a new team manager, Adolf Hitler, who set out his Views in a Book called *Mine Camp*. In it, he claimed that Arians were the master-race. Churchill, who was Sagittarius, naturally disagreed with this and decided to fight them on the beaches. The War started because of a mistake by Chamberlain, who foolishly did not take an Interpreter with him to Munich. Chamberlain's German was very Bad and when he said 'Please do not start a major world war' it came out as 'My country is facing an acute shortage of fresh vegetables.' It was for this Reason that he returned bearing a Piece of Paper which promised Peas in our Time.

Eventually America decided to end the War by using The Bomb. This meant that Britain was definitely no longer Top Nation since now there were two Superpowers, but Britain nevertheless demanded that it be allowed to have an Independent Nuclear Detergent. This arrived in the form of the Polarised Missile and led to the Aldermaston Marches, which led to Michael Foot.

It was some while before Technology was put to Peaceful use. It was President Kennedy the Memorable President, who

before he was shot (by John Harvey-Jones) in Dallas (or perhaps it was Dynasty), vowed to put a Man on the Moon. This was because the Russians were Beating the Americans in the Space Race. The first Man in Space was a Russian, Yuri Gargling. The Americans instead put a Chimpanzee into orbit, proving that Darwin was Right. But in the End they had to use Humans since the Chimpanzee could not master the Weightless Banana.

The Sixties also saw Planning Blight. Large areas of Britain's cities had been bombed in the War by the Luftwaffe, and Urban Planners decided to build Monstrous Carbuncles to replace them. Despite this, London became Swinging and four young men changed the face of pop music – The Beadles, four bearded pranksters who charmed the nation.

Perhaps the most Memorable invention of this century is the Electric Golf-ball Warmer (available from the Innovations catalogue, battery not included) but running it a close second is television, which was invented in 1926 by John Yogi Baird who, on 27 January, managed to project flickering and indistinct pictures of two ventriloquist's dolls onto a screen. (He had, in fact, picked up a Channel 4 film season.)

Meanwhile in America there had been a Wall Street Crash and a great Depression (which is why Americans started going to Psychiatrists) then a Big Deal, then a War, and then a Consumer Age. However, in the early Seventies the country was rocked by a great Scandal – Watergoat, in which Tricky Dicky and all his Men got caught playing silly Buggers.

At the end of the Seventies everybody stopped wearing flared trousers (except Open University lecturers) and there was a Swing to the Right. *Punch* was now nearly 140 years old, as was Ronald Reagan, who became President and suggested everybody watch *Star Wars*. In Russia lots of Old men died and then Gorbachev took over and began Glasnost. In Britain, the Chanel Tunnel began to get bored and the M25 was finished. (Before it started.)

1066 And All That first appeared in Punch in 1930. Steve Punt first appeared in Punch in 1990 and is a member of the Mary Whitehouse Experience.

1860: The great diet craze begins

1890: Transylvania donates blood donor clinic to Britain

1948: The National Health Service is introduced

1965: Mass protest meeting of patients on NHS waiting list

I'm tired of Picasso, I think I'd like a Miro nose and a Dali chin now.

1975: Cosmetic surgery becomes fashionable

1985: Doctors discover heart failure is the most common cause of death amongst private patients

plus VAT!

AAARGH!

I think they're part of the new waste disposal system!

1990s: Privatisation of the NHS begins

Memories

Norman Tebbit MP

Only two and a half times my age, wearing much better and providing more laughs.

Russell Davies

Former Punch deputy editor and contributor

I reckon I must have hosted about ten Punch Lunches in all and they tend to blur into one. I do remember the occasion when about four *Punch* editors turned up at the same time. Quite a frightening experience. And then there was the strange occasion when I found myself sitting next to Rolf Harris. Who invited *him*? Actually he was quite a success, as was Kate Adie who tends to give better than she gets.

Guests believed that at some embarrassing moment they'd be expected to launch into a prepared monologue – that is, until they were told to sit down and not be so daft. One or two inevitably would get drunk and a colleague and myself found ourselves one afternoon having to cart a cartoonist blinded by ale off to Euston for his train back north. To get a wheelchair from British Rail we had to pretend he had a rare degenerative disease.

The pretence that he was immobile, however, could only be sustained until we got him on to his train, whereupon he promptly got out and staggered across to enter a train waiting on the other side. I see he's still working, though, so he must have got home eventually.

Another memorable event was the Duchess of York carving her name on the Punch Table in an improvised sort of way. I am not sure whether she was asked but, of course, we all pretended to be delighted. I suppose we didn't know any better at the time.

Country Life first appeared under Bill Davis's editorship on 6 August 1969 with the aim of covering bizarre British news stories. Readers were paid £1 for each clipping used. Over the years, the emphasis moved from oddity and eccentricity to misprints and ill-chosen phrases. And the reward is now £5.

Left out of the magazine for a while, the column was reinstated in the late Eighties. Then, in 1989, the title was dropped and included in the letters pages. Readers took no notice and kept sending entries marked Country Life. The title was restored the following year. It remains one of Punch's most popular features.

The best of Country Life

1969

A Chertsey man found lying in the road was 'lucky not to have been run over,' Staines magistrates were told on Monday…'Some unfortunate motorist might have come along and run you over,' said Mr Slagg. 'That would not have mattered but the motorist would have been upset.'

T MOORE (*Chertsey News & Herald*)

Dennis Shamblin, 102, who recently applied for a marriage licence to marry Mamie Gibson, 60, says he does not plan to have children. 'My eyes are giving me trouble,' he explained.

A ROGERS (*Los Angeles Times*)

After spitting in a policeman's face, hitting him in the face and kicking him, Michael Hobbins (38) of Rochdale said: 'I love you, officer.'

R FOSTER (*Rochdale Observer*)

One million people in Australia can't read. Are you one of them?

J WOODS (*Commonwealth Employment Service Notice*)

1970

A moment of complete and utter silence at the conclusion of a performance of great music is a sure sign that an audience has been moved.

H J OWENS (*Surrey Mirror*)

Power demand went up by 1,200 MW when BBC screened the Miss World Contest. The biggest increase in demand was during the cabaret act by Frank Ifield when people switched kettles on.

B G DOBBS (*Power News*)

ROME – Maria Marcon, 24, told police she accepted a ride from a dark-haired stranger and was robbed by a three-foot dwarf who popped out of a cardboard box on the back seat.

G M W ADAMS (*Regina Leader-Post*)

LOST – Bull Terrier, has three legs, blind in left eye, missing right ear, broken tail, recently castrated. Answers to the name of Lucky.

P BUTLER
(*Trinidad Guardian*)

I was attacked by a little girl…

An unemployed Harrow man suffered a fractured cheek, broken nose and severe bruising to the eye after being attacked by three youths outside the Goodwill To All pub in Headstone Drive last Friday.

K BERNSTEIN (*Harrow Independent*)

1971

Before he rushed back to his interrupted schedule, the professor chipped away at the bark of six trees, pronouncing three definitely alive, two definitely dead, and one half-dead and half-alive.

E BELCHEM (*Jerusalem Post*)

Early the following morning, Burton approached his wife. She expected a kiss, but he hit her on the head with a spanner, said Inspector Bentley, prosecuting.

J F CLARKE (*Nottingham Post*)

A word with the doctor: A fat baby is almost universally admired. The dimples in the cheeks, on the back of each hand, the second chin, and the legs which look like up-ended melons are regarded as evidence of beauty and wonderful fitness. Those same features in the infant's mother would put her bottom in any beauty competition.

C POOLE (*Scarborough Mercury*)

He said Littleton, in a cell by himself, cut his throat with a razor blade, but said Littleton did not answer when asked why he did it.

F SCOTT (*Memphis CA*)

CARTOONS: GRAY JOLLIFFE

Someone left a seven-foot shark in a telephone kiosk at Mudeford Quay, Hampshire, early yesterday. It fell on the first caller to open the door.

B A LACEY (*South Wales Echo*)

As Hannibal urged his 40,000 men and 37 elephants across the Alps in 218 BC, he could have had little idea that he would be followed 2,200 years later by a party of 20 boys and four masters from Oswestry School, among them 14-year-old Stephen Jones, from Bulford Camp.

D PETTIWARD (*Salisbury Journal*)

Kirchner told the court that, after his divorce, life on his isolated farm had become very lonely. He said he had made the wrong friends, mostly policemen, and they had regular drinking parties on his farm.

E J MACKENZIE (*Johannesburg Star*)

1973

African municipal bus drivers in Springs will get a bonus each month if they refrain from hitting their passengers.

F A INGRAM (*Johannesburg Star*)

A self-employed lorry driver who was said to have told police he had Fred Astaire in the boot of his car was fined £25 at Portsmouth Crown Court.

S J BRIGGS (*Portsmouth News*)

Mr Kanso Yoshida, cousin of Emperor Hirohito of Japan, has died in Liverpool aged 78. Since he came to Liverpool in 1912, Mr Yoshida has been known as Paddy Murphy.

R W BRANCH (*Liverpool Post*)

He had been eating tomatoes and drinking milk, and the woman may have mistaken this for an offer of sex. It was not, he said.

A THOMAS (*Rhodesia Herald*)

An Irishman who was claimed to have said he was Welsh and allowed himself to be held in custody for three weeks on a charge of stealing a car that turned out to be his own was fined a total of £25 in Leeds.

G SMITH (*Yorkshire Evening Post*)

After his girlfriend said she did not want to go out with him any more, a photographer sent her a sack of potatoes, rang her up 50 to 60 times a day, and sent a fire engine to her office.

R J EASTWOOD (*Yorkshire Post*)

Said chairman Alderman Jack Margrett: 'But, of course, if there are any further cases of indecent exposure, then we shall look at it very carefully.'

R CLACK
(*Rochester & Chatham Post*)

Mr Ross's flab-fighting efforts, which reduced his 15-stone frame to two stone, won himself a buffet banquet for 80 and a portable colour television.

M LAWRENSON
(*Harrogate Advertiser*)

1974

One indignant stripper, whose tools of the trade are a bottle and a whip and rejoices in the unlikely stage name of 'Smokey Joe', protested to the magistrate that her routines were not all that different from those she performed at police balls.

M MORGAN (*South London Press*)

Inspector Wardop said on 23 February at 12.30 am PC Murphy found Miss Nickerson in Sandle Road, banging her saucepan. When he asked her to go home quietly she said: 'I'm only looking for my *@&*@$* cat. I have to bang hard: he's been missing for two years.'

D ANDERSON (*Herts & Essex Observer*)

Picketing miners who have stood round the clock at one Yorkshire power station have now withdrawn their guard. The men braved this week's cold and rain outside Halifax's power station until ☞

The former head chaplain at Brooke Army Medical Centre has pleaded guilty to charges of adultery, sodomy and wrongful use of a government telephone.

W H GORDON
(*Express News, San Antonio*)

a kindly policeman told them the truth: the power station closed down three years ago.

M J ROBINSON (*Yorkshire Post*)

A week after a brick had hurtled through a shop window in Grange Mount causing £64 of damage, a 19-year-old youth returned to the shop and asked for his brick back. He then complained to a police officer that the shopkeeper would not return it, said Inspector Cooke, prosecuting.

G P HIGGINS (*Birkenhead News*)

Sri Lanka moves to curb violence by telling force: 'Shoot on sight.'

G ROBERTSON (*Montreal Gazette*)

1977

Former Navy officer now in business, late 30s, seeks sincere lady, late or early 20s. Ex-nuns or athletes given priority, any religion.

P WALBRIDGE (*Irish Independent*)

When Frank Rea, a club entertainer who astonished audiences as 'The Amazing Memoranda', was asked by a social security officer how much work he did on the side, he said he did not remember.

G GITTINS (*Altrincham Guardian*)

There were 26 people there, 22 men and four women, drinking beer and spirits. Four full 11-gallon canisters of beer, five empty ones, one part full, 415 cans of pale ale and lager, 22 partly full cans, 68 empty cans, and several dozen beer and spirit glasses were found.

'I came to the conclusion that this was a place used for drinking,' said the inspector.

A FAIRRIE (*The Scotsman*)

Thirty women moon worshippers met on a hill on Wednesday night to dance naked in an ancient pagan ritual, but called off the ceremony when 150 men turned up to watch.

R LOCKIE (*Saskatoon Star*)

A visually impaired San Francisco man argued he wasn't driving solo in the commuter lane reserved for cars carrying two or more people because his dog, Queenie, was helping him navigate.

R GOTTLIEB
(*Seattle Times*)

I said turn right or are you deaf too?

We have been unable to publish a letter on vandalism from Mrs Elizabeth Stewart of Oak Road, Abronhill. It arrived badly charred after vandals set fire to a letter-box in Abronhill.

G HAGGERTY (*Cumbernauld News*)

Her book is full of the most delightful pieces of information. 'Hang mothballs on your peach tree' is advice we're certainly going to follow.

B SAMPSON (*Here's Health*)

GOATS! On a special occasion something special counts. A goat for a cake on your wedding day counts. For a bite during parties a goat counts. Enjoy with your family to slaughter a goat on a weekend. Get one today – for slaughter or breeding. Fantastic varieties, reasonable

prices. So easy to produce. So easy to slaughter.

J FREYBERG (*Tanzania Daily News*)

1986

The steamy film *9½ Weeks* has been temporarily banned from Worthing's Dome Cinema until it has been privately viewed by Worthing Council's moral watchdogs. The film *Body Lust, Best Bit Of Crumpet in Denmark* will be shown instead while the committee decide the fate of *9½ Weeks*.

A GOVER (*Worthing Guardian*)

Detective Constable Patricia Basely (30) said today she was 'a very lucky woman' after being hit by the car, carried ten yards on the bonnet and then having her leg run over.

J FITZPATRICK
(*Northampton Chronicle & Echo*)

1987

HARD OF HEARING? HAVE YOUR HEARING TESTED FREE AT G C BATEMAN OPTICIAN.

M BALSTON (*Portsmouth Journal*)

In view of all the complaints received from women who've had their feet accosted by a toe-sucking man, Los Angeles County Sheriff's Detective Loyace Mauldin says: 'I never wear open-toed shoes to the market any more.'

G PENLETT (*Los Angeles Times*)

(Interview with Yannick Noah)
Q: Weren't you in direct line for tribal leadership?
A: Yes, for the Ewondo tribe. My great-grandfather was a chef.

I LYNCH

Inspector Keith Hill from Amersham police said: 'We have received a complaint from a nursing sister to the effect that he was riding his motorbike up and down the corridor without wearing his crash helmet.'

R HUNTER (*South Bucks Star*) ☞

Pensioners in South Wales tried to cash their AIDS warning leaflets for a fiver thinking they were the heating allowances forms.

They had been sent the 'Don't Die Of Ignorance' leaflet in Welsh, a language spoken by less than one in five in the south, and could not understand a word of it.

B KAY (*Golden Age*)

1989

To our readers – the *Korea Herald* will not be published tomorrow as the paper closes today in observance of Newspaper Day. We regret any inconvenience to our readers.

P MORRISS (*The Korea Herald*)

The Minister for Water and Planning, Michael Howard, said lots of people had the idea that water fell God-given from the skies.

T B O'BRIEN (*The Age, Melbourne*)

Because of unforeseen circumstances, the *Niugini Nius* Astrologer became suddenly indisposed this week and was unable to provide his usual horoscopes which are so helpful to our readers.

J MILLS
(*Niugini Nius, Papua New Guinea*)

Prostitute Linda Clelland thought she had picked up just another client until the couple undressed in a Bayswater hotel bedroom. 'I realised there was something weird about him when instead of getting into bed he produced a can of corned beef, opened it and began eating it.'

R RUBIN
(*Hampstead and Highgate Express*)

Today there are many more superbly skilful soccer players. It is no longer only the exceptional players like Diego Maradona who can use their feet like hands to control the ball.

P COUGHLIN (*The Jerusalem Post*)

SEVEN SAMURAI (1954): Akira Kurosawa's epic masterpiece about 16th century Samurai warriors who are hired to defend villagers against the bandits who are depressing them.

P HOWE (*The Citizen*)

1990

Robert Leys, a taxi driver who wears an SS cap and long boots, dresses in black and entertains his passengers with tapes of

Gerald Harris, whose name was incorrectly given as Harold Morris and who is 39 and not 93 as stated in the story, is an associate professor of Tort Law School and not a janitor at the public library as the story incorrectly stated.

L LEVERT (*Dalhousie Gazette*)

Nazi party war songs has had his licence to drive a taxi revoked. Mr Leys said he would fight any attempt to take away his licence. 'This is the sort of thing that happened in Nazi Germany,' he said.

R S MOUNTSTEPHENS (*Sydney Herald*)

Well, nothing wrong with your reflexes Ms. Gitting...

He kissed my right breast first and then he started to suck them. I asked him whether all this was necessary. It was an odd situation. I had only come to get a prescription.

G M GITTING
(*Altrincham Messenger*)

A green scarf and green folding umbrella were left behind after the professional negligence seminar.

P D WOODS
(*Manchester Law Society Messenger*)

The police thought he was disposing of a body, but found the pair very much alive, romping on a blanket near Luton, Beds. Detective Inspector Gerth Pestell said yesterday, 'We withdrew at once, but I am not sure what the young man did.'

T HOPKINS
(*Herald and Post*)

WRITING WELL ISN'T EAST AND NO-ONE SHOULD PRETEND IT IS. Write now for a free prospectus to the London College of Journalism.

W STANNARD ALLEN (*Weekend Guardian*)

Defence lawyer Ian Pearson said: 'It is accepted that kissing privates is not a sensible course of action for a captain or any other soldier.'

O ROSE (*The Sun*)

1991

I can't read in bed because it disturbs my husband. Are there any books on the subject you could recommend?

D BEAVERIDGE (*TV Times*)

A man stole the TV while the occupants of the house were watching it, a court heard. The 42-year-old man calmly unplugged the set, told the occupants he was taking it for 'forensic' and left.

L SCOTT (*Staffordshire Evening Sentinel*)

Police investigating a break-in at the home of Norman Fowler MP had no difficulty in identifying the culprit, magistrates heard last Thursday. One of the three burglars, a 19-year-old Irishman, left his birth certificate behind.

J BROCKINGTON (*Sutton Coldfield News*)

Memories

Gerald Scarfe
Cartoonist
When I'd bring my drawings into Bill Hewison in the Sixties he always told me my noses were too big and my arms were too long and that I should go away and re-do them. Instead, I'm afraid I went on drawing bigger and bigger noses regardless. And then I went on to join *Private Eye*.

Bill Hewison
Illustrator and Punch art editor 1960 – 1984
No cartoonist ever forgets the first cartoon he got into *Punch*. In my case it was two caryatids – one frowning, the other offering a bottle of aspirin. When I joined the staff in 1957, I felt there was nowhere higher that someone in my position could aim to be. It was one of those rare jobs where you rubbed your hands at the thought of going in.

Hunter Davies
Punch columnist
I began my 'Father's Day' column at a time every other column was being written by women who wanted to run the world. I think Alan Coren saw it as a chance for a man to answer back. In terms of reader identification, I soon realised I'd hit a gold mine. If only I hadn't mentioned my children by name – they could have stayed the same age forever in it and I could still have been writing it.

I have collected quite a bit of *Punch* memorabilia over the years, including an 1854 pocket book diary. Twenty-eight quid I paid for that. Must have been bonkers.

..HERE AM I SITTING IN A TIN CAN...

'Can we have another tape on, please?'

'It seems like it's a giant step for mankind to get off his butt and take his empties out to the kitchen'

'When you've done a couple of years researching the effects of cigarette smoking, space flight's a doddle'

'First of all, we have to get our pet Germans to stop the rockets heading for London as soon as they blast off'

'We had such great plans – McDonald's on the moon, Disneyland, Mars…'

'Oh no! Two weeks in orbit and now I'm going to get seasick'

'One of the main spin-offs from the space program; the Teflon-coated President!'

'Comrades – I can't find anything in the complete works of Marx and Lenin that has any bearing on the current emergency!'

Memories

In the days before they grew up these people worked for *Punch*.

Michael Parkinson

One of the greatest things about sitting down at the Punch Table was that you never knew who was going to row with who.

Sometimes it was Bill Davis and Alan Coren – whereupon fellow diners experienced that creeping discomfort you can get in a restaurant when married couples start to fall out. I attended the famous lunch to which Margaret Thatcher – prior to becoming Prime Minister – was invited. It seemed to me that a bunch of some of the cleverest, brightest and most formidable hacks – such as Bill Grundy and Keith Waterhouse – had been assembled for the occasion, like a pack of pit bulls, to run rings round her. But instead she was quite brilliant; those she didn't completely charm she thoroughly defeated with logical argument. I said to Keith Waterhouse afterwards, 'What did you think of that then?' Keith said he might forget that the lunch ever happened.

Malcolm Bradbury
Novelist

I sent my first article in to *Punch* when I was a tiny lad of about 18. Everyone said, once you've got something into *Punch* it makes you a comic writer. I think I did about 30 pieces in all throughout the Fifties and Sixties – mainly on my experiences teaching in America, and it was as a result of those that I was approached by an agent and got my first book – *Eating People is Wrong* – published. The last Punch Lunch I went to was hosted by Alan Coren, who always set a cracking pace. But isn't it funny how, when you try to recall particulars, all the lunches you've ever had all seem to blur into one?

Mitch, Critch and Titch

Austin Mitchell   *Labour MP and Punch contributor*

Punch Lunches started to go wrong when the humorists started stealing the politicians' jokes and the politicians started listening to the *Punch* writers' views on policy. Now that Critch, Mitch and Titch have displaced Roy Hattersley as guests on the grounds that we only need the same amount of food, I'm expecting a reversal of trade. This will make John Major look to be the wittiest man in the House of Commons and *Punch* better than the Labour Party Manifesto. As the latter is now being published as a weekly part-work in competition with *Punch* I think some differentiation is essential.

Julian Critchley   *Punch contributor and occasional Conservative MP*

My earliest encounter with *Punch* was as a schoolboy at Shrewsbury; reading bound Forties volumes of it in the library – but only if it was raining. If not, we had to be out running somewhere. Actually, what everyone wanted to find most in the library were dirty books – a pretty pointless exercise, as any that were even faintly dirty would have already been stolen. What I mostly did was not so much read *Punch* as look at the cartoons. It was a great comfort in those times.

Funnily enough, my most recent Punch Lunch took me back to my schooldays, I think it was the food. I might say it wasn't exactly a gastronomic experience – but I wouldn't want to sound ungrateful.

Charles Kennedy   *Punch Luncher and minority party president*

Mitch, Critch and Titch they have taken to calling us at Radio 4 – owing to the fact that myself, Julian Critchley and Austin Mitchell seem to appear so often as a threesome. But I have never attended the same Punch Lunches as Julian. My memory of them is that they have always been pretty excellent occasions – there weren't any other politicians there.

Peter Snow was at the last one I attended and I still remember one of the hottest topics of conversation – whether or not it was a good idea to give away his sandpit in a readers' competition.

# of Punch

and became important, all of CAROL PRICE plays Boswell

Simon Hoggart
Punch political correspondent

Alan Coren asked me to do a column for him around about the time that there was an absolute explosion in political gossip. The great thing about my *Punch* column was that it gave me the freedom to put down material I couldn't necessarily use elsewhere. I could operate in the hazy area where people would tell me fascinating things without realising that, unless they specifically requested otherwise, it would all get jotted down to go into print. MPs, however, remain as odd as ever when it comes to what they react and object to in print. Say a chap's the most horrific politician since Caligula and nothing happens. Say the same chap's got halitosis and he goes raving mad. Most MPs, though, can tolerate you being a bit rude about them. They see it as the price they pay for the absolute joy they can subsequently experience when you are ruder still about their colleagues.

Katharine Whitehorn
Columnist

The thing that sticks in my mind most about *Punch* was how extremely narked I was that Arianna Stassinopoulos got to make it to their Lunch table before many other women who had already been contributors for some time. Here was someone who had built a whole doctrine round a woman's place being in the home; a living example of a person who didn't practise what she preached if you ask me.

Ann Leslie and I always had a policy of writing just enough for the magazine to keep getting invited to the Lunches, but there were also pretty jolly outings to the races and Christmas and summer parties.

Alan Coren
Punch writer and Editor

After I graduated from Oxford I thought I'd be a serious writer. I went off to the States on a Harkness Fellowship, ostensibly to do a PhD, but when I got to Yale I discovered that America was terribly funny and that I could write comedy. So I started contributing pieces of embellished reporting to the *New Yorker* and *Punch*.

When I came back to England I went to lunch with Bernard Hollowood, who said, 'Why don't you come and be an assistant editor?' I joined the staff in June 1963.

The offices were in Bouverie Street. They looked like an Edwardian hotel. There was an oak-panelled hall, with a marble floor and a porter. *Punch* took up four floors and everyone had huge offices with Persian carpets and 19th century partners' desks.

Even though Hollowood was a socialist all his life, you couldn't come to work without a jacket and tie. Most of the staff were reasonably left-wing. But they were the sort who would give you a hard time at a Punch Lunch if the wine wasn't good and the pheasant didn't have lead in it. They were quite extravagant in their sexual behaviours – a little bit naughty, really.

The next editor, Bill Davis, thought he could teach himself humour like he taught himself everything else. And he almost could. He sent his secretary out to buy all of P G Wodehouse, Thurber and so on. Then he'd speed-read through three books before lunch. When he wrote, you could see this strange pastiche of other people's styles, and along the way he made one or two jokes, fabricated out of other people's spare parts. Because Bill had *High Life* in his domain, he had a vast supply of BA tickets. You'd get calls from Kinshasa or Anchorage because he'd just decided to go off there. Then he'd come back and write a piece on the socio-economic state of Alaska. Bill carried this Jim Hanson or David Frost-style patina of success with him – tremendous energy, a tremendous suntan, Italian lightweight suits. He was very hard, very tough on the outside, but underneath he was very sentimental. I like the bloke a lot.

By the time that I became editor (in 1977), the atmosphere was much more open-plan, in attitude if not in geography. I was a hands-on editor, but David Taylor was an absolutely marvellous deputy. He was instrumental in introducing leisure pursuits – cars, property, drink and so on. The thought was, 'We've got to do them, but let's do them in an entirely individual way and seduce advertisers even when we're taking the piss out of them.'

Michael Heath was very important. He was wonderful in the office – a constant irritant: bitchy, sarcastic but so engaging and so witty that everyone else honed themselves against him.

The thing I enjoyed the most was the printing strike of (I think) 1985, when we took the magazine to France for printing. Every week, five of us would go off on a plane with all the copy and artwork. Then we'd have it all set and printed in France and drive it back on a lorry. We managed to turn around copy to news-stands faster than when it was printed in England, and we had fewer misprints. We felt rather heroic – in a continuum of 25 years of enormous enjoyment, they were the best half-dozen issues we ever produced.

More reminiscences can be found throughout the magazine starting on page 45.

'Why not invest that money in "Tooth Fairy plc"? Send for a prospectus now'

'Just for the minutes, did anyone manage to catch the chairman's parting words?'

*'You call **that** going bump in the night?'*

*'I'd recognise that illiterate scrawl **anywhere** – it's Zorro!'*

WHO GIVES A MONKEY'S?

A CRITICAL LOOK AT MODERN LIFE
by *Richard Littlejohn*

No. 10 Cycling Shorts

It used to be Sloane's Liniment. No self-respecting Sunday morning soccer player would dream of taking to the field without first smearing his legs with the creamy elixir. (In my time, I've even seen one horribly hungover half-back take a quick swig from the bottle before kick-off.)

You might not look like a footballer, you might not play like one. But you sure as hell smelt like one. It was the magic ingredient which park poseurs thought would transform them into stylish sportsmen.

Today it is cycling shorts, the athletic equivalent of GTi badges and go-faster stripes. Skin-tight Lycra leggings have become as ubiquitous on the playing fields of England as orange cones on the motorways.

Admittedly they may have helped Linford Christie shave a millisecond or two off his personal best. But not everyone is Linford Christie. And contour-hugging cycling shorts can cruelly expose anyone whose performance falls an inch or two short of an all-comers' record. You need a full kitbag to get away with this particular garb.

That might explain why so many men wear their cycling shorts *under* their regular strip.

Of course, they will never admit that they are wearing them in the vain hope it will improve their game. They will try to convince you it is either to nurse a hamstring or prevent groin strain. Don't believe a word. The only groin strain they are likely to suffer is when they are trying to put the damn things on.

Inevitably, cycling shorts have followed shell suits and running shoes out of the locker room and onto the streets. And, equally inevitably, they are now being worn in public by the very people who should never be *allowed* to wear them.

The hideously fat squeeze into cycling shorts in the absurd delusion that they will somehow look thin. Instead they look like the Michelin Man. The anorexic look even worse, resembling returnees from the River Kwai.

We are not fooled. We know the last bike they rode was built by Moulton and had stabilisers and a basket over the handlebars. And, frankly, we don't give a monkeys.

Richard Littlejohn is a Sun columnist.

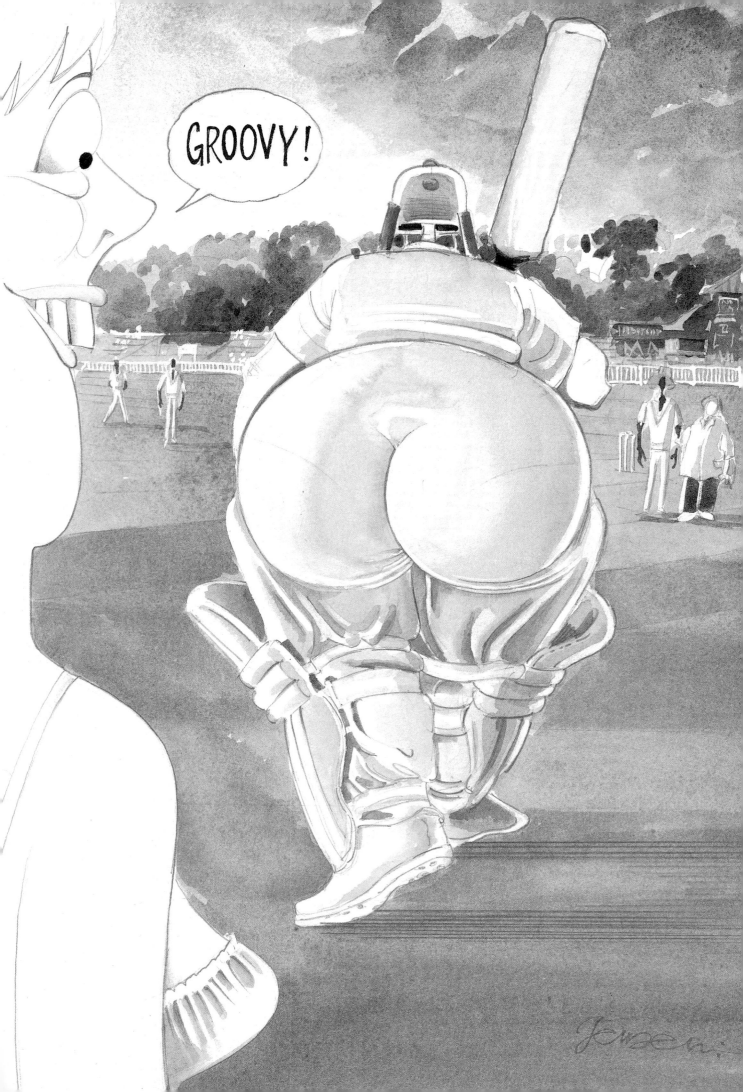

Well padded

Why do Test stars need big bottoms?

Say what you like about England's cricket team – and most people say things like 'they're not very good, are they?' Or, if you're my girlfriend, 'Phwoarr! that Mark Ramprakash is a bit of all right, isn't he?' – but one thing they don't lack is bottom. I mean, just compare the West Indies' fastest bowler, Curtley Ambrose, and England's swiftest operative, David Lawrence. Ambrose is slender, lithe, athletic. Lawrence waddles along as though there's something rather nasty in his trousers. And indeed there is. An enormous bottom.

England, of course, have always been well endowed in the posterior department. Mike Gatting has a whopper. Graham Gooch is not what you might call underequipped. And Ian Botham's is about as big a bottom as you can get without falling over.

'So what?' you may ask, or possibly, 'How much has he had to drink?' But as I shall prove in my forthcoming book *Choice Cheeks: Test Selection and The Importance of Huge Bottoms 1960 – 1991*, the dimension of your *derrière* has long been of vital importance when it comes to playing Test matches.

How has Lamb managed to play 75 Test matches with an average of only 35, when Derek Randall played just 47, and was usually put in at number two because no one else wanted to go there? Because Randall has barely no buttocks to speak of, while Allan Lamb, though born and bred in South Africa, is about as English as they come in the hindquarters department.

Why, similarly, did Phil Edmonds play so many fewer Tests than his Middlesex spin-twin John Emburey? Because Emburey was so much better a bowler? Because Edmonds didn't 'get on' with Mike Brearley? Just take a gander at their trouser padding before you come to any conclusions.

Of course, it could be said that a large bottom provides a vital second line of defence, especially against fast bowlers, and reduces by some margin the chances of being bowled around

your legs. Few bowlers appeal for 'arse before wicket', and even if the ball ricochets off into the hands of short leg, most fielding sides will recognise the unique elastic qualities of a huge set of haunches, and won't even appeal for a bat-bum catch. Colin Cowdrey, for one, was very rarely bowled around his legs – he knew where his wicket was, and he knew where his bum was as well.

But what's remarkable is that this strong belief in the powers of the bottom appears to be a purely English phenomenon. The West Indies, as you'll probably have noticed, have perfectly normal-sized bottoms. So do the Australians. And the Indians, when not being described by commentators as 'wristy', are always called 'slender-hipped', with just, I sense, the merest hint of derision. W G Grace, after all, had a gigantic set, and they never did him any harm.

PADDING UNDER HIS SHIRT AND TROUSERS? HE HASN'T GOT ROOM FOR IT!

Well, so theory has it. In real life, of course, there's no evidence whatsoever that possession of a comfortably proportioned behind improves your cricket in any way at all. Indeed, if anything, the reverse seems to be true.

Certainly, the rise and fall in Ian Botham's fortunes throughout the Eighties could be directly correlated to the rise and fall in his bottom. When he was slim, fit and youthful, he scored loads of runs, took millions of wickets and dyed his hair silly colours. But as the years and the pork pies took their toll, his form began to suffer, his whites visibly expanded, and before long he was bowling his now customary lollipops to all-comers and being wellied to every part of the ground.

It was a sad spectacle, and one entirely bottom-related.

But the selectors have their traditions (such as the one that states that new batsmen should only be picked just after they have lost all form and got out to the touring side for a pair), and they seem likely to stick with bottoms for the foreseeable future. Players like Ramprakash and Atherton, who look like normal human beings, will never be able to feel entirely secure in their side – not unless they start piling on the pounds, that is. For the time being, they'll only be able to keep their places by the tiring and time-consuming process of scoring runs.

Who, then, will be the next substantial candidates for preferment to England colours? Certainly, if you're looking for a shock selection for this winter's World Cup squad, you could do worse than Warwickshire's doughty opening batsman Andy Moles. Against him is his record – huge numbers of runs against everyone, and a career average over 40. In his favour, however, is a noticeably substantial bottom. This is a man for whom diets are merely a bad dream. Just the man, I'd say, to open the batting for England... 🦔

This Is Spinal Tap was the cult film that sent up heavy metal music. But, says ANDY BOOT, the truth about metal turns out to be even more ridiculous than the fiction

The Spinal countdown

The film *This Is Spinal Tap* has been hailed as the best rock spoof of all time. Since its release nearly ten years ago *Tap* has become an enduring cult. The film charts the downward spiral of ageing heavy metal band Spinal Tap and their 1982 American tour. The band lurch from one disaster to another under the watchful eye of documentary – 'rockumentary, if you will' – maker Marti de Bergi. Their new album – *Sniff The Glove* – flops disastrously. One of them is apprehended when the foil-wrapped cucumber he has secreted in his trousers sets off an airport security device. They order a gigantic Stonehenge stage set, only to be given scenery that is 18 inches high.

Any sensible person would conclude that this is an outrageous spoof that has nothing at all to do with the reality of life on the rock road. After all, more than 20 years after Led Zeppelin and Vanilla Fudge first turned their amplifiers up beyond the pain barrier, heavy metal remains a monstrous, multi-national industry. Its long-haired, acne-scarred adherents are as fanatical now as speir predecessors ever were. Whole generations are united by the guilty secret that they once bought a record by Emerson, Lake and Palmer, or played air guitar to the sound of 'Smoke On The Water'. Could they ever have devoted themselves to the cult of metal if it was really as ridiculous a. Spinal Tap suggests?

You betcha. For not only does Tap turn out to be chillingly accurate, many real-life rock bands have even claimed to be the inspiration for the film. Harry Shearer, who plays Tap's bas: player in the film, accompanied Bradford-based metal-basher Saxon on the road for part of a US tour in 1980. Aerosmith': Steve Tyler is reputed to refuse to watch the film on the ground: that it's based on his band. And UK veterans Uriah Heep have also put forward their case. Certainly, Heep are bad enough to be Tap. A *Rolling Stone* journalist once said of them, 'If thi band are successful, I'll kill myself.'

Until now, these suggestions have been little more than pur speculation. But, as our exclusive survey (below) reveals, Spina Tap turns out to have been a straightforward, scrupulously researched look at a musical genre which brings new depths o meaning to the word 'ludicrous'. Let's start with…

The Tap logo The lettering the band use for their name, i its use of metallic type and the lightning slash 'S', is reminiscen of several bands, most notably US rockers Kiss and English sta

Tapping a vein

Tufnell dreams of working in a haberdashery store. This is a spooky premonition of the fate that was to befall Saxon, the retired members of which now run – *inter alia* – a stripped-pine warehouse and a chain of ladies' hairdressers.

The gnomic, moustachioed bass player **Derek Smalls** is an uncanny double of Deep Purple's Jon Lord. It is his Bacofoil-encrusted trouser-stiffener that causes such airport mayhem. This codpiece fetishism is all-too common in rock. Stephen Piercey of Ratt was even photographed stuffing rolled up sweat socks down his spandex strides. Blame Elvis Presley, who started it all with a length of hosepipe.

Tap do have a habit of losing drummers. One died in 'a bizarre gardening accident', another 'choked on someone else's vomit', and **Mick Shrimpton** spontaneously combusts at the end of the movie. Uriah Heep have gone through enough drummers to start an employment exchange, and Led Zeppelin drummer John Bonham did choke on vomit – alas it was his own.

Stage designs The band's stage show – especially the model of Stonehenge that ends up 18 inches not 18 feet high – is strongly reminiscent of Black Sabbath. They too suffered problems of scale with their set – but in the opposite direction. Having spent a fortune on a gigantic pseudo-Stonehenge, they set out on a tour of America, only to find that their backdrop was too big to fit into any auditoria. Tap's use of dwarves as onstage dancers recalls the ex-'Sab' Ozzy Osbourne, the celebrated bat-biter. Mr Osbourne, however, used to suspend his little people from the scenery. Finally, those beard-laden bards ZZ Top once toured with a stage set the shape of Texas, complete with its own menagerie of local species. This stopped when the animals began to eat each mid-gig.

The manager Ian Faith is a pukka Englishman and the spitting image of Alan Niven (son of David), manager of US rockers Great White and Guns 'n' Roses. His habit of carrying a cricket bat ('sometimes in rock 'n' roll it helps to have a good solid piece of wood in your hands') echoes the strong-arm tactics of Led Zeppelin manager Peter Grant, who wielded a golf club, and legendary Sab boss and hard man Don Arden.

Album covers Ian has a lot of trouble over the sleeve of Tap's *Smell The Glove* album with Polymer record company (whose head, Sir Denis Eton-Hogg, suggests ex-Decca head Sir Edward Lewis). The original design has a greased naked woman on a leash smelling a gloved hand. Such sexism is typically meta-lesque. One Ted Nugent album had a nude woman in a boxing-ring. The title? *If You Can't Lick 'Em, Lick 'Em.*

Few record-sleeves, however, can compete with the sheer tastelessness of the debut album by a short-lived Seventies band called Boxer. It featured a semi-naked woman. She was spread-eagled across the cover. A large, boxing glove-clad fist could be seen travelling north between her legs. ☛

*Left: Tap's leopardskin-laden fretster Nigel Tufnell in satirical full-throttle axe posture
Above: The real stuff – Saxon singer Byf Bifford and strumming sidekick. Did their antics inspire Tap?
Right: disaster-prone Spinal Tap's 1982 line-up*

...warts Black Sabbath. The absurd use of umlauts when they're not required also brings to mind the solecisms of Blue Oyster Cült and Motley Crüe.

The band members Pretentious lead singer **David St Hubbins**, with his blonde coiffure, is a dead ringer for Moody Blue Justin Hayward. The silly name is derived from one Derek St Holmes, an ex-Ted Nugent singer in the Seventies, who later formed his own Whitford St Holmes outfit of which not a lot was ever heard.

David's desire to record his acoustic songs with the London Philharmonic was actually achieved by Mr Hayward, although his album disappeared without trace. Deep Purple teamed up with the London Philharmonic for a 'Concerto for Group and Orchestra'. The Phil have felt little need to revive this ground-breaking opus for the benefit of the nation's concert-goers.

Guitarist **Nigel Tufnell** has similar classical ambitions. We see him composing at his piano and he explains, 'I'm influenced by Mozart and Bach – it's sort of Mach'. He then reveals the piece is called 'Lick My Love Pump' – a similar theme to Kiss's 'Rocket Ride', a sensitive ode to riding their pocket rockets.

🐍 Tapping a vein

Lyrics Tap's lyrics are actually too witty to be mistaken for the output of most metal bands. The metaphorical imagery of 'Sex Farm' ('Working my pitchfork/Tossing your hay') and 'Big Bottoms' ('The looser the waistband/The deeper the quicksand', and 'My baby fits me like a flesh tuxedo/I want to sink her with my pink torpedo') are far too bright and imaginative for the likes of Heep: 'I was only 17/I fell in love with a gypsy queen/Her father took me to a shack/And put a whip across my back'. But AC/DC recorded a number called 'Sink the Pink' and Aerosmith's 'F.I.N.E.' has the memorable line, 'I haven't made love for 25 weeks/I tell you she's so tight her loving squeaks.'

Instruments Nigel Tufnell delights in showing his guitar collection to de Bergi (Steve Howe of Yes collected guitars in this way), and shows him the amp on which all the switches are set on 11, because: 'When you're all the way up, where can you go? This is one louder than ten'. US band Manowar made the single 'All Men Play On Ten' and Deep Purple are in the *Guinness Book Of Records* for being the loudest band of all time. Some modern manufacturers have taken the Tufnell principle a stage further: their amplifiers go up to 20.

Backstage mishaps Nigel complains about the food at one gig: the meat in his sandwiches is round but the bread is square. It is explained that the meat can be folded to fit the bread more neatly but Nigel remains unconvinced. This incident was lifted, without exaggeration, from a similar nutritional mishap which befell Saxon bassist Steve Dawson backstage at a concert in America. Nor is food the only problem area. While playing the Xanadu Star Theatre in Cleveland, Tap are unable to find the stage door. This actually happened to Dave Stewart of Brit rockers Egg. The band waited on stage at Newport while he blundered around, having emerged from the toilet and become hopelessly lost.

The girlfriend Janine (a perfect choice of name) is David's *amour*. She tries to take over the management of the band, a move that suggests Aerosmith, whose song 'Sweet Emotion' is based on guitarist Joe Perry's outspoken wife.

Above: Tap's July 1967 performance of 'Listen to the Flower People' on the Jamboree Bop show. Note that Tap's drummer was then Eric 'Stumpy Joe' Childs
Below: Eeriely Tapesque heavy rockers Uriah Heep

hour strummathons. One band, Mountain, actually released a live album of which three and a half sides consisted of one song.

Reunion Tap are, of course, saved by the return of Nigel after 'Sex Farm' is a hit in Japan. Bad Company and Deep Purple have re-formed in recent years, and Japan, whose teenagers lap up metal, has kept many a career going after Occidental record buyers have lost interest. Even Saxon recently re-formed when a surprise revival in Germany led to cash-laden concert offers. Many observers feel that this alone is a powerful argument against European unity.

Left: Tap bassist Derek Smalls has problems with his foil-wrapped cucumber at customs. Right: those Barnsley power chorders Saxon relax with spookily Tap-style taste, restraint and panache

Bust-ups One result of Janine taking over the management of the band is Nigel's onstage walkout. In the last days of Deep Purple (pre-reformation, of course), Ritchie Blackmore and drummer Ian Paice often had to be restrained from throttling each other. David Byron of Uriah Heep was sacked after careering head first into the mike stand in front of 20,000 screaming Americans. Mistaking their cheers for jeers, he promptly told them to 'f*** off' before storming offstage.

Nigel actually storms off during a gig at an airforce base where his radio-miked guitar picks up air traffic control messages. The Hammersmith Odeon is notoriously bad for radio mike users – Angus Young of AC/DC once found his entire solo guitar spot consisting of mini-cab messages.

Concert disasters Without Nigel the band are unable to do a full set, so they resort to 'Jazz Odyssey', a 'free-form jazz excursion'. Shades here of Hawkwind's mammoth jamming sessions and the Grateful Dead's legendary four

Who is the real Tap? It is a tie between Saxon and Uriah Heep, but Heep probably clinch it if you look at the band's eeriely Tapesque names: David Byron, Mick Box, Gary Thain, Lee Kerslake and Ken Hensley.

Spinal Tap made a recent appearance as guests of honour at *R.I.P.* magazine's birthday party. And there is also a rumour that a sequel to the film will be made, picking up where the first left off: the band's Japan tour. So don't throw out those spandex pants just yet. 🐍

Additional research by Raw's Paul 'Chesney' Rees.

ALBERT

'Bang go his chances of man of the match'

'*Sometimes I feel he over-disciplines his dog*'

'He was a gentleman to the core'

'Bad news from my dentist. I've got to have 127 fillings'

How to be a has-been...
EAST BLOC CHIEF

The hey day

You're the Marxist with the mostest, the leading Leninist of your limping people's republic. 'Glory, glory, glory' shout 'spontaneous demonstrations'. But it's all downhill from here...

The slippery slope

1. The shops are half empty. You announce an 'advance from socialism to communism'. The shops...
2. Become completely empty. You erect an 'anti-fascist protection barrier'. All the guns...
3. Point the wrong way. 'Political prisoners have been released,' you tell Amnesty International.
4. 'To mental homes,' they suggest. You are re-elected 'Hero of the People'. The people...rebel.

The futile gesture

5. You promise reforms like the closure of your hunting estate. But the politburo...
6. Are hunting for your head. You resign for 'health reasons'. 'Yes,' says your successor, 'a firing squad is unhealthy.'
7. 'He's an unscrupulous demagogue,' you retort. 'Unscrupulous, but elected,' says the *Independent on Sunday*'s Neal Ascherson. You attempt entry to a Russian-run hospital.
8. 'Any hard cash?' asks Gorbachev. You contact the Cuban embassy.
9. 'No way, José,' replies Fidel Castro. You make a comeback...

The killer blow

10. In the dock. Your sentence is the 'ultimate punishment' – release into the community.

The cruel twist

After your death, from your country's polluted atmosphere, the new 'market republic' lurches from inflation to unemployment, deficit and chaos. 'Under him, we weren't like Britain,' say your former subjects.

MIKE CONWAY

'Now will you use a deodorant?'

Mixed Blessings

♪ OH, THE GRAND OLD DUCHESS OF YORK, SHE HAD 10,000 MEN... ♪

'Shouldn't that be powdered?'

An on-air vasectomy, a dad at 92, and a street-walking Cleopatra. We select the best of those desperate space-fillers that pass for news when it's the...

silly season

When no news is, er, no news

SHORT TERM

Inmates at Dartmoor Prison have switched to making boxer shorts and chef's hats after the Post Office stopped ordering mailbags.

Daily Mail, 6 August

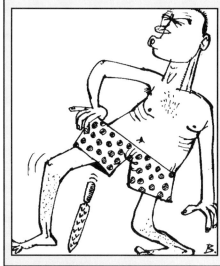

999! HE'S SCOFFED MY APPLE CRUMBLE

Hungry Peter McCormack looked a right pudding when wife Pam shopped him to police for scoffing her apple crumble.

Pamela, 35, called the law and told them to give 53-year-old Peter his just desserts. She stormed out of the house near Dundee, Scotland and walked 1½ miles to the local police station. When officers drove her back, Peter locked the doors until the PCs left.

Sun, 27 July

DJ HAS SNIP LIVE ON RADIO

Talk-show host Dan Patrick had a vasectomy yesterday live on the radio. 'If I can do this guys, you can,' he told listeners to station KSEV-AM in Houston, Texas.

Afterwards, Dan declared, 'I feel fine.' But the surgery wasn't completely painless. At one stage Dan yelped: 'Ow! What are you looking for down there, doc?'

Sun, 8 August

'GODDESS' SLEPT WITH 2,000 MEN

A woman from Santa Clarita, California, who claims spiritual lineage from Cleopatra and said she offered sexual intercourse as a 'purification ritual' (the going 'sacrifice' was £60), has been jailed for a year for prostitution.

Mary Tracy, 48, who said she slept with more than 2,000 men, claims her First Amendment right to freedom of religion is being violated.

Daily Telegraph, 31 July

Kiss my asp!

DEAR ANYONE, PLEASE TELL US WHERE WE HAD A GREAT TIME!

Absent-minded Ray and Joyce Elkeron had a great time on a day trip – but haven't got a clue where they went! Now they have put an ad in the paper asking people if they recognise their description of the beauty spot.

It was only after they got home and planned a return trip that they realised they had no idea where they had been.

Sun, 5 July

PUSHKIN PORNOGRAPHY

A Dutch Magazine, *De Tweede Ronde* yesterday published what it claimed to be a pornographic poem by the young Russian writer, Pushkin. The poem tells how an Orthodox priest is struck by impotence while visiting a brothel, but cured by the ghost of an 18th-century writer.

Guardian, 6 August

BRIT WAS PAINTED WITH TAR

A drunken prank nearly killed holiday-maker Simon Walker when he was daubed from head to foot with tar. Friend Stephen Parkinson painted him for a joke after they had both boozed the night away at a disco.

Simon passed out and Stephen, 21, thought it would be a laugh if he woke up 'looking like a black man'.

Sun, 5 August

DID FLO CARRY A LAMP FOR THE GENERAL'S AUNT?

According to one Major General Frank Richardson, Nurse Nightingale was gay. And not in the genteel sense. She was apparently, to use a fitting though most unfortunate military phrase, as camp as a row of tents.

'Florence Nightingale was a rip-roaring old lesbian who tried to have an affair with my great aunt. But my great aunt wasn't like that,' he said.

Sunday Express, 28 July

TELLY NUDES FLASH

Late-night TV viewers were stunned when a hard-core porn film interrupted their show. The clip, 30 seconds long, showed a couple 'in a number of positions'.

A spokesman for the TV3 Channel in Wellington, New Zealand, said several viewers complained. The station has ordered an inquiry.

Sun, 6 August

LES A DAD AT 92

Old Rascal Leslie Colley has become a dad for the sixth time – at the age of 92.

'The hardest thing was breaking the news to my 71-year-old son, Norman,' said Les. Norman, who has 12 great grandchildren himself, admitted he was shocked: 'My wife and I are on walking sticks. My father's never been afraid of hard work. But I bet this is the hardest job he's done for a while.'

Sun, 2 August

DUGGIE HOT FOOTS IT FROM PAIN IN SPAIN

Stand-up comedian Duggie Nichols had to hot-foot it from Spain after he burnt his feet in the midday sun – and couldn't stand up. Two days later after performing his act sitting down, he gave up his 'big break' tour in agony and returned to Dudley in the West Midlands. 'I tried to do the act Dave Allen-style sitting on a stool, but the feet were giving me such gyp I had to pack it in.'

Sun, 29 July

CALL MY ROAD GAY? NO WAY, SAYS RAY

Builder Ray Mitchard is going up the wall over plans to call one of his new roads 'Gay'. Company boss Ray was horrified when the local council came up with a pansy-sounding nameplate to honour their past chairman Horace Gay. Now Ray has demanded that councillors rename Horace Gay Gardens, telling them: 'Gay? No way.'

Sun, 5 July

(Silly Season research by Giles Wilson)

MIX'N'MATCH THESE TALL TALES TO WRITE YOUR OWN SILLY STORY

HAVE-A-GO hero Fred Tufnel	got into a teething rage	his choppers fell *IN THE LOO!*
STUNNING blonde glamour model Veronica Forward, 19,	found her saucy underwear dissolves in rain	her trickster fella switches them *FOR RICE PAPER!*
PLUCKY Preston pensioner Alfie Smegg, 103, **HAS**	unleashed his rottweiler, Tyson, onto a passing postie **BECAUSE**	he refused to deliver his *OAP GIRO CHEQUE!*
HUNKY Radio 1 medallion man DJ Diddy Syrup, 38,	been left foaming mad at his local laundrette	his knickers got in a twist and *JAMMED THE MACHINE!*
HEARTBREAK tug-of-love tot Jamie Nipper, 18 months,	driven his mum, Pat, 30, wild with rage	he put the family goldfish *IN THE MICROWAVE!*

'And now for Ian's team...'

'We're just good friends'

'Hello we're Jehovas party gatecrashers'

'Looks as though we're not the first team he's played for'

'That's him, he's the one who keeps ringing my doorbell'

'I bet you it's a toupé'

'Mmm…flatulence. I like that in a woman'

'Mmm…like the white tux!'

MANIC DEPRESSIVES SOCIETY

'You've got to laugh, haven't you?'

HÔPITAL

'Don't complain, I said. Leave it, I said. But oh no, not you…'

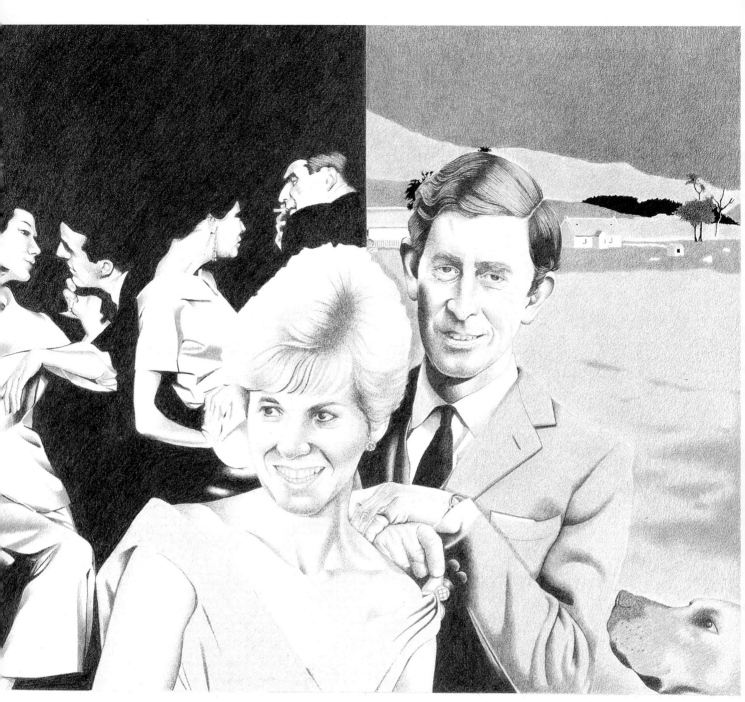

Charles and Diana
A *Punch* survey tribute

I t's over! The Prince and Princess of Wales might as well decide who gets custody of Cornwall and call it a day. Last week saw the clearest indication yet that the royal marriage is heading for serious trouble. There were no public rows, no frosty glances, it was much, much worse. Last week saw a 324-page full-colour Tenth Wedding Anniversary Special edition of *Hello!* magazine, 'illustrating every aspect of the magnificent wedding celebrations of the Prince and Princess, plus a year-by-year account of their lives.'

Jane Seymour, Donald and Ivana Trump, Andrew Lloyd Webber and Sarah Brightman, Bill Wyman and Mandy Smith have all spoken to *Hello!* about their fairy-tale marriages. And

the first thing that you notice about all these marriages is that they're all over.

But all is not lost for the Waleses. The Princess of Wales announced recently that she suffered from back pain. At last, royalists noted, the couple have something in common.

There is just the wildest chance that the Prince and Princess don't hurl saucepans at each other, but skip about hand-in-hand gazing into each other's eyes with Harry Nilsson's 'Without You' playing in the background. Perhaps they don't quarrel at all. Perhaps the papers just make it up.

It doesn't seem very likely, does it? So here is a headline-by-headline guide to the royal marriage as seen by Fleet Street.

The Royal Marriage-o-Matic

1981　1982　1983

Fairy-tale marriage

The *Hello!* magazine fantasy of the royal marriage

The real thing

In love

That day, that magic, that smooch. The fairy tale begins

Happy

William born and all's well

'The vulnerable, nervous young bride who emerged from St Paul's Cathedral on 29 July, 1981, in a cloud of apprehension and silk taffeta, is now a poised public personality and a radiant young mother. Her husband has been transformed from a boisterous bachelor into a mature monarch-to-be, a caring father and supportive husband,' gushes the *Daily Express*.

They travel to New Zealand, Australia and Canada and reach a 'new height of happiness'.

World tours and still in touch

Separate tables

'The age gap just does not matter,' Diana says on the day their engagement is announced. Charles jokes: 'Diana will certainly keep me young.'

At the wedding, the princess brushes her tears of joy away...it is a touching, emotional scene, despite the fact that she's forgotten to iron her dress.

Dancing Di lovingly clings to her handsome prince

Separate beds

'Neither of us will ever forget the atmosphere,' says an emotional Charles. 'It was electric, I felt, and I know my wife agrees. The noise outside my bedroom window (in Buckingham Palace) was almost unbelievable.'

'So in love and not afraid to show it,' says the *Daily Express*.

Despite Di's suspected anorexia after Prince William's birth, the couple are still in good spirits. Charles often shows his concern for her in public.

Separate lives

During the royal honeymoon, on the Royal Yacht, the Royal Marines band plays 'Romeo and Juliet'.

'That moonlit night, Charles and Diana set up a barbecue for two on their lovely, lonely beach,' says the *Daily Express*.

On Remembrance Day Di turns up five minutes later than the Queen – a major breach of protocol.

All smiles but have our cuddly crown-meisters got too much on their plate?

The Royal Marriage-o

The next four years of the *Hello!* magazine fantasy

Fairy-tale marriage

In love

Happy

Separate Tables

Separate beds

Separate lives

A double shock for the royal couple. Diana is stunned to find herself so ill with morning sickness. And with the arrival of Harry, Charles confesses that he finds fatherhood 'a grown-up thing…rather a shock to the system.'

A leading Chinese horoscope expert generously offers his own forecast that 'the bliss' is ephemeral. 'Rats and Buffalos are very attracted to each other, but the happiness does not last.'

Charles confides to friends that his marital problems are 'minor ones thrown up by their age difference.' 'Princess Diana likes discos and he doesn't,' says an insider.

Lady Dale Tryon, once banished by Diana from their circle of intimate friends, is spotted driving Charles's car around Balmoral.

The couple disagree over how to bring up their sons. He wants old-style nannies to keep the boys in their place; she wants to be more involved with their education – like winning the Sports Day mothers' race.

Charles is pals again with Kanga

The Prince and Princess of Wales apparently reach 'a special agreement' to keep their five-year marriage from 'floundering'. She is said to be celebrating her new-found freedom after the Prince and his Princess 'agreed to go their separate ways'.

Charles takes early lead in frantic crown jewels search

Agree to differ pact

At a marquee party 'Saucy Di' is said to have 'pecked Superman lookalike Philip Dunne on the cheek and ran her fingers through the City banker's dark hair.' Not to be outdone Charles and old hunting pal Anna 'Whiplash' Wallace are spotted 'whispering sweet nothings outside.'

'Charles and Di barely speak to each other,' a Royal insider says. 'They are thought to have seen each other only once in the past month.'

Diana is said to be 'dating a tall, dark, handsome stranger' behind Charles's back – even kissing him (on both cheeks) in the street outside the home of one of the Prince's most trusted pals, TV mogul David Frost. The Princess's detective is said to be so embarrassed by the scene that he walked away and sat in the car.

Charles and Diana are apart again after a reunion lasting only 21 hours. But later he puts his arm around her saying 'darling' loud enough for the Press to hear.

Princess Diana makes a determined attempt to show the world that all is right with her marriage.

Doomed! Press go mad

Would-be thronester Di in beefcake lusting scenario

Matic, continued

1988	1989	1990	1991

Ten years on and *Hello!* know this wonderful couple are still as devoted as ever!

The Princess's father, Earl Spencer, dismisses rumours of marriage problems as 'trivial'. She's still 'very much in love with Prince Charles. Charles and Diana have their rows, What couple doesn't?'

Maria Molett of the Marriage and Counselling Centre says, 'If this was an ordinary couple coming to see me I frankly don't think they'd have a very good chance of making it.'

Fleet Street editors are called to Buckingham Palace and kindly asked to rein back on the intrusive attention to protect Diana's mental health.

'Now the name "Diana" rarely crosses his lips,' reports the *People*.

Editors rapped

'Prince Charles stepped out at the society wedding of the year and, once again, Princess Diana was nowhere in sight,' says the *Sunday Express*.

Diana undergoes marriage guidance training twice and expresses a desire to be a counsellor. Or so claims a friend who says that Diana is 'concerned about married couples and their awfulness to each other'.

'Is it? Could it...? I know her – Selina Scott!'

Holidays apart

'I can't wait to get hold of your mallet,' trills Di

United by Charles's polo hell

When the Prince is asked if he is in love, he mutters: 'Whatever love is.'

'One in three Britons believes that Princess Diana no longer loves Prince Charles,' says *Today*.

One aide says: 'He still lives the life of a bachelor. He wants the best of both worlds. He has made no compromise for Diana's youth or her interests,' says the *Sun*.

The title of Di's favourite singer Phil Collins's 'Separate Lives' 'comes closest to describing her marriage,' says the *Star*.

'Sex is definitely a problem here, so is discoing, wining, dining and sport. Indeed, anything to do with physical activity is biorhythmically out for this couple,' says the *Express*.

Charles and Diana's ten-year marriage is stone dead,' proclaims *People* magazine.

'This is no fairy-tale royal marriage, it never was. But as they approach their tenth anniversary, Charles and Diana have a special kind of new and warm relationship. They still make each other laugh. This is no great love affair, but it is working,' says the *Daily Express*.

Diana tells a friend: 'People jump to conclusions so easily. It is so easy to judge my marriage, but they don't understand. I am never going to get divorced and that's that.'

In the waiting-room at Relate? And no Punch to read

'Sometimes he takes things too seriously. I help him relax,' she says.

Di snubs Charles's birthday party offer and heads for the Savoy. He stays home to live it up with a church restoration committee. 🐾

'Uh oh...'

Robert Winter · Christopher Wright · John Wright · Thomas Percy · Guido Fawkes · Robert Catesby · Thomas Winter · Bates

Westminster eight retrial shocker
Baker to review Bomb Plot Case

HOME SECRETARY Kenneth Baker has announced that he is to review the convictions of the so-called Westminster Eight, sentenced to death 386 years ago for conspiring to blow up the Houses of Parliament.

Baker has ordered a retrial after doubts were cast on forensic evidence offered by the Weft Midlandf Feriouf Crimef Fquad. One of the eight, Mr Guy Fawkes, was executed, dragged through the streets, then cut into four pieces while in custody. A police spokesman claimed this was 'an accident'.

VATICAN ACCENTS

Fawkes, 35, was arrested after he was spotted wearing a 'silly pointy hat and a beard'. Another conspirator, Bob 'The Nutter' Catesby, 32, was later rounded up for having a 'beard' and a 'pointy hat'. The eight men all spoke with Vatican accents.

According to contemporary reports by Sir John of Cole, 'the police somply wanted a onvoction. They jost arrested the forst eeyt non with beards and pointy hats they saw.'

It was around 8pm on the evening of 5 November, 1605 – with most of the county celebrating Bonfire Night – that a vigi-

by Nick Davies
Ohio correspondent

lant security man at the House of Commons noticed the sophisticated device – 50 large barrels of gunpowder and a lighted match.

The bomb disposal squad was called and swiftly disabled the device by sweeping away the fuse with a broom.

Police claimed that the plotters had been sold gunpowder by the Spanish government. Detectives later found three empty bottles of San Miguel in Fawkes's house.

ANNE BOLEYN

Home Office officials are also investigating claims that other convictions may be unsafe, notably that of Anne Boleyn. Her conviction is in question after new doubts on the admissibility of the prosecution case that 'Henry fancies Jane Seymour'.

NHS Charter: those ten points

1 Wards being visited by the Princess of Wales will contain the genuinely sick.

2 Nurses should be able to carry out their normal duties without patients saying, 'It's not like *Casualty*, is it?'

3 Cabinet ministers will be able to use private medicine without having to explain themselves to Brian Redhead afterwards. (No change here.)

4 Doctors will have the right to drive expensive cars while moaning about how badly they are paid. (No change here either.)

5 Doctors should be able to go to dinner parties without people asking them to take a look at their knee/lump in their back/athlete's foot.

6 When doctors ask patients how they are, they need no longer reply 'Very well thank you, doctor' and feel embarrassed.

7 Doctor David Owen will go back to having a proper job as a GP.

8 Nurses will not necessarily be compelled to marry policemen.

9 Gazza will get his knee fixed.

10 Then maybe at last he'll bugger off to Italy so that we can all settle down and forget all about him.

PhotoSynthesis in conference *Caplin & Jeremy*

The libel

Have you suffered an insult at the hands of a hack? RICHARD LITTLEJOHN says: 'Relax! You too can sue for fun and profit.'

It has been a most profitable year for Mr George Graham, manager of Arsenal Football Club. Not only did he win the Football League Championship, he also got a result in the High Court. The *Daily Mirror* paid Mr Graham 'substantial' damages over a critical article which foolishly questioned his popularity at the club.

Perhaps the *Mirror* was distracted by the fact that Mr Graham's reputation as a disciplinarian has earned him the affectionate nickname of 'Gaddafi' amongst some of the fans. Those of us who regularly attend First Division football matches have of course heard him called a lot worse. Allegations are frequently made concerning his parentage, not to mention certain solitary sexual practices. Though to the best of my knowledge he has no legal means of instituting defamation proceedings against the vociferous habitués of The Shelf terracing, White Hart Lane.

Libel is all about reputation. If the *Mirror* case had made it into open court, Mr Graham would have had the task of persuading a jury that the article had brought odium, ridicule and contempt upon him.

A jury would have had to decide whether publication of the article had lowered Mr Graham's public esteem. The arguments would have been fascinating. Could anything, for instance, in the eyes of a 'right-thinking member of society', never mind those of the adoring North Bank, Highbury, have damaged the standing of a manager who has won two championships in three years?

Or would the opinion of Mr Graham held by supporters of Tottenham Hotspur FC be likely to change as a result of hearing that he is allegedly nicknamed after a barking raghead?

Whatever, the *Mirror* opted to settle out of court and Mr Graham is somewhere between £5,000 and £50,000 better off. That's what 'substantial' usually means in legal parlance. 'Very substantial' is normally over 50 grand. Most libel actions are settled before they get anywhere near a jury. Fewer than ten per cent ever see the inside of a courtroom. That is largely because of the horrendous cost of trials. As soon as you flag down Mr Rumpole the meter starts running like Ben Johnson on speed and by the time your journey through the highways of the defamation laws is complete, you will find you have been over the river and round the M25 a few times. The wheels of justice do not acknowledge the back doubles.

And, as Mr Anthony Mudd recently discovered to his expense (roughly £400,000's worth of award and costs) when sued by Teresa Gorman MP, libel is also a hazardous lottery. There are no fixed penalties. The size of any award is quite arbi-

NEWSPAPER FOR THE NINETIES

trary and depends on the mood of the jury. The outcome of a convoluted trial can be influenced by whether or not the foreman got his leg over that morning. Some of the amounts handed out to successful litigants have been the stuff of Pools wins.

The likes of Jeffrey Archer and Koo Stark caned the tabloids for hundreds of thousands, fuelled by a groundswell of public opinion that press excesses must be punished where it hurts. Meanwhile, tycoons such as the late Armand Hammer, who successfully sued both *Private Eye* and TV-am, discovered that the threat of litigation was enough to discourage publication of potentially hostile articles or books. For a while, libel damages rose into the stratosphere with the litigious Mrs Sonia Sutcliffe, wife of the Yorkshire Ripper, taking *Private Eye* for £600,000, causing editor Ian Hislop to famously remark that if this was justice he was a banana.

The Sutcliffe verdict was eventually reduced to £60,000 by agreement amid a backlash of concern that if awards continued to escalate like game show prizes, Bob Monkhouse would be in

belt

ne to become Master of the Rolls. Even Peter Carter-Ruck –
ritain's foremost libel lawyer (see page 24) – has written that
ney cast doubt over the current nature of jury system.

Until then, Mrs Ripper had enjoyed unbroken success in a
series of libel actions. The wheels on her particular gravy
train only came off this year with a successful defence by
ne *News of the World* that landed her with frightening costs.
nce judgment went against Sonia, Fleet Street lawyers report a
aling off in writs. Persistent litigants who'd fire off a solicitor's
tter every time their name appeared in print are thinking twice.

Encouraged by the *News of the World*'s success, more news-
aper lawyers now fancy their chances in front of a jury where
ney feel an article, however defamatory, is either true or can be
stified as fair comment.

Peter Carter-Ruck is reported to advise his clients not to go to
urt unless they have an 85 per cent chance of winning. Faced
ith absurd costs of a full defence, even a successful one, many

newspaper lawyers still prefer a quiet life with the emphasis on
damage limitation.

Commercial considerations are a substantial determining factor. It is invariably cheaper to give a complainant a small drink
to go away, without prejudice of course, than to pursue the matter to the bitter end. Payments of between £1,000 and £5,000
are commonplace in borderline cases. Quite often no apology is
ever published. A number of determined folk have earned well
out of this hush money over the years. Newspaper lawyers are
understandably reluctant to say just how much is paid out in
this way, for fear of encouraging copycat actions but it must run
into hundreds of thousands, maybe millions, a year.

There are some names which always set alarm bells ringing
in newspaper legal departments. They include the aforementioned Miss Stark, Chelsea FC chairman Ken Bates, film director
Michael Winner, composer Andrew Lloyd Webber and Captain
Robert Maxwell, who are said to scour the public prints for
alleged defamatory references to themselves. If they find any-

🐾 Sue and cry

thing promising, notice of action lands on the newspaper lawyer's desk before the offending newsprint is old enough to wrap cod and chips in.

There has also, of late, been a trend among journalists and politicians to sue for libel. Neil Kinnock, a man with a ready jibe within the privileged confines of the House of Commons, and who has been known to settle other disagreements with his fists, at the last count had seven writs outstanding against Fleet Street. The late-night phone call from members of the Labour hierarchy threatening legal action after the first editions drop has become a common and tiresome feature of the political correspondent's life. Fortunately, most politicians and journalists who sue end up looking ridiculous, even if they win.

Edwina Currie was awarded a derisory £5,000 after complaining that an *Observer* film review likened her to a Charlotte Rampling character who sacrificed her family and committed murder in pursuit of her political career. If she hadn't gone to court, hardly anyone would have known about it.

Labour's Michael Meacher ended up with a bill for £200,000 costs after losing an action against the *Observer*'s Alan Watkins, who had accused him of covering up his middle-class origins to gain acceptance by the hairy-arsed sons of toil tendency. Derek Jameson spectacularly lost a libel action against the BBC and Andrew Neil got a paltry £1,000 when he sued rival editor Sir Peregrine Worsthorne over criticisms of his young, free and single lifestyle.

Left-wing journalists, particularly those who bleat loudest about the freedom of the Press, tend to be the most sensitive, as I discovered when I presented *What The Papers Say* and was forced to moderate criticisms of a litigious leftie hack by the programme's lawyers.

Funny, they never bother about preventing journalists from the unpopular Press ridiculing me. (Not that I give a monkey's, of course, as regular readers are well aware.) 'But you're on record as saying journalists should never sue,' they replied. True, true. But then I know a lot of dockers. I find them far more efficient at exacting recompense than men in gowns and wigs.

In Britain, the libel laws favour the rich and powerful. In the USA it is quite the reverse. The Americans take the healthy view that those who voluntarily dive headfirst into the cauldron of publicity and self-promotion have only themselves to blame if they suffer first-degree burns. Consequently, in a country where Joe Ordinary can expect to be awarded hundreds of millions of dollars compensation for breaking his nail opening a soft-drinks can, it is virtually impossible for any public figure to win damages for defamation. Mere inaccuracy is not enough. The key is in proving malice on the part of the writer.

Tom Selleck won an out-of-court settlement from the *Globe* after it claimed to have outed him as a homosexual and Liz Taylor won millions after a supermarket tabloid made allegations that were excessive even by the standards of her personal mythology. But they are the exceptions to the rule.

This may explain why writs are flooding into Britain from overseas, especially from Hollywood. Jack Nicholson is testifying in a case against the *News of the World*, Harrison Ford, Clint Eastwood, Sylvester Stallone and Arnold Schwarzenegger have sued or are in the process of suing other British publications. The other scam is to sue an American newspaper which circulates over here, however few the copies sold, under English law. The *National Enquirer* may yet live to regret launching over here. Can we look forward to Colonel Gaddafi instructing his lawyers to issue a writ against the *Daily Mirror* for comparing him with George Graham? 🐾

Where there's Ruck, there's bras

Former *Punch* legal adviser, **Peter Carter-Ruck** is the head of Britain's leading libel firm Peter Carter-Ruck and partners. He is to libel what Ollie Reed is to fisticuffs. He has represented Edwina Currie, Teresa Gorman, Winston Churchill (Jnr), Armand Hammer, Cecil Parkinson, the Bruges Group, Euro MP Lord Bethell, and Norman Lamont.

Gavel Row: meet thos

↑ See you in Rio

= Volume of settlements in £s

Note: Out-of-court settlements are difficult to confirm. Libel jackpot winners are often, oddly enough, shy of declaring their cash gains. Neil Kinnock's office, for one, is particularly reticent.

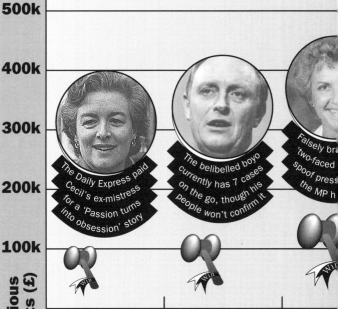

12m
6m
500k
400k
300k
200k
100k

Prodigious payouts (£)

The Daily Express paid Cecil's ex-mistress for a 'Passion turns into obsession' story

The belibelled boyo currently has 7 cases on the go, though his people won't confirm it

Falsely bra two-faced spoof press the MP h

Sarah Keays   **Neil Kinnock**   **Ter Gor**

He is not in favour of the US laws where all a publication need say is it published in 'good faith'. He says: 'In Britain, lawyers are not allowed to take a slice of the awards, unlike the US. It is possible, acting quickly, to settle cases in just half an hour [his record for a libel case], and this is the most amicable way to do things. But gold-diggers are a thing of the past, which is due to the expense of litigation. Libel, alas, is the province of the rich.'

In the past 20 years Mr Carter-Ruck has won an estimated £200,000 in damages from *Private Eye*. He is 77.

Top libel tips
Carter-Ruck's Golden Rules

1. Act quickly in filing that suit.
2. Only sue when there's 85 per cent chance of success.
3. Stress the terms of the complaint very precisely.
4. If defending, delay and wait for tempers to cool.
5. Keep calm, don't respond provocatively.
6. Always consider settling to save costs and time.
7. Always ask for an apology so it looks like you're not just after money.
8. If you just go for money, the other side will say they were prepared to apologise all along, but won't pay.
9. Beware of the expense; people of middle income and less can't afford to sue.
10. Political cases are dodgy; juries may have strong feelings. You never know whether you will get a 'South Kensington' or 'Brixton' jury.

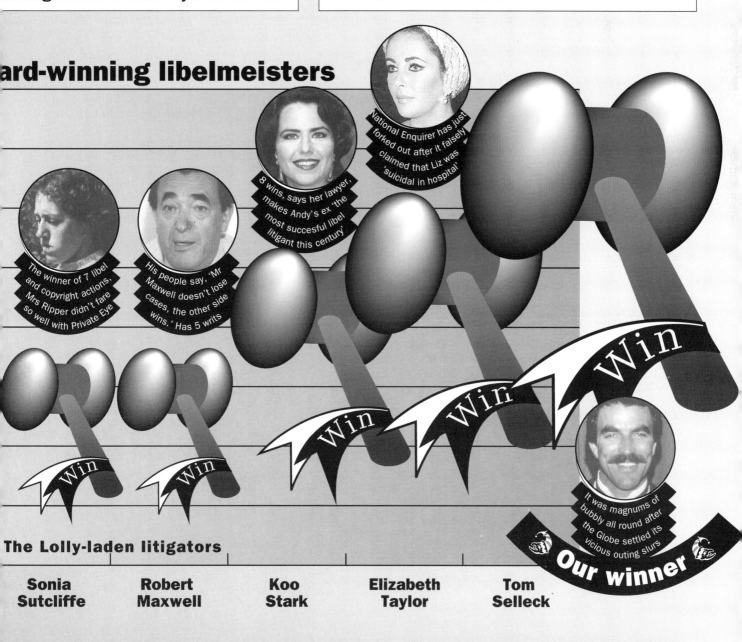

ard-winning libelmeisters

The winner of 7 libel and copyright actions, Mrs Ripper didn't fare so well with Private Eye

His people say, 'Mr Maxwell doesn't lose cases, the other side wins.' Has 5 writs

8 wins, says her lawyer, makes Andy's ex 'the most succesful libel litigant this century'

National Enquirer has just forked out after it falsely claimed that Liz was 'suicidal in hospital'

It was magnums of bubbly all round after the Globe settled its vicious outing slurs

Our winner

The Lolly-laden litigators

| Sonia Sutcliffe | Robert Maxwell | Koo Stark | Elizabeth Taylor | Tom Selleck |

McLachlan

SELLAFIELD DINNER & DANCE

WITH DANNY & the BLUE STARS

BLUE STARS

'I just hope we don't have the hokey-cokey this evening'

'I've not made up my mind about the new neighbours yet'

'It's no use, Yuko – we're hopelessly lost in this bonsai forest'

'Moscaow? Take the road to Yeltsinpol, turn left in the centre to Yeltsinsk, right at Yeltsinforsk, then the through road to Yeltsingrad…'

'Stubborn, eh?'

'Good morning – I am a Jehovah's Witness, fourth dan'

'You've been found guilty of a breathtaking fraud that cheated thousands of people. Is there any reason why I should not send you to prison for a very long time?'

'The shoe was repossessed so we're living in the box now'

The Coucho club

Psycho-analysts take all of August off. So by now their patients are feeling the strain. JOHN HIND and STEVEN MOSCO seek out alternative therapy

Posted in many parts of the country are stickers asking: 'Depressed? Call the I Care Prayer Help Line! We will listen, pray and help you 24 hours a day'. As insomniac consumer watch-dogs we telephoned all three numbers advertised, in search of spiritual and anti-suicidal solace – at 1am, 3.45am and 5am, two nights running. Alas, despite leaving all lines ringing for ten minutes, not one I-Carer picked up the receiver once. No holy hello, no paltry prayer, not a single sausage of sympathy on offer.

So who is going to help you?

Feeling in a helpful mood, we decided to investigate a variety of therapists advertised in the classified sections of popular journals. Posing as depressive, angst-ridden folk, we rang an assortment of problem practitioners in search of the cream of the professional carers. We told them we had a washing phobia (thus possessing 'a rather rough smell') and went on to get personal – personal about ourselves and personal about them.

It is on the telephone that therapists first woo their clients. And full marks must go to Conchita, the Brazilian 'Creative Psychotherapist Offering Individual Sessions' who had the most soothing voice on offer. 'Helloooo-o...My approach is more humanistic and Ju-ng-ian, it's more in terms of interpretation of body,' she charmed. Even the declaration 'I'm currently studying Jung and astrology...astrology is something we could use – where you were born for instance,' didn't detract from her lush terms. 'I don't charge for my first interview,' she announced, which made her even rarer. 'I don't have a Freudian approach – I would actually say "Good morning"'.

'Does my previous crush/counter-transference onto a female therapist bother you?'

'No.' She now turned sterner. 'Because our relationship will be entirely business-like.'

Spiritually mortified, we phoned the Gurdjieff Ouspensky Fellowship Of Friends Center (sic) in London, advertised as 'now accepting students for the inner evolution of man'. An American woman answered and explained that, in the Gurdjieff Ouspensky way, 'each person follows his/her own natural path within our system and becomes more of what he/she is.' Furthermore, she added that refreshments were on offer after each meeting. But what will evolution set a person back, financially? 'The first meetings are no-fee-paying. But after that, you see, Gurdjieff felt payment was a principle. That you pay for everything, that nothing is free and that you don't value the free...You pay slowly by giving up your unnecessary suffering.'

Do you have a free leaflet of information? 'We don't have any literature at all. Everything is acquired and felt by passing it on verbally...So should I put you on our list, then in a month we'll call you, and then you'll call us, and then we'll get back to you with the address?'

> '*I don't charge for my first interview,*' said Conchita. '*I don't have a Freudian approach. I would actually say: Good morning*'

Anxious, not least over time, we instead called The Alexander Centre, Bloomsbury, who were advertising 'The Alexander Technique'. They were more forthcoming with literature, but their enticements were a touch left-field: 'Are you standing up with your throat? Holding your shopping bag with your shoulders? Talking with your feet?' it quizzed. 'An overwhelming 80–90 per cent of the population are habitually indulging in such unlikely sounding methods of body use...and these cause their personal problems. The Alexander Technique is not supposed to be a therapy. It's a way of being, and undoing of bad habits to uncover the relaxed ease inbuilt in the 'action blueprint' we were all born with.' Jean, the lady taking our call, enthused: 'It makes you feel nice, the Alex technique, very nice!' Unfortunately, the next introductory lecture would set us back £35 a head, and was not for three weeks; three weeks in which we would have to go on walking with our collar-bones.

No worries, because phoning therapists can be a therapy in itself – at least if you can get through to them. Otherwise it exacerbates your symptoms beyond belief. Some therapists have receptionists, some have answerphones in the corner of their office. Sometimes, while they're with a 'patient', they'll pick up

"... And they say they won't be coming back till you've resolved this fear of washing"

the phone, most times they'll phone back (at their expense), other times they'll tell you to phone them back, usually at a time like '9.05pm' or '10.18am'. When you do this more often than not you'll get an answerphone message.

Therapists leave entertaining answerphone messages about 'unforeseen circumstances' and 'unfortunate availability'. One answerphone message (left by Dr Franklin Wenham) asked potential clients to please state on tape: 'whether you are interested in Primal Therapy or Foreign Languages.'

When we called one therapist in London, his five-year-old daughter answered the phone and, Daddy being out, she conversed with us for eight minutes in soothing tones, the motives

of which we knew were young and pure. Slightly more cynically – not least because it's reported that Sigmund Freud once battered the side of his couch and exclaimed to a patient: 'The trouble is, I am an old man and you do not think it worth your while to love me!' – we turned our attention to the eight prime-movers in the London listing-mag therapy ad-section. We wanted to turn the couches on them and cut to the caring quick. To know who they were, whether they had regular bowel-movements, whether they served coffee, and exactly how (financially) caring they really were.

Over the page we present The *Punch* Couch-Consumer Survey, complete with The Big Eight's responses to our bad-smelling, inquisitive and demanding potential-client, Bob. ☛

The Punch bark-o-thon guide

Therapist	DESCRIBE YOUR TECHNIQUE	DESCRIBE YOURSELF	WOULD IT BOTHER YOU THAT I DON'T WASH?	WHAT WOULD YOU DO TO HELP JOHN McCARTHY?
1. Peter Wanless Individual Humanistic & Analytic Psychologist £25/hr 071-328 7641	I use transference situations and material from your everyday life. I see your externality and how it relates to me – they form a dynamic.	I suppose I'm what you'd call middle-aged – in my forties. I have experience of psychodynamic, primal and body gestalt approaches and union and object relation.	Er, no, it's not a problem for me. How does it affect you – is it a fear of water?	(No response.)
2. 'Yvette' (real name Adele) Reflexologist £15/hr 081-805 8949	You take your socks off and roll your trousers up! You get 40 minutes of reflexology – which is where the talcum-powder comes in.	In the mornings, I work at the technical department of Neville Russell Chartered Accountants.	Yes.	I could only give him reflexology. Of course, some clients don't enjoy it. They go into a trance-like state and are left with a high – like being drunk.
3. Dr Hans Laufer German Hypno/ Psychotherapist £25/hr (£10 assessment) 081-348 3556	I'm psycho-dynamically orientated. I use hypnosis to draw out vot ve need at a more economical speed, ja?	I think you vil just have to come along for a consultation and see me, ja? It's £10.	That's probably something ve should look at, ja?	Vat do you mean? Listen! He vill be looked after by loads of therapists. He needs counselling not psychotherapy and it will take over a year.
4. Morris Veale Gestalt Therapist £123 for ten group sessions £18-27/hr for one-on-one 071-263 4079	It emphasises your experience of feelings, fantasies, memories and 'awareness' at that juncture. It's Mind Expression!	Generally – this is a way of me answering and not answering your question – I show and share a degree of me yet I don't see it as a scenario to explore my own feelings.	I would think it very strange if a therapist wouldn't see you for that. But I couldn't tell without having a consultation first.	I would have to speak to him personally and explore those experiences which were attempting to emerge and discuss his feelings toward the future.
5. Michael Perry Shiatsu/Stress Counsellor £25/hr (£30 for home visits) 081-690 5413	It's acupuncture without the puncture, just the acu. Stresses and sicknesses are just an imbalance of energy lines through your body.	I'm 37, married with two kids and spend three days a week looking after them. You can hear them now…Will you go in and shut the door!... That's basically me.	Ummmm, no, that's not a problem for me. Hearing you talk, my mind goes into thinking you have to build up different areas of your life, yeah?	(No response.)
6. Christopher Hansard Psychophysical Therapist £20/hr (neg) 071-603 7712	(Stuttering) I use l-l-lots of techniques, not just one! I combine alternative and, shall we say, establishment processes.	I'm 34, run a psychiatric ward and trained in Tibetan medicine – a synthesis of Indian, Greek, Persian, Nepalese and other 8th century systemology.	I treat someone who's in a similar situation to you! It's quite a common thing. I know this doesn't help much, but you're not the only one who doesn't wash.	I would be concerned primarily with connecting his body with his physical surroundings. I can't go into more detail because treatment is a personal thing.
7. Janet Armitage Primal Therapist £975 for 15 days (in Brighton and London); or £30/hr 0273-500647	It's about re-living repressed traumas to the full so you can make freer choices in your here and now. Based on Janov but less destructive.	I'm in my thirties, travelled widely and lived in France. I have a colleague called Franklin, a post-grad dip in counselling and I've Primaled.	It's not something that puts me off. No, not at all!	I would help him relive suppressed emotions, but if the patient is not too far removed from his experiences it can be dangerous.
8. 'Paul' Black Male Masseur £35/hr (£60 for home visits) 081-766 6049	I'm a relaxation massage therapist, yeah? Most people come for massage, then relief, then a few porn films, y'know, and basically have a good wank.	I'm 24, a weight-trainer, quite muscular, black, smooth-skinned, clean-shaven and very good-looking.	If you haven't had a bath I'll stand you in the shower, mate, because I'm not going to work with someone who's filthy.	(Lots of laughter) I really do think you're taking the piss. I can't help you. Sorry. Bye!

to therapists' mental health

DO YOU HAVE REGULAR BOWEL MOVEMENTS?

Pardon? I don't particularly wish to discuss my bowels! But the work I would do is knit together your bowels with other elements of your life.

I don't have that sort of problem, no. But how exciting for you. Both massage and reflexology are successful in moving your, um, toxins along.

Vy do you vant to know zese things?

I beg your pardon!?

No real problems personally. But I have worked on constipation patients. Just to stop and have a shiatsu is a bowel-relaxing experience.

Is th-th-that something you consider im-im-impor-por-por-tant?

That's a very strange question from a total stranger. But I would say that Primal can help people shed their, er, excess baggage.

I don't usually have many problems – no. If that's your scene, massage could relax you a little, it could get them going, I suppose.

DO YOU THINK DAVID ICKE IS A HAPPENING GEEZER?

I certainly believe there is a spiritual dimension in life. I haven't read much about David Icke, but everything is relevant, a part of The You.

He's not my scene to be honest.

I do not know of zis man.

No comment.

I'm not mystical, per se, but part of the West's problem is that in this stress-filled Nineties it's difficult to approve of illogical others. Yeah?

I don't know of him. I couldn't comment until we meet. I have certain religious and astrological interests, of sorts, but we should talk.

I'm afraid I'm not a mystical person. I would add, though, that several of our clients find Primal Screaming interlocks with their spirituality.

Yeah, yeah! I'm a bit religious and that. Do you know what I mean?

DID YOU HAVE A HAPPY CHILDHOOD, DOCTOR?

mOne requirement of being a therapist is to go through therapy oneself. So you can conclude that having done it myself I had reason to do it, yes?

As can be expected.

Zis really isn't the time or place for zis, Bob!

I don't really think we can conduct a session on the phone. I think you're going to have to come. Are you looking for day or evening appointments?

The older I become the more happy it was. My parents didn't fulfil my emotional quota as a teenager, but then what teenager gets that, yeah?

It was quite special in that it was very happy and very relaxed. I know that many people didn't have what I had, so that's why I want to see them happy.

It's usually the case, of course, that we have been clients ourselves. So I think it's sufficient to know that I did therapy for my own good reasons.

Haa-ha!

CAN YOU LEND ME 50 QUID?

No, absolutely not! I prefer to be paid after each session. Once there's trust, I may bend the rules, but it's not something I've done before!

No, of course not! I usually relieve clients of the money before the treatment. It saves bouncing cheques etc, and makes everyone happy.

(Slams the phone down.)

I find that a very strange question.

Credit depends on how regular my clients are – if I've seen them for two years, I know they're going to pay me. Otherwise I'm strict and unbending.

No. How bad is your financial situation? Payment can be according to your needings. But I'm not in it for the cash, I can tell you that.

Pardon? We're not a bank or a friend. But I would say that the £975 is essentially negotiable.

Certainly not! No. Don't be a silly bitch. I don't do finance terms, credit or anything. If you can't afford a good job, go out on the street and pay a tenner, OK?

Ross

'Honey, I can't seem to get through to Rentokil'

'Oh hell! Look what I've trodden in'

'The Crowleys are having another barbecue'

'I made the cache when they first started debating muzzles in the Commons'

'Lucky I joined the AA – I've got a flat'

'It's a disgrace. The animals are so bored that they're trapped in the same routine every day'

THE BLOKE WHO GIVES IT TO YOU STRAIGHT

Jason

ALRIGHT, MATES! HI KIDS! It's the technicolor dreamboat here. You know what gets me mad? It's when I don't, as we say Down Under, get a fair suck of the sauce stick. I like a fair deal, me. But these Pom journos keep poking their sticky beaks in and suggesting that I'm not a lairy larrikin. The nerve.

Jeepers, cobbers, I mean, fair goes, mates. That's all I need – a bunch of root-faced media wowzers not giving me the credit I deserve for being an Ocker pants man through and through. Listen, mates, I'm as red-blooded as the next bloke,

me. You know, I'm the kind of bloke who's not averse to bit of aggro, who likes to strop his mulligan, twang his wire and entertain a sheila back at his drum.

If there's one thing I can't stand it's being called a mattress-muncher. I

work out in the gym, you know, mates. It ain't exactly hard for me to feature with a chorus girl, if you get my drift.

Down Under

Strewth! I don't mind telling you that when it comes to dropping me daks with a sheila, I'm non-stop once I crack a fat. That's non-bloody-stop. None of this drilling for vegemite nonsense.

Sheilas, eh, don't you just love 'em?

Cliff Richard hasn't had a woman in years but no one doubts he's a fair dinkum ladies' man. I, on the other hand, have dated Kylie Minogue and Denice Lewis and they still claimed I was going to be outed. It's a funny old world, isn't it, mates?

Technicolor yawn

There's only one thing my mates like more than sheilas, and that's lager. When they go round the chunder circuit they drink so much VB and Tooheys, they spend half the night in a dunnee aiming Archie at the armitage or leaping into the lala to pray to the porcelain god. Now I'm no two-pot screamer, but I'd rather be sober. So I drink fizzy pop. Don't you just love it?

Jace

Here's one of my favourite jokes. I often have a chuckle over it as I share a few Cokes with my bodgie buddies. It goes: Why do Ocker men come so quickly? So they can get down the pub and tell their mates!

Pub-crawling's not my scene. I'd rather grapple with a great pair of funbags and give my pigskin bus a guided tour around Tasmania! Geography, don't you love it?

spot

Jason pops his cork

CHOCKABLOCKA WITH THE OCKER ROCKER

The Punch guide to
SEX
and laughter

Our special, horizontally-inclined issue begins with the definitive survey of sex surveys, compiled by STEVEN SMETHURST and introduced by DAVID THOMAS

What about me? Don't you ever think I may resent being treated as a sex object?

Frankly, no

There isn't a Citizens' Charter For Sex yet. But it can only be a matter of time. These days, sex is agonised over and complained about as much as Telecom or British Rail. So, to help John Major, here are *Punch*'s suggestions for the three key clauses of the Charter...

1. All people conducting sexual liaisons must wear name tags. This will avoid embarrassing morning-after amnesia.

2. Anyone who has had a bad sexual experience will be able to sue his or her partner for the money wasted in persuading them into bed in the first place. And...

3. Everyone must come on time.

By now, many readers may feel that this is just typical of *Punch*'s decline into teenage smut, not to mention the pathetic male obsession with sex. All of which is probably true, but we're not alone. This year has seen a media explosion of sexual investigations, polls and probes. Such traditional sexual stalwarts as *Cosmopolitan* have been joined in their pursuit of the perfect orgasm by newspapers from the *Sun* to the *Observer*, numerous TV channels, and every women's magazine that can still afford ink and paper. Nor is this obsession with matters genital confined to this side of the Atlantic. The latest edition of the American movie magazine *Premiere* is devoted to an examination of sex in the cinema. It reveals, amongst other things, that regular viewers of pornographic films have 'more positive attitudes towards women than does the general public'; that Amanda Donohoe felt 'an enormous sense of pride' when she first saw herself naked on screen (how, one wonders, did she feel the next 58 times?), and that *Henry and June* – the recent film about Anaïs Nin and Henry Miller – was given an X-certificate because one shot showed a postcard depicting a woman 'in a compromising position' with an octopus.

What is it that has provoked this sudden rush into panting print? Why, even as these words are being written, the *Daily Express* is tantalising its audience of late-middle-aged Tories with a series called 'Sense and Sexuality'. Needless to say, there isn't much sense in it, although it does have the astonishing revelation that kissing has less to do with the traditional tongue-wrestle and is actually all about the desire to smell our partners as intimately as possible.

Women, it says, have a much more powerful sense of smell than men, which is why, 'When her lover is away, an anguished woman goes to the laundry basket and takes out his shirt, presses it to her face and is overwhelmed by tenderness.' If she can get that kind of a hit off a shirt, what sort of high will she get from a whiff of his football socks? And where, if men are so insensitive to smell, does this leave the pervert and his bicycle seat?

The *Express* series, by Diane Ackerman, is a treasure trove of corny prose. 'We still ache fiercely with love, lust, loyalty and passion,' she gushes, breathlessly, before adding, 'The mind doesn't really dwell in the brain but travels the whole body on caravans of hormone and enzyme.'

Speak for yourself, Diane. The rest of us, whose minds remain obstinately stationary, might be tempted to say, 'Piffle!' or even 'Bollocks!' Which reminds me...the readers of this month's *Marie Claire* magazine are currently being treated to a feature on sex aids.

The article, which is to be found in the mag's health column – well, it makes a change from another high-fibre diet – lists and illustrates an astounding variety of means by which a woman can be brought to orgasm. Amongst these are a pair of plastic 'love balls' which are inserted and then left to clank around in an erotic sort of way whilst the user goes about her daily business; an assortment of pink, white, black, smooth, knobbly and finger-shaped vibrators, and an inflatable male doll, complete with erect, vibrating penis.

All this, mark you, is to be found on the pages, not of a top-shelf, brown-envelope, filthpacket rag, but of a respectable magazine for open-minded young women-about-town. Presumably, it – like this whole issue of *Punch* – is there because sex shifts

copies. But it also raises the possibility that – as Bargepole implies elsewhere in this issue – the female of the species is not only more deadly, but also more sex-crazed than the male.

After all, if men are the ones who think about sex all the time, why is it that the pages they choose to read in the nation's newspapers are full of football, whereas the women's pages are – *pace* the odd spot on fashion or feminism – packed with nothing but rumpy-pumpy?

And what is it that people want to know about sex? Or – to put it another way – what don't they want to know? Here, taken more-or-less at random from a selection of recent surveys on the subject are 20 bizarre facts about the beast-with-two-backs...

- The first sex manual was commissioned in 2,600BC by the Chinese Emperor Huang Ti.
- The Muria people of India lose their virginity at six years old.
- At any given moment, 6,000,000 people are having sex.
- There are an estimated 30,946 prostitutes in Britain.
- Insurance companies have found that an early morning kiss reduces your chances of a car accident.
- Today's young woman allows petting at the age of 14 years 10 months.
- Ten per cent of people have had sex at work.
- Twenty one per cent of people have had more than ten lovers.
- Ninety three per cent of 18-24 year-olds have had oral sex.
- Northern women appear to be less likely to insist that men wear a condom.
- Nothing beats good clitoral stimulation.
- As long ago as 3,000BC men were wrapping their organs in sheaths to prevent conception and keep off flies.
- One hundred and forty seven million condoms were sold in Britain last year.
- Mickey Rourke is the ultimate male sex symbol.
- The Spanish believe that octopus, simmered in its own ink, is an aphrodisiac.
- Neolithic hunters achieved orgasm by sticking barley stalks into their own members.
- Fewer than 20 per cent of married men have ever revealed their favourite forms of sex play to their wives.
- Twenty nine per cent of women say that intercourse does not last long enough.
- Italians are the world's sexiest men, and...
- Women find small penises amusing. ☞

Words of wisdom
quality writing from the sex surveys

Whatever blue movies' demerits from an artistic or a feminist viewpoint, they are very effective at inducing genital tumescence.
Observer Magazine

She's got the look that turns you on, whether it's the red dress, her hair, the way she walks. Whatever it is – bingo! Your underwear starts feeling the strain. *Cosmopolitan*

I've always been rather attached to my penis. It is a reasonable size, but frankly that isn't good enough. I would be happy only if my penis was monstrously large. *Company*

Arriving in casualty with a vibrator several feet up your colon is a most embarrassing experience. *Marie Claire*

How to pull a Euro-hunk...To a German: 'Are you into sport? I bet you play a great game of tonsil hockey!' The *Sun*

If you think a desk job is boring you're not doing it right

If *Company* magazine is anything to go by, women find all penises amusing. The magazine printed a spread consisting of 36 close-up photographs of male organs. Accompanying each shot was one of the many nicknames associated with that particular body part, viz: Joystick, One-Eyed Trouser Snake, Blue-veined Piccolo, Bald-Headed Hermit, Hampton Wick, Hamster, Love-Trunk, Knob and so forth.

Some commentators remarked that there was little difference between this sort of stuff and the male pornography which women's magazines condemn as being demeaning. On the principle that what was saucy for the goose might well be saucy for the gander, we at *Punch* decided to parody *Company*'s well-hung pages with a similar feature on female genitalia.

The idea was to print a series of punning pictures: a beaver, a pussy-cat, President Bush, Mrs Thatch, a fur hoop and so forth. We even had a certain diminutive, balding, satirical magazine editor marked down as a little twat.

The project was abandoned for a number of reasons (apart from simple good taste). In the first place, none of us fancied a lifetime of revenge in the pages of *Private Eye*. But also, jokes about women are assumed to be inherently sexist. Men, on the other hand, are always a fair – and easy – target.

The same principle applies to many of the 'how-to' sex guides. *Sex Now*, the recent ITV programme, whose poll results were published in the *Mail on Sunday*, spent most of its series bemoaning the inability of men to satisfy the ever-more intricate sexual demands of modern womanhood.

The general assumption upon which the programme – and most newspaper sex series – was based was that the sole female task was to turn up and say 'Yes'. Male sexual needs were considered to be so simple that any old orifice would do. As *Blitz* magazine put it, shortly before its untimely commercial demise, 'All men really want is two tits, a hole and a heartbeat...men will have oral sex with a labrador if it's going.'

By contrast, the girls at *Blitz* felt that, 'We women are outrageous creatures who probably have more sexual knowledge than we'll ever use.'

An informal poll conducted amongst the men in the *Punch* office, however, revealed that most regarded the first assertion as inaccurate. Nor would any *Punch* staffers have oral sex with any breed of dog under any circumstances. The general tone of most conversations on the subject, however, would tend to indicate that men and women are equally likely to be good, bad or middling when attempting to make their respective ends meet.

But for those of our readers who still wish to achieve a new personal best, we have compiled a compendium of the cream, as it were, of this year's media sexology. Please ensure that you have a condom to hand before you start to read it...

Additional research by John Walker and Giles Wilson.

Of all the journalists working in the field of human relationships, none is so devoted to the subject as the redoubtable Jaci Stephen. This pint-sized dynamo from the Valleys has set Fleet Street alight with her frank and fearless approach to modern sackrobatics.

Her most remarkable achievement is the way in which she has converted her TV review column in the *New Statesman and Society* (hardly the world's sexiest publication) into a non-stop torrent of erotic analysis.

We checked her first 30 columns of 1991 and discovered that
● Twenty four mentioned sex, and...

We wanted the answer. So we made a ten-point comparison of Cosmopolitan, the mag for sex-crazed secretaries everywhere, and GQ, the rag for their boyfriends. These were the results...

1. Just turn the page and think of England: *Cosmopolitan* magazine's sex-crazed cover lines, January-September 1991...

● What's the formula for grand passion?
● How come you're in love after one night of sex?
● Why some men can't bear to be alone
● Keep it up! The care and feeding of his erection
● Is he a sex mate or a soul mate?
● What gives a man that heart-stopping feeling?
● The condom: what's in it for you?
● Why charming men can be dangerous lovers
● What men do wrong in bed! (And we could use some sex tips too!)
● When exactly is the right time to sleep with him?
● The new rules for oral sex
● Learner lovers: don't wait to be chosen, ask him out!
● Yes, yes, oh yes! Men fake orgasms too
● Can you lead a normal life after incest?
● Take a condom, not a cardie...and other things Mummy should have told you
● When your mind wants sex but your body says no
● Stop kidding yourself about married men
● Porn again! A man sheds new light on the eternal attraction
● Read all about it! The 60lb penis, multiple orgasms, the sex with the sensitive nose

- Thirteen mentioned sex in the first paragraph, but...
- On average it took her 2.78 paragraphs to mention TV. Amongst her many revelations were the statements that she would never sleep with Gazza *(18.1.91)* and...
- David Jason's sexuality is not of the 'knicker-ripping kind' *(7.6.91)*, but...
- Harry Hamlin 'could have me for a tenner' *(5.4.91)*.
- Then again, she has yet to witness 'anything remotely resembling a good bonk', and...
- Only Clive from *Chancer* registers anything on the 'bonkability scale' but...
- John from *Twin Peaks* gives her goose-pimples where she thought none existed *(all 7.6.91)*.

Also, TV detectives don't have sex any more *(22.2.91)*; there is a 'public school predilection for sticking your dick up your mate's bum,' *(29.3.91)*, and the trouble with psychiatry is that 'the meter is already at £10 and so far not a whiff of your father's penis.'

Ms Stephen's weekly column in the *Daily Mail* (on sex, actually, since you asked) reveals a profound dissatisfaction, to wit:

'On the whole, men spend the first half of their lives full of energy, but delivering mediocre, if not downright incompetent sexual performances; and the second half performing a great deal better but rarely having the energy to do so.'

Ms Stephen, however, has compiled a plan for male sexual self-improvement, viz:

- The British national average for sex to be increased from 6.2 minutes to 90.3 minutes.
- No stopping during intercourse to read the *Spectator*.
- Men to wash their bedding at least biannually.
- The phrase 'I'll call you,' to be followed by a phone call.
  To which we have two responses...
1. Six Minutes? It's supposed to take *that* long? And...
2. She's absolutely right about the *Spectator*. ☛

Does sex sell?

- Leg-over lads: men who treat women as sport
- Every man has one: Could you be the woman on his mind?
- GREAT SEX is crazy positions, silly noises, odd odours and other undignified things

2. **Men think about sex every ten minutes (or less than once a month, depending): The complete carnal cover-lines of *GQ* magazine, 1991**
- Why women leave you
- Susan Sontag on AIDS
- 51 ways to leave your lover
- Bare essentials: the clothes you want her to wear
- The nasty girl: she may drive you crazy, she will drive you wild
- Girl Talk: revealed, what they really want

3. **Total number of sexy coverlines in *Cosmopolitan*: 23**
4. **Total number of sexy coverlines in *GQ*: 6**
5. **Factor by which Cosmo exceeds *GQ*: 383 per cent**

6. **What GQ sold instead of sex...ten genuinely rumpo-free cover-lines from Britain's top men's glossy**
- Gabriel García Márquez in action
- Real men don't use mice: computer protocol
- Street-cred capitalists
- The last days of Nicolae Ceausescu
- Politics takes a walk on the mild side
- Simply great suits
- Work-outs that work
- What's so cool about Bryan Ferry?
- The theory and practice of a real close shave
- Everyone who's anyone at the Groucho Club

7. **Current audited monthly sales of *Cosmopolitan*: 450,285**
8. **Current audited monthly sales of *GQ*: 71,229**
9. **Factor by which Cosmo exceeds *GQ*: 632 per cent**

10. **Conclusion:** *Cosmopolitan* has nearly four times as many sexy coverlines as *GQ*. But it achieves more than six times as many sales. Sex is therefore a disproportionately effective selling tool and should be used as often as possible. Given *GQ*'s predilection for stories about business, snobbery and suits, we suggest the following as sure-fire circulation boosters...

- **Shagging your secretary: is her slowhand as good as her short-hand?**

- **How to get your kit off without creasing your clothes**

- **Pump up that penis: the ten-day wanger work-out**

Our invoice is in the post.

Bad Company?

We compare the holiday habits of Viz's Fat Slags with the readers of Britain's raunchiest glossy for go-getting girlies

In August 1991, *Company* magazine published a survey of the holiday habits of its young, female readership. Among its findings were the revelations that ten per cent of respondents had a fling whenever they went on vacation; that 68 per cent felt sexier on their hols and that 34 per cent had a boyfriend at home at the time of their holiday romance. These attitudes seemed incompatible with the stern, condomised morality of the AIDS era and they attracted considerable media interest, particularly amongst the over-heated sexperts on the tabloids.

No one, however, noticed the extraordinary resemblance between the *Company* readers and a couple of other well-known young women. To wit...

● More than one woman in eight, according to the *Company* survey, has sex 'within a couple of hours' of meeting their man.
The Fat Slags, on holiday, had sex within four frames of coming across a bunch of squaddies.

● Sixty seven per cent of women sunbathe to look healthier.
Tracy, looking at her rear says, 'Eeh, San. Me arse looks like it's seen a ghost! I could do wi' a tan.'

● 'It's just not a holiday without a fling!' said one *Company* reader. And one in ten of them have a holiday romance every time they go away.
San and Tray, looking at a hunk in the travel agent's, book two tickets 'to wherever he's going. Same week, an' all!'

● Eighty five per cent of women would not turn down a second, third or fourth fling on foreign shores.
The Fat Slags have the soldiers lining up, trousers down, 'standing to attention'.

● Sixty per cent of the respondents go on holiday with a friend, and the same number do not use a condom.
Naturally, the girls fit into both these categories.

● Twenty five per cent of readers buy a new wardrobe to take on holiday.
The sombrero-wearing San and Tray get 'friggin' knackered' carrying their four suitcases.

● Over 40 per cent of *Company*'s readers spend above £300 whilst on holiday.
***Viz*'s stalwarts take a rather more parsimonious approach, preferring to earn a free meal by bestowing favours on the squaddies' bodies in return for a bag of chips each.**

How often do you do it?

At least once per issue	*Company*
Most times	*Cosmopolitan*
Sometimes	*Marie Claire*
Rarely	*Blitz*
Never	*GQ*

Have you ever faked it?

Yes	Nearly everyone
No	*GQ*

(None of our sample would want to admit to faking, but several participants were distinctly over-enthusiastic. *Esquire*'s cover story 'The Best Sex in Britain' was little more than a guide to beaches, museums and village cricket. The *Mail on Sunday*'s was 'the most remarkable survey you will ever read' and 'there's never been a survey like' the *Express*'s.)

And what's more, they fart in bed...

Why British men are such lousy lovers, in 12 easy stages

1. The wait-till-I-tell-the-guys factor can ruin a relationship.
Observer

2. Men who call women 'baby' should have their peckers cut off.
Observer

3. Most men are like those spiders who are willing to sacrifice their lives for sex. At the sight of a woman in a miniskirt they become a seething mass of hormones.
Cosmopolitan

4. You've got to feel sorry for men. They perform cunnilingus as if they were weather-proofing someone, instead of drawing the alphabet.
Blitz

5. Women are getting more sex, but it's not the kind they want. They want men to become more feminine in their approach.
Sunday Express

6. Many women remain silent about their

Well, last night was an education. Went to a great restaurant, got harangued about male attitudes, got insulted, got kicked, got a huge bill and got rejected. A lot of rabbit but no pussy.

I'm glad you can joke about it

lack of orgasm to protect their men from loss of face.
Daily Express

7. Men are the victims of porn: they think

women will be like that.
Blitz

8. British men seem largely ignorant of what women want in bed.
Cosmopolitan

9. Men suffer from penis envy. They're concerned theirs doesn't match up.
Cosmopolitan

10. Women are bored; 'You don't know your romance from your camshaft and telling us to roll over is nobody's idea of foreplay.'
Esquire

11. Men treat sexual encounters as a contest they will win or lose.
Daily Express

12. Nearly two out of three women think that men's lovemaking is too mechanical; one in four report their partner penetrates too early for them; one in five regularly fake orgasm.
Mail on Sunday

So just how sexy are you, gloss-features?

The tables are turned as the magazines go under the microscope

How long does it normally last?
N/A	GQ
Up to 5 pages	Cosmo, Marie Claire
Between 6 and 15	Esquire, Blitz
Above 15	Company
Three days	Sun
A week	Daily Express
Three weeks	Mail on Sunday
One month	Observer Magazine

Are you a 'New Mag'?
Yes	GQ
Not any more	Everyone else

(A couple of years ago the concept of the non-sexist, emotionally-open 'New Mag' was all the rage, but it came to be regarded as wimpish. Post New Mag, therefore, is not afraid to talk about sex openly, or even having nude pictures 'if we want them. We're not scared'.)

Can you be satisfied?
Two per cent of *Express* respondents never achieve orgasm

Ten per cent of *Cosmo* respondents never achieve orgasm

Thirty three per cent of *Mail on Sunday* respondents never achieve orgasm

All *GQ* readers achieve orgasm, but only so long as it does not mess up their suits.

These figures, except for *GQ*, are taken from published surveys of female readers. So if you see a woman leaving the newsagent with a happy smile and a warm glow, chances are she doesn't read the *Mail on Sunday.*

ARE YOU SICK?

Well STEVEN APPLEBY certainly is, and he concludes that the rest of us are too

Say when...

Stir me!

eat me!

That was marvellous darling!

Thank you, darling...

Cover me in French dressing!

● More and more people these days get hours of healthy enjoyment from a good honest fetish. Roger and Gillian X, for example, enjoy drinking cups of tea off each others bodies - are they abnormal? ● Mr and Mrs W like to make love in separate rooms, which some people regard as odd. ● A rural man, who prefers to remain anonymous, gets pleasure from dressing as a lettuce, being watered, forced under glass, thinned out and re-potted in the greenhouse - who are we to pass judgement? ● The Bingleys like nothing better than to spend a pleasant evening wrapping one another in brown

paper and sticky tape, after which they lick stamps and post themselves to an address selected at random. Mr Bingley is a member of the local Round Table. ● Mr P from Herne Hill thrives on dressing as a bedside lamp and being turned on. ● Reading is an interest which many people develop, and Janet B frequently curls up with a good book or takes a magazine to bed, while David L - dressed as a large wasp - chews his copy of The Times into a paste and uses it to wallpaper his room. ● In fact, you can have a fetish about virtually anything, but some people go too far! For reasons of public decency we are unable to print in the pages of *Punch* a picture of the perverts who derive some sort of disturbed pleasure from the wearing of brightly coloured nylon sportswear.

It's getting a bit gloomy in here...

BUZZ...

A CAR FETISHIST POLISHING:

I can see my entire body in it!

disgusting!

HOW DOES IT START? Here we see that the beginnings of some sexual fetishes are rooted in childhood:

No more ice cream!

AGE 7   AGE 30

Eat your greens!

goo...

AGE 7   AGE 30

Do your homework

AGE 7   AGE 30

BORED with YOUR sex life? Add a little something with one of these non-toxic SEX TOYS...

A vibrating Something-or-other. Available in flesh colour (dead) or purple. Batteries not included.

A large washable thingy — One size only.

A realistic doo-dah — in presentation case. Instructions enclosed.

A set of 3 edible what-do-you-call-its. Just what the doctor would order if he knew!

A superb whatsit — and good value at the moment — HURRY while stocks last! Blue only.

SPECIAL OFFER Glow-in-the-dark 'His 'n' Hers' ™ underwear! Putting out the lights won't extinguish the passion! Now you can find one another in the dark! Guaranteed...

A 'HOOVERIST' DEMONSTRATES 3 INTERESTING CLEANING POSITIONS:

a: whooo...

b:

whooo...

c:

whooo...

FOOD AND FETISHISM:

You've had your cake, Simon — now go make your bed and lie in it!

A DOUBLE PERVERSION:

How do you do?

A man, dressed as a woman, dressed as a man.

FOOD & FOOTWEAR: exotic sexual appetites can sometimes be satisfied with shoes made out of pastry, chocolate and fresh cream.

1:

2:

SPLUDGE!

Remember: PEOPLE ARE UNDERSTANDING AND IT IS ALWAYS BEST TO BE OPEN AND HONEST ABOUT YOURSELF...

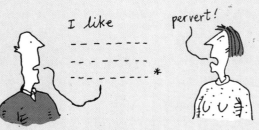

I like
- - - - - - -
- - - - - - -
- - - - - - - *

pervert!

* Fill in your sexual deviation here. (Continue on separate sheet if necessary).

The Guttersnipe guide to carnality

By Mr Kent Dorfmann

'It has been brought to one's attention,' writes our garrulous gossip, 'that many periodicals now opt for the sequential presentation of trivial information. Thus, when one was invited to contribute to this special issue, it was agreed that this contemporary style should be adopted. Normal services will be resumed next week.'

Speaking of which, one might ask, 'Who, pray, is Miss Victoria Hodge?' (See p46.) She is a baronet's daughter whose amorous adventures enthralled the nation's tabloid 'hacks' some years ago. Her family's motto is, 'Glory is the reward for virtue.' Quite.

Ten tabloid newspaper expressions with respect to carnality and how they translate into the Queen's English

Lovemaking session: Carnality
Sex romps: Carnality on more than one occasion
Secret love tryst: Appointment for carnality
Secret love nest: Venue for carnality
Sun-soaked hideaway: Overseas venue for carnality
Love child: Illegitimate baby
Vice girl: Courtesan
Rent boy: Male courtesan
A night of shame: Carnality with a courtesan
Sordid night of shame: Carnality with a male courtesan

That's right sir... all arranged with absolute discretion and guaranteed Tabloid exposure.

SUNSOAKED HIDEAWAY ⋆ Secret love Trysts ⋆ Sordid Nights of Shame

Ten gentlemen who indulged in homosexual practices

Cole Porter
W Somerset Maugham
André Gide
Errol Flynn
Socrates
Walt Whitman
Maurice Chevalier
Jean Cocteau
Marcel Proust
Michelangelo

Ten ladies who indulged in Sapphic practices

Queen Christina of Sweden
Tallulah Bankhead
Billie Jean King
Bessie Smith
Ivy Compton-Burnett
Janis Joplin
Martina Navratilova
Colette
Virginia Woolf
Gertrude Stein

Ten carnal liaisons of which you may not have previously been aware

Elvis Presley and Jayne Mansfield
Leopold Stowkowski and Greta Garbo
Eva Peron and Aristotle Onassis
Howard Hughes and Jean Harlow
Mike Todd and Gypsy Rose Lee
Marilyn Monroe and Orson Welles
Farrah Fawcett and Sylvester Stallone
Frank Sinatra and Natalie Wood
Rita Hayworth and David Niven
Howard Hughes and Errol Flynn

The age at which ten famous people first experienced carnality

Louis XVI: 23
Loretta Lynn: 13
David Niven: 14   Joan Rivers: 20
Havelock Ellis: 32
Tennessee Williams: 28
E M Forster: 31
George Bernard Shaw: 29
Victoria Principal: 18
Cleopatra: 12

Ten foodstuffs which experienced carnal practitioners claim have aphrodisiac properties

Watercress   Lobster
Truffles   Cucumbers
Asparagus   Carrots
Chocolate   Peaches
Avocados   Honey

Ten gentlemen who experienced carnal relations with Marlene Dietrich

Yul Brynner
John Gilbert
Gary Cooper
Mike Todd
John Wayne   Michael Wilding
James Stewart   Jean Gabin
Erich Maria Remarque   Burt Bacharach

Ten women of whom Mr Warren 'Bunny' Beatty has had carnal knowledge

Brigitte Bardot
Joan Collins
Michelle Phillips
Julie Christie
Natalie Wood
Kate Jackson
Leslie Caron
Goldie Hawn
Candice Bergen
Diana Ross

Warren Beatty's first sexual experience...

Here Kitty Kitty...

PORNO LISTS

Ten other substances which carnal practitioners claim have aphrodisiac qualities

Beeswax
Ginseng
Strychnine
Henna
Spanish fly
Vitamin E
Marijuana
Silkworm pods
Caterpillars
The word 'the' (If puzzled refer to the works of Messrs Derek and Clive)

Ten women (Ms Farrah Fawcett apart) whom Mr Ryan O'Neal has serviced

Margaret Trudeau	Bianca Jagger
Joan Collins	Britt Ekland
Barbra Streisand	Anjelica Huston
Anouk Aimée	Jacqueline Bisset
Ursula Andress	Mia Farrow

Ten gentlemen who have tasted the fruits of Miss Victoria Hodge

Elliott Gould
Gordon Waller
 (of Peter and
 Gordon)
John Bindon
George Lazenby
David Bailey
Yul Brynner
Prince Andrew
Jimmy Mitchum
Ringo Starr
Jamie Niven 🦎

Jamie Blandford

HE'S THE HARD-DRIVING PEER WITH A NOSE FOR TROUBLE!

My God, what's Britain coming to? Just what the bloody hell is going on? I mean if a chap can't take his motor out for a quick spin when the fancy takes him, what's the point of calling this a free country, eh? Eh?!? What? What!!!

I know you're going to say that a chap needs insurance forms and driving licences and endless other bits of boring paper doled out by spotty narg at Post Office counters.

Rubbish. You may need that sort of thing, because you're a grotty little pleb. But I don't. I'm a peer, a marquess actually. I can do whatever the bloody hell I like. And don't you forget it.

> Nigel Mansell is a thoroughly decent British chap who drives incredibly fast and the whole country adores him. I, too, am a thoroughly decent British chap and I certainly know where to find the accelerator. But I am slapped into jail. It's a funny old world, isn't it?

NOB IN SLAMMER SHOCK

Some of the other chaps here in chokey like to put pictures up on the wall. You know the sort of thing – saucy little totties from the lower orders who can't think of anything better to do than whip their kit off for the filth-merchants.

There was one particularly trouser-warming snap on the wall of my cell. A skinny little blonde number, she was, with not much on apart from her undies and tights. Not unnaturally, I took a closer look and…*bloody hell*! It was my wife, the Marchioness!

Tatler Oct '91

BAPS OUT FOR THE TOFF

'Look at the pins on that,' said my cellmate, one Fat Jack Slagdon. 'I got 'er out that *Tatler* magazine. It woz ordered special for you, Lord Blandford. Or should that be *Banned*ford? Oh you gotta laugh, chief, incha? Look at this – underwear special wunnit? That is a pretty tasty sort, squire. Pity you can't see 'er baps.'

'Well you can bloody well put her back, you *noxious* little yob!' I replied.

'I'll have you know that she's my wife, the Marchioness of Blandford. If you want a girl on the wall, pick on someone from your own bloody class.'

PROLES PASTE PEER

Do you know what happened next? The *ghastly* prole gave me a couple of black eyes and removed four of my front teeth. Really – what on earth is this country coming to, eh? What??!??

Inherited titles must never be mocked

I CAN'T TELL YOU HOW pleased I was to hear that Margaret Thatcher had put an end to all that silly talk about her becoming the Countess of Finchley. We can't have *jumped-up* grocers' daughters entering the Lords. It would lower the tone.

And can you imagine the horrors of having Mark Thatcher as an Earl? I ask you. It would make a mockery of the whole system. Eh? What??!!

HE'S BRASH, HE'S BLUFF, HE LIKES HIS SNUFF!

Dillie Keane

Going in foetus first

Some of the green judgments in Ireland's abortion case

The moment John Major stepped into Margaret Thatcher's shoes, he was instantly plunged into the Gulf War. Albert Reynolds, Ireland's new Taoiseach, could have been forgiven for thinking that Major had a cushy number, because no sooner had he succeeded Haughey than he was pitched headlong into a moral war, ie the abortion case. The man was boxing shadows.

Ireland is no stranger to civil war but this was emotional warfare on a grand scale. The flak flying about at the time of the referendum on the eighth amendment to the constitution, protecting the life of the unborn child, was small beer by comparison. This time, a sexually-abused 14-year-old girl had been made a victim twice over; once by the abuser (and whether her allegations of rape are true or not, it is still a crime to have sex with a minor) and again by the law. Even though the Supreme Court eventually ruled that the girl could travel to England to have an abortion, it is totally impossible to regard her as a winner.

No one could talk of anything but the case here in Dublin. Ben Dunne, one of Ireland's most famous and successful businessmen, admitted taking coke with an escort girl in a Florida hotel, where he was spotted having the screaming abdabs and trying to hurl himself off the balcony. Sensational stuff. Did anyone care? Not a lot. Sure, it made the headlines, but only a visit from the Virgin Mary herself would have eclipsed the abortion case.

The airwaves were jammed with it. I was doing publicity for my show, and with every journalist and presenter, the conversation returned inexorably to the subject. Never before had the *Irish Times* devoted whole pages to 'Letters to the Editor' on one topic alone. Yet the press behaved well: they didn't hunt her down, nor identify her and they turned down substantial cash offers from British tabloids to reveal all.

The ramifications and repercussions are extraordinary. The Protestant extremists in Northern Ireland must be throwing their hats in the air at the mediaeval and barbarous practices of the priest-ridden south. Thus, they must be saying, will the world see the real Ireland from which we ever wish to be sundered. On a wider scale, but not of earth-shattering moment, it is rumoured that the King and Queen of Sweden might be forced to cancel their visit in April due to public outcry at home. More serious is the prospect for the referendum to be held later this year on the Maastricht treaty and it is whispered that Ireland might even vote itself out of the EC.

This country is riddled with inconsistencies. A woman can have her tubes tied in some hospitals, not in others. Vasectomies, on the other hand, seem to be widely available. You cannot get a divorce, but married persons leaving the country to get an English divorce are not hunted down and barred from leaving the country. Nor do those who remarry in England and then return home find themselves thrown in chokey for bigamy, which, technically, is their crime.

The feminist argument – and many of the women in Ireland are very angry indeed – is that the eighth amendment is yet another example of male control. This argument is undermined, however, by the fact that many of the most virulent anti-abortionists are women. It also fails to take into account the innocence of a foetus that cannot plead its case: a powerful emotional factor. It all depends on who is perceived as the victim: the mother or the unborn? In this case, both are victims: thus the dilemma.

While individual members of the clergy are predictably vociferous in support of the original ruling, the church itself has been remarkably cagey. It seems that they felt the girl ought to be able to go to England for a termination, in order to avert the possibility of another referendum which might bring about the deletion of the controversial amendment. This is known as the Irish Solution: as long as it doesn't happen on Irish soil, it's OK.

There are some who think the girl was a bold puss who got no more than she deserved and ought to be made to live with the consequences. They miss the point that even after the abortion, she will never stop living with the consequences.

Finally, there is the conspiracy theory: the girl was got pregnant deliberately and it's all a satanic plot to bring about a change in the constitution. Some normally sensible folk are more persuaded by this argument than I care to admit.

The President broke her queenly silence early on in the debate to say that it was a tragedy and that it must be resolved. Normally sensible folk were up in arms that she didn't obey protocol and say nothing. What they failed to see was that she had said nothing very successfully. But what she seemed to convey was sympathy towards the girl's cause, which had the pro-life crowd in paroxysms of rage.

What baffles me, as someone who was born and raised a Catholic, and who still paddles about in the shallows as a collapsed Catholic, is this: whatever happened to the Free Will we were all told about, the greatest gift that God could give us and so fundamental to the Catholic faith? A lot of troubled people here find the idea of abortion obscene, but feel that freedom of choice is essential and know that abortion is going to go on whether it is legal or not. Nobody in their right mind could want to return to the dark days of knitting needles, perforated wombs, sterility, death and babies on doorsteps. And yet they do. And yet they do. ❧

'This spring cleaning's a lark'

What he doesn't know about sex could be written on an oral contraceptive tablet. He's BARGEPOLE and he's here to share his secrets with you

Lights, camera, Kleenex, action

It is a grey morning. We are high above London Bridge. Dirty gusts eddy about the pale shanks of innumerable office women and flap the trouser-legs of their pallid male colleagues. As we zoom in we see among the tight-lipped, frowning faces, a single tight-lipped, smirking face. It is the face of Mister Colin Figment. Mister Figment works in the Small Claims department of an insurance company.

Now, Mister Figment *should* be thinking about the SC(D)22 backlog, because it is Wednesday. But Mister Figment's mind is not on SC(D)22s, Wednesday or not. Mister Figment is Master of the Universe today, because last night he got *Wuthering Heights* out by mistake, and while Mrs Figment watched it, he made a delicious boil-in-the-bag cod in cheese sauce with some Batchelor's Savoury Rice and Mrs Figment said, 'Well, that was nice, Colin,' and later on she didn't edge away when he nudged her buttock under her C&A nightie...and then after a bit she said, 'Well, that was nice, Colin,' and today Mister Figment is Master of the Universe.

This is how it goes. Horrible, isn't it? Yet every day, thousands of Britons write to me with sexual anxieties which make Mister Figment seem like one in the grip of terminal satyriasis. They cannot get it up. They cannot get it down again. If they do get it up, they don't know what to do with it, or they don't want to do it with the one person who will let them. They want to know how to pick up men. They have strange urges, wrenching desires that leave them flopped like starfish in the hours before dawn. They buy appliances from Soho stores, then hide them in the bottom of the wardrobe. They buy contact magazines and highlight the interesting box numbers in fluorescent pen, but take it no further because they would have to send off a postal order, and smirking Mr Patel at the Post Office would Guess Sunnink.

Britain in 1991 is a sensory Gehenna of thwarted lubricity.

Even in London, there is nowhere you can go for a couple of Thai girls, a bottle of mescal and a 5:1 Varispeed power hoist. The dreadful furtiveness of the British assumes it is wrong. The dire unconfidence of the British assumes it is their fault. The grisly resentment of the British declares that It Is All Right For Some. And they expect me to tell them what to do.

Right. I shall.

Let us clear up a few things so that we know where we stand.

1. The British are the most unattractive race in Europe.
2. They are to the pleasure of the bed what dogs are to the pleasures of the violin.
3. British men are unwholesome and frigid.
4. British women are feverish and nasty.
5. It is their fault.
6. It is all right for some.

It is, for example, all right for me. While the rest of you were Getting On, playing office politics, going to the right sort of dinner parties, planning your career moves, taking out top-up mortgages, arranging pensions and Doing OK, actually I was sunk, wallowing, in a squirming pit of ceaseless venery, save for a brief hiatus in 1987 – 89.

Here are the fruits of my knowledge, the answers to the questions you most frequently ask. You won't be able to do anything about it because you are cowards and fools but by God it will make you feel bad.

What do women want? It is extraordinary how many people ask me this. What a foolish question. Do you really believe that 'women' are so indistinguishable that they all want the same things? Hah. Actually, they all *do* want the same things. The main thing women want is a man who knows what they want. They also want to be told what to do, but only at the right time. 'Put your hands behind the back of your neck. I am going to

to take the top of your head off!' Men do not realise this and it makes them uneasy. On the other hand, men should be quite clear in their minds that if they say 'Turn over and grit your teeth; this is going to take the top of your head off!', they had better damned well deliver the goods or leave the country.

Why do men talk about sex all the time? They don't. Men don't actually talk about sex very much at all. Men boast to each other and carefully avoid personal intimacies. This should not be discouraged. Just as most men have no clue how jolly it is to spend an evening gossiping with the girls about everyone's private lives, women don't understand how *relieving* an evening of plumage display, whisky and gratuitous bullshit can be.

To be sure, it is women who talk about sex. All the time. In complete detail. If every man were aware that all his mistress's friends know (a) how he goes about it; (b) how big it is; (c) his deficiencies and (d) the exact timbre of the silly, grunting, 'ooof' noise he makes at climax, man would learn an appropriate degree of respectful circumspection and might be much happier.

How do I talk to women? Fourteenth-century Croatian? Oh, for God's sake. If you adhere to the principle that you do not have to bed every woman you meet, that should answer the question. If you adhere to the principle that you *do* have to bed every woman you meet, you should already know the answer; if you don't, change your principles rather than your conversation.

How do I make a pass at a woman? This is one of the questions I am most commonly asked. It is easy. Touch her. If she moves away, forget it. If she moves towards you, good. Women just want a little tenderness, a little…

No, I mean how do I get her into bed? Aha. She is…in your flat. She says 'I really ought to go now.' You say 'Go? What do you mean, go? Don't be daft. Get your gear off.' This works. Signed testimonials on view at our offices. Thousands of satisfied customers. Politely but firmly refuse all imitations.

Sex is bad. Damn right. Good, isn't it?

My woman has gone off it. Why? Probably because you are useless. Try having a bath occasionally, and stop wearing that dreadful grey suit. Your aftershave lotion is wrong. You stoop. You look diffident, as if expecting rejection, yet you are a bully. And don't be so damn moody. As for all this office nonsense, do you really think she likes knocking around with a bloke who pushes paper for a living? At least pretend to be intrepid. And get your teeth fixed, for heaven's sake. And don't take insurance proposals to bed with you. Grow up, pull yourself together.

I've done all that and she still won't. OK. Have an affair. If you can't be bothered to have an affair, go to a hooker. Hookers are fun. Lots of fun.

But I've never paid for it in my life. Well, let me tell you, nobody likes a cheapskate. I suppose you wouldn't pay for a meal in a restaurant, either? Listen: for three hundred quid you can have two good hookers, a noseful of cocaine, a few good joints, and you can use all those odd little gizmos clanking around the bottom of the wardrobe that you're too cowardly to show your woman, although you bet she'd love it. What would you rather spend it on? A lawnmower, for heaven's sake?

Actually, yes. Sorry. We don't do lawnmower stuff here any more. Things have changed.

What about AIDS? Phooey. Fuss about nothing. Had it myself. Cleared up on its own. You can't get it twice, you know…🐉

handcuff you,' is all right. 'No, no, make the incision *there*, you fool. Call yourself a surgeon?' is wrong.

Women are, however, not unreasonable. They are amenable to compromise. But it has to be the right sort of compromise. If you do not know what they want, it is a bad idea to guess. It is an even worse idea to ask in a sort of sheepish way 'Is it all right if I tie you to the bedposts and whip you with this velvet cat o' nine tails?' It is not erotic. Deciding what a woman wants (providing it is interesting, stylish and likely to please) then gently insisting upon it *is* erotic.

Women like being given one tablet of Ecstasy when they are pleasantly, woozily aroused or when they are in a roaring frenzy of rhinoceros lust. Women do *not* like being given two tablets of Ecstasy when they are drunk, cross and confused particularly if accompanied by the words 'Go on, doll, go on, darling, do it for me, go on, you want to, you know you do.'

Finally, women do not like being raped. They do not even like the *idea* of being raped. What women *do* like, occasionally, is the thought of the idea of being raped. Do not even contemplate meddling with this harmless fantasy unless you are an expert, or you will find yourself in chokey before your feet touch the ground, and serve you right too.

What do men like? Julie Burchill offended the sensibilities of any number of duplicitous New Men – the ones who really like women, no, really, all my close friends are women – by declaring in her muck novel that all most men really want is silk teddies, black stockings and blow jobs. Julie Burchill writes a lot of rubbish. But it's not all rubbish. The suggestion that all most men really want is silk teddies, black stockings and blow jobs is *absolutely true*, and the sooner women realise this, the better.

What men *don't* like is all the stuff about respect. Women know that the correct answer to 'But do you *respect* me as a person?' is 'Hell, no. Turn over and grit your teeth; this is going

The female of the species can generally be divided into two categories...

This is not the case with the male, whose readiness to mate is often denoted by his distinctive plumage.

① ... those who don't

SEX EQUALITY

SEXY QUALITY

and... ... those who do

②

QUALIFIED SEX INSTRUCTOR APPLY WITHIN

IF I SAID YOU HAD A BEAUTIFUL BODY WOULD YOU HOLD IT AGAINST ME

⑤ ... while the males make their selection from a discreet distance, making appropriate signs to signal their interest...

⑥ A pecking order is established and the dominant male exercises his authority...

I DON'T FANCY YOURS

... though he will often assist the less experienced male.

LISTEN — SHE'S GOT THIS FRIEND...

⑨ Sometimes, the mating process is not carried through to its normal conclusion...

'ELLO 'ELLO

... e.g. COP-US INTERRUPTUS

⑩ When it is, a soft glow will soon suffuse the countenances of the male and his mate.

WANNA FAG?

YEAH, TA

⑪ Oddly, in this species, procreation is not necessarily the main object of mating.

PREGNANCY TEST RESULT

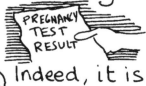

Indeed, it is sometimes...

The mating season normally lasts for 12 months of the year – with a short break every 4 years during the World Cup.

YES! YES! COME ON! YES! YES! AGHHHHH!

HE USED TO SAY THAT TO ME

③

Surprisingly, the courtship dance is often performed solely by the female and commences with the ritual placing of the handbag on the floor.

④

Prior to mating, the male can be observed engaging in the 'ritual feeding' of the female.

ANOTHER TRIPLE GIN AND LEMONADE — EASY ON THE LEMONADE

⑦

Soon afterwards, a suitable location is chosen and the overtures to the actual mating begin.

OOOH — ERIC!

ARE YOU TAKING PRECAUTIONS?

YEAH – I LOCKED THE DOOR

GIVE OVER DOREEN, YOU'VE SHIFTED THE GEAR-STICK INTO FIRST

YOU SHOW ME **YOUR** HIV TEST RESULT AND I'LL SHOW YOU **MINE**

LAY BY

⑧

... undesirable.

YOU'RE WHAT ?!

⑫

There's one sure sign of a successful union, however...

AIRPORT

⑬ ... the *EARLY MIGRATION* of the MALE.

Botham: just how sensitive is he?

Gerry Connolly upset our Ian in Oz

Australians were shocked when their burly hero, beefy Ian Botham, stormed out of a cabaret show on the eve of the Cricket World Cup. The cabaret, by Aussie drag artist Gerry Connolly, had satirised the royal family and made jokes about the Duke and Duchess of York. 'I love my country,' said Botham, 'and I don't have to put up with any of this crap.'

'He's being over-sensitive,' said one Australian observer. Amazingly, it took an Australian to notice this hitherto overlooked side of Ian's character.

In England, Ian Botham is frequently portrayed as beery, boorish and builder-bottomed. How unfair, and how far from the truth. Only the British could have overlooked the quiet, sensitive side to Ian Botham's nature. Just look at the evidence:

1981 Ian leaps on top of Geoff Boycott, pins him to the ground and bullies him with Chinese torture. He later de-bags Boycott and

A typically polite umpire appeal from Beefy

pours wine over his private parts. He is later reported to have run around a swimming pool, pulling everybody's shorts down and throwing clothes into the pool.

1984 On tour, Botham describes Pakistan as a place 'you wouldn't send your mother-in-law'. He is fined £1,000 by the Test and County Cricket Board.

1986 Former Miss Barbados talks of wild orgies with Botham. Yes,' she says, 'We did break the bed.' He later refers to the Test selectors as 'gin-swilling old dodderers'.

1987 Botham puts shaving foam into cricketers' boxes and squirts jam on telephone receivers.

1988 A Chepstow golf barman claims Botham head-butted him. In a different incident, he is fined £200 for offensive language, and later fined £325 after assaulting two passengers on a flight, 'He had already reduced a bar-

England hero Ian Botham bathes his sensitive bits in hot water

maid to tears during a rowdy binge,' reports *Today*.

1990 On a lecture tour, he tells students about the products he endorses for advertisers. The endorsement is less than warm. 'Don't drink that gnat's piss Dansk LA,' he advises. 'It's a hell of a waste of time drinking 18 pints of it then driving home. And I wouldn't eat any Shredded Wheat either. I don't like sawdust with milk all over it.' The *Sunday Express* calls him an 'oaf'.

1991 Botham claims the England Rugby Union team should not be rewarded for their wins because 'they're amateurs'.

1992 Geoff Boycott allegedly takes a tape measure to Beefy's midriff. In a familiar revenge, Botham whips off Boycott's trousers and 'measures his middle stump'.

Now who says Guy the Gorilla isn't a sensitve, caring individual? 🐾

'He's your cat…you take him into the kitchen and rub his nose in it…'

Tee Hee Titter Tee hee Snigger Smirk

Exterminate me.

BURNIE

'The hospital describes Mr Ronay's condition as "stable"'

BURNIE

Th

Amid the Mirrorgate spy controversy SEAN MACAULAY probes the secret world of suave media tycoon Robert Maxwell. And discovers that the handsome captain is an uncanny double (oh-seven) for sexy spy James Bond

People have made a big mistake about Robert Maxwell, the millionaire publisher and rotund philanthropist. For years he has been compared to a Bond villain and, admittedly, the evidence was strong: he is an immigrant who took a new name (like Dr No); he is used to brokering with superpowers (like Hugo Drax in *Moonraker*); and he once, in a scene reminiscent of Ernst Stavros Blofeld's treatment of his cats in *You Only Live Twice*, dragged an unwilling puppy for a walk. Maxwell also commands a growing empire, bidding for world domination, and boasts a mighty army of goons and henchman in his Holborn fortress. He even dismisses employees who fail him with the no-nonsense precision you expect from a superior Bond villain. Take, for example, the sacking of *Daily Mirror* columnist John Diamond which Maxwell reportedly executed with a cry of 'Terminate him!' How eerily this compares with Donald Pleasence's shrieking injunction as chrome-domed twisted genius Blofeld: 'Kill Bond *now*!'

However, with the Mirrorgate brouhaha and the 'termination' of Maxwell employee Nicholas Davies for 'untrue' denials over his whereabouts amid allegations of arms dealing, attention has shifted. One of the accusations being made is that Maxwell is a spy for Mossad, the Israeli secret service. Secret agent Bob Maxwell? This is patently ludicrous. But if one looks at the material again, there is one fictional character with whom Maxwell has some uncanny resemblances. But it's not an Ian Fleming villain like Dr Julius No or Francisco 'The Man With The Golden Gun' Scaramanga; it's the Ian Fleming hero.

It is quite clear, if you consider the evidence on the opposite page, that Captain Bob works not for Mossad but Her Majesty. It may even be that Sean Connery based his portrayal of 007 on the young Maxwell. After all, the compliment may well have been returned when Maxwell's daughter Anne appeared in the Connery film *Ransom* in 1974. Maxwell even has a Felix Leiter figure in the form of *Mirror* sidekick Joe Haines to assist him in despatching decriers. So step down Commander Bond and step forward Captain Bob – jet-set patriot, fearless death-defier, and gourmet sex symbol. 🐾

How our two superheroes match up

Captain Robert Maxwell MC	**Name**	Commander James Bond CMG, RNVR
French wife Elisabeth Meynard	**Spouse**	Italian wife Tracy di Vicenzo (deceased)
Orphaned in late teens	**Upbringing**	Orphaned at 11
Bentley, private helicopter, a Cadillac when in New York	**Vehicles**	Mark II Bentley, Little Nell one-man copter, Cadillac in New York
On a Qantas flight, Maxwell was brought a cigar and brandy. Discovering them to be Australian he stabbed one into the other and said to the stewardess that the first deserved the second. She broke down	**Epicureanism**	When dining with Felix Leiter at the Royal Bahamian in Nassau, Bond complains of 'inflated bogosity of tourist-hotel food…[it] has certainly been in various deep-freezes for at least six months'
In the days when Maxwell smoked, he only smoked du Maurier cigarettes at a rate of two packs a day. Lung trouble made him stop	**Tobacco**	Smokes Morlands, of Grosvenor Street, a Balkan and Turkish mixture with three gold bands at a rate of 60 a day. Later switches to low-tar brand
'Extremely good-looking, thick shock of dark hair, heavily arched eyebrows, expressive, sensuous mouth, alert, observing eyes. Overwhelming impression of masculinity…etc.' Description of the young Maxwell from his friend Brian Straton-Ferrier	**Looks**	'Very good-looking…but there is something cold and ruthless in his…' says Bond girl Vesper Lynd in *Casino Royale*, sadly interrupted by an explosion. Fleming is more specific: 'A dark clean-cut face…long black brows…cruel mouth'
'He moves fast and not ungracefully…[has] apparently inexhaustible stamina…[like] a marathon runner who can do the course twice.' (Joe Haines)	**Fitness**	Bond is an outstanding athlete, able to swim a couple of miles without tiring. He exercises daily until 'his stomach muscles scream'
Changed his name from Ludvik Hoch, after using Ivan du Maurier (after his favourite brand)	**Name change**	Uses pseudonym Peter Franks in *Diamonds Are Forever* and poses as *FT* hack in *A View to a Kill*
Maxwell was once held at gunpoint for half an hour by a Mexican policeman after escaping from an overcrowded plane. Also active in World War II	**Gunplay**	Uses Walter PPK but often held at gunpoint – *Goldfinger, Russia, Diamonds* etc – 'I'm afraid you've caught me with more than my hands up'
Loves a bold risk and is a good poker player – has even beaten Rupert Murdoch	**Gambling**	Loves the 'dry riffle of the cards' and sees luck as a woman, 'to be softly wooed'
Seymour Hersh	**Enemy**	Smersh
Ian Hislop	**Dwarflike assailant**	Nick Nack

The Eye's omunular ular enchman

Midget man-servant Hervé Villechaize

Those Captain Bob 007 remakes in full

- **From Liechtenstein With Love**
- **A View to a Writ**
- **The Spy Who Left Me**
- **Moneyraker**

- **Muckflinger**
- **On His Majesty's Secret Shareprice**
- **Licence Revoked**
- **Mirror Let Die**

- **The Man With The Golden Gut**
- **(John) Diamonds Are Not Forever**
- **Octopushy**

PIRATE EYE

No. 001
Wednesday
23 Oct '91

BANANA TO APPEAL

EYE OF SORROWS

BY
SYLVIE CRINGE

THE STORY SO FAR: Having handed the control of the magazine 'Private Eye' to his dwarf-like sycophant Ian Hislop, Richard Ingrams has retired to Rye to lead a life of penmanship and gentle contemplation.

Now read on...

Richard lay back on his antique Fantoni divan and stuffed a plug of Old Booker's Virginia Shag into his beloved meerschaum, which he had bought from Balon's in Dean Street in the days when Ian Hislop was just a babe in arms and the *Eye* was still his alone.

In the background, Richard could hear Silvester, his portly, red-faced butler, singing Cole Porter songs to himself as he polished the leather-bound volumes of old back numbers. Silvester's voice was flat and tuneless, but there was something deeply comforting about the sound of the tone-deaf old retainer as he went about his work.

The doorbell rang, and Richard felt his heart leap as Silvester came into his study and announced, 'There is a Miss Bordes to see you, sir.'

Could it be true? After he had sat next to Pamella at a lunch which Hislop had organised for *The South Bank Show* ('Believe me, Richard, old boy,' he had said, 'there's a lot to be gained from sucking up to the TV Johnnies') Richard had been consumed with a heartfelt longing for the lustrous Indian houri. Could it possibly be that she felt equally strongly about him?

All his doubts vanished as Pamella walked into the room. Her body clad in a stunning minidress by Kinnochio of Milan, her dainty feet teetering in a pair of Jacques Delors high heels, she exuded femininity. The soft afternoon light that poured in through the cottage's old leaded windows danced about her thick black hair, cut for her by Francis at Michaelheath. Her eyes sparkled with feminine mischief and there was an unmistakably seductive smile playing around those pouting lips, painted in a delicate shade of Pinter Pink as she made an invitation Richard could not refuse. *(Get on with it. Ed.)*

'Why don't we go for a walk along the shore?' said Pamella. 'Just the two of us.'

Pausing just long enough to put on his old Wheen and Beadle countryman's jacket, Richard strode out of his cottage and made his way towards the seafront.

The touch of Pamella's hand on his arm was enough to send the blood surging through his elderly veins. Suddenly he was tingling with sensations he had feared were gone forever. He felt young again, all his old energy had returned. Why, he might even tell young Hislop that it was time for the master to return to the helm at the *Eye*.

In the distance, Richard could see a balding man in an expensively cut suit pointing at him and Pamella. From time to time he would write things in a little

notebook. Richard thought little of it. He was in love and nothing could come between him and the woman at his side.

The next day at breakfast, Richard was still feeling wonderful. Pamella had had to leave before dinner. She was taking some photographs for *Hello!* magazine, she said, and needed a good night's sleep. But Richard knew that she would race back to him as soon as her work allowed, and he had passed the evening in a long and cheerful telephone call with Nigel Dempster, with whom he had worked so happily, back in the good old days.

Silvester entered the dining-room and coughed respectfully. 'You might care to look at the *Daily Mail*, sir. I believe that you feature in Mr Dempster's diary.'

With mounting horror, Richard's eyes scanned the column: 'Sad old man... walking arm in arm...half his age...' until he felt the cruellest blow of all from his own dear Pamella. 'He's a sweet old boy,' she had told Dempster, 'but I'd never go out with him. He's ancient enough to be my grandad.'

Finally came a line which struck at Richard like a hammer-blow. 'Sources close to *Private Eye* say that the whole "love-affair" was dreamed up by Ian Hislop to publicise his ailing organ, whose fortnightly sales have slipped by 10,000 over the last 12 months.'

Richard ran to the phone and dialled the *Eye*. 'Hislop here,' said the voice at the other end of the line. 'Oh, hi, Richard, did you see the bit in the *Mail*. Great PR, wasn't it? Nothing Dumpster likes more than a good bit of sauce.'

Down the line, Richard could hear a woman's voice in the background. 'Poor old Dickie-baby fell for it hook, line and sinker,' it purred. And the mocking laughter that followed seemed to Richard to be striking at his very soul.

(To be discontinued)

🐸 *Pete Dredge*

'They're making the film of the book!'

'Masons!'

'...So that's a glass of Chardonnay and
a bottle of your house fire-water'

'I think it's time we had that dog done, dear!'

'We've taken in a mature student!'

'I can never remember – do clocks go forward or back an hour?'

'Who's the bastard in the black?'

'I'm going inside now and I may be some some time!'

King sneer

Fat. Bald. Ugly. And that's just what he says about other people. We give Clive James's victims a chance to return the compliments

Presumably as a warm-up act for his third novel out next month, *Clive James On Television* has recently been published. This is the collected TV reviews of the much-loved Aussie funnyman. And yet according to Picador: 'Nobody seems interested. Although Mr James is doing his new BBC series we're not getting any reviews.' How strange.

The reasoning for re-packaging his TV criticism is explained by James in his preface to the hardback preface to the paperback preface to the collected reviews. 'It is now,' he writes, 'a good moment…to remember the good moments.' Indeed it is now so good a moment that James seems to have forgotten about all the bad moments. All the moments when he insulted anything behind a newsdesk, in front of an autocue, or under a wig. All the moments of abuse, put-downs and insolence which earned him the nickname 'TV's Mr Sneer'.

James has suffered what can only be an attack of sentimental retrospection. In the same preface to the preface to the preface, he apologetically explains, 'If at first, I was slow to realise just how good they [the good moments] were, at least I got excited by instinct.' This can be interpreted as a subtle disclaimer of his decade of savage wisecracks: ie, if I didn't give you a good review, I'm sorry folks, I just wasn't thinking.

But on TV, in his new series of *Saturday Night Clive*, James is as insulting as ever to those who aren't guests being toadied to. The problem is that his lack of self-knowledge rather gets in the way. When James crowingly sniggers over a photograph of Robert Maxwell on a mini-bike for being a real fatso, there is a multiple problem here – James's chins. These days the undercarriage beneath his jaw sways like a custard-filled hammock. TV'

The biter bit: TV's Mr Sneer

Square boobs?

Clive said of Jilly Cooper: 'One day someone cleverer than her is going to describe her as she describes other people and say the bridge of her nose has caved in, she's got rotten skin, square boobs and shouldn't wear a low neckline, and she writes very bad prose.'
Jilly Cooper replies: 'Is it the one about me having square tits? I really don't want to start that row up again. We've agreed to forget it now, after the *Spectator* party last year. I think he looks alright, like a very nice pig. But then I've always been fond of pigs.' *Conciliatory!*

Clive said of Barbara Cartland: '[her] mascara-laden eyes are like the corpses of two small crows that have crashed into a chalk cliff.'
Barbara Cartland replies: 'Clive who? Yes I know him. What did he say about me? Oh, is that all, I suppose I'm quite lucky really. He's said that for years. He's very witty and

A dead crow?

amusing. His appearance? He's unique on television; that's enough now dear.' *Tactful!*

Clive said of Vincent Hanna: '*Newsnight*'s inquisitor at large, sounds so aggressive that you start sympathising with the poor harried politicos, even when they are being evasive. Vincent achieved the difficult feat of making Eric Heffer sound hard done-by.'
Vincent Hanna replies: 'His knowledge of British politics has remained relatively static. People and ideas change but the jokes do not. Perhaps even after all this time, he is still a visitor to Britain.' *Politique!*

Clive sneered at Japanese television especially the gameshow *Endurance*. Mrs Yamagata of Nihon Keizai Shimbun Europe replies: 'It doesn't bother me, most of them are really silly programmes anyway. He uses English black humour but I don't think he shows any deep understanding for the Japanese people.' *Diplomatic!*

Japanese Embassy spokesperson replies: 'Yes, well, he's gone over to flattering us now, hasn't he.' *So there!*

An oily duck?

Clive said of Paul Shane: 'With his hair arranged in a messily glistening Tony Curtis cut that looked as if a duck had just taken off from an oil slick, he fills the lower half of the close-up with serried chin while his trained eyes search for campers who need jollifying and his mouth unreels an unbroken ticker tape of triple-tested patter.'
Paul Shane replies: 'What's he said about me? It's OK, it's a journalist's right, he's entitled to his opinion. Mind you, 'e's not an oil painting 'imself. Tell him to keep wearing the see-through wig! I hear he's lost a couple of pounds recently; that'll put him down to the size of an elephant!' *Fighting talk!*

Clive said of Kenny Everett: 'He looks like a rat peering through a bog-brush.'
Kenny Everett replies: 'He's eyeless,

Lofty frontman Clive: Is he the BBC's biggest star?

Mr Sneer is now chunkier than he has ever been. When he gets on the scales the needle hits the 15-stone mark like a garden rake being stepped on in a Tom and Jerry cartoon.

The James face, with its disappearing eyes and melting clay texture, tells the full story. Here is a man who bravely gave up fags and booze in 1977 only to replace them with food. Big Clive does have a basic diet plan which involves eating Lean Cuisine – the only snag is he eats three packs at a time.

Sweet snacks are his danger zone. BBC legend (doubtless apocryphal) has it that when on location for James's *Postcard* series, an advance party has to purge his hotel rooms of any hospitality gifts to prevent him bingeing on the chocolates. But still he expands. So it seems only fair to let some of the victims of his TV reviews have their say. They may even wound the portly funster because, despite his adipose torso, James is still a touch vain. For his wife's birthday he gave her a portrait of *himself*. And he has often instructed cameramen on the right angle to avoid highlighting either his baldness or his chin(s).

Maybe one would find it easier to embrace Cuddly Clive, paunch and all, if he'd come clean about being trivial. Ten years ago he said that one of the TV critic's tasks was 'to see the inadequacy and bogusness of much that claims the status of quality.' How disappointing it is to see James himself now making such inflated claims for his own TV show, a frenzy of wacky adverts, foreign trash, jokey picture captions and celebrity guests:

'I can't think of anything more serious than mass communication,' he says. And, 'There's nothing slumming about writing the links between clips of peak-time Japanese torture-show TV.' Even, 'Trying to work for a large audience is the most valuable thing there is. I do not regard myself as slumming.'

It has been said of him that he is the thinking man's Rolf Harris. But after James's new BBC1 direction, could it be that Rolf is now the thinking man's Clive James? ▧

gets a taste of his own medicine

neckless and benign…do I really look like a rat?' ***Bemused!***

Clive said of Mrs Thatcher: '[She] sounded like the Book of Revelations read out over a railway public address system by a head mistress of a certain age wearing calico knickers.'
Bernard Ingham, her former press secretary, replies: 'That sounds like just the sort of thing Clive James would say. He's a man who has only achieved success through the disparaging of others. Mrs Thatcher handled criticism in the same way I do – she laughed at it.' ***No nonsense!***

Clive said of Murray Walker: 'Even in moments of tranquillity he sounds like a man whose trousers are on fire…like a blindfolded man riding a unicycle on the rim of the pit of doom.'
Murray Walker replies: 'The man who can destroy more people with fewer words than anyone else I know. He's bald and tubby and a toupé would certainly help!' ***Robust!***

Clive said of Peter Marshall: 'Showed all the signs of having been passed through that famous BBC processing

room where front-men go to be deprived of charisma…can speak endlessly without meaning anything.'
Peter Marshall replies: 'Clive had a go at me *two weeks* after the Miss World competition because I had pointed out that he wasn't as good as Michael Parkinson at presenting *Cinema*. Clive obviously feels that if you call yourself fat and bald as a coot first, you steal everyone else's thunder, and indeed I can't really add to that description. I think Miss World will be around a long time after he will.' ***Take that!***

Unsubtle?

Clive said of *The Glittering Prizes*: 'All the aphoristic subtlety of Montaigne… [Characters] emitting one of the clever things Frederic Raphael once said (or else would have said, but thought of too late, and so is saying now)…precious little sense of anything special going on. A dull start.'
Frederic Raphael replies: 'The best response to this appears in the film *The Fountainhead*. In it a critic ruins

the life of Gary Cooper, a genius architect, who winds up walking the street of New York. When they meet, the critic confronts the genius and asks him, 'We're completely alone. Now you can tell me exactly what you think of me.' And the genius turns and says, 'I don't think of you. [And you're Gary Cooper?] Of course. Clive just doesn't matter to me.' ***Quid pro quo!***

Clive said of Lord Longford: '[His] struggle to attain humility would be somewhat eased by a self-appraisal which faced the fact that he is one of the most conceited men alive.'
Lord Longford replies: 'Forgive me, but if I know he's coming on the television, I switch it off. It's ridiculous. I have many faults but conceit's not one of them. I knew *Punch* under Malcolm

Muggeridge, you know. Is this all you can manage? Really, being rung up about this James fellow is like being rung up about the World Ludo Championship.'
Conceited? ***Touché!***

'He modelled himself on Brian Robson'

ROBERT THOMPSON.

'Waddle...to Waddle...'

'Hello, I've run out of dog biscuits'

'...then we lost the Andrex account'

'Now, let me see, Ronald red is naughty,
but Billy blue's a good little boy...'

'Don't worry. Whatever it is, it's not serious'

The *Punch* guide to
SPORT
and alcohol

Do you speak sport?
MARCUS BERKMANN begins our survey
with a diploma course in the bizarre
language of the sports pages

FIRST RULE OF FOOTBALL JOURNALISM, SON, – NEVER LOSE POSSESSION

Sometimes you have to feel sorry for foreigners. (Not often, I know, but sometimes.) Eager to flourish in an English-speaking world, they can spend years assiduously learning the language, practising their vowel sounds, trying to say 'th' without flobbing vast quantities of Europhlegm over whoever they're talking to – and then some entirely unfamiliar form of the tongue comes along with which they simply can't cope: Cockney rhyming slang, computer jargon, legalese, Scottish tramps wandering up to you in St James's Park asking for ten pence for a cup of tea in broad Glaswegian accents; all can easily confound real English people, let alone poor Johnny Foreigner, over here on holiday with his rucksack and his wispy beard.

But of all the nation's most obscure and incomprehensible dialects, none is quite as opaque and stylised as that of the sportswriter. Most of us who customarily turn to the back page of a morning to see which First Division manager has been fired today have, over many years, become used to this strange hyperbolic prose, in which titles are invariably 'clinched', defences 'bolstered' and crosses 'converted'. But what about someone coming across all this bilge for the first time? How would a Martian react to the news that a player had been 'axed'? With a machete? Is summary execution of inadequate sportsmen legal in this barbarous land?

Those big questions answered: what does Richie Benaud do after his TV Test Match intros? Who's column is angry and read? Can footballers read? And who the hell is John Sadler?

Have pen, will drivel: *10 modest sporting by-lines*

- **Norman Gillers:** 'Looks at the funny side of sport' *Sunday Express*
- **Johnny Giles**: 'The man the players read' *Daily Express*
- **James Lawton**: 'The column that tackles the big sporting issues' *Daily Express*
- **Peter Shaw**'s 'Angry Column' *Daily Mirror*
- **Mike Langley**: 'Voice of *People* sport' *People*
- **Richie Benaud**: 'The voice of cricket' *News of the World.*
- **John Taylor**: 'The voice of
- rugby.' *Mail on Sunday*
- **Tony Lewis**: 'The voice of racing' *Daily Star*
- **Bob Driscoll**: 'The real voice of sport' *Daily Star*
- **John Sadler**: 'The man who gives it to you straight' *Sun*

In an attempt, therefore, to untangle this linguistic labyrinth, *Punch* now presents its own detailed guide to the gentle art of sportswriting. No one need ever again gasp with horror and incredulity on reading of a player who 'slices open' defences.

FOOTBALL

Of all sports, football perhaps has the most colourful vocabulary and unusual turns of phrase. This is mainly due to one of the unwritten rules of sports journalism, which is that football is the most interesting sport in the world. Every day, pages and pages are devoted to it, whether or not anything interesting has happened the previous day. Sadly, interesting things happen only very rarely in the world of football, and then, such as Gazza's altercation with a mystery assailant in a Newcastle nightclub, only on

Oh, I say!
10 ways of describing that crucial ball-in-back of net scenario

- Pierce the defence
- Convert a cross
- Strike sweetly
- Crack in a goal
- Notch a hat-trick
- Force home
- Lash home
- Drive home
- With a rapier thrust
- With a crisp header

But where were the big men at the back?

And with little or nothing actually to write about, the language has to take the strain. Players, when not being 'axed', are instead 'banished', either to Outer Darkness or, if they're lucky, to the reserves. Teams don't lose, they 'crash' or 'slump' to a defeat. Goalkeepers who don't let any goals in have 'clean sheets', which presumably saves on detergent. And managers do not buy players, they 'splash out' on them, although whether they do so on the clean sheets is rarely specified.

Managers, of course, are the lifeblood of the modern game. Twenty years ago, managers were like Bertie Mee and Bill Nicholson, reserved figures who simply got on with managing. The newspapers were more interested in the players. Now, with all these pages to fill, managers have turned into sharp-suited quote machines. Matches, sorry, 'top-table clashes' between sides are now seen as the battle of the managers, with the players merely there as decoration. But then very few players give good quotes. When Paul Merson is quoted as saying 'I hope my call-up repays the people who stuck by me in the bad times,' we all know that he never said that, partly because no one in the world would ever utter a sentence like 'I hope my call-up repays the people who stuck by me in the bad times,' and partly because to a footballer 16 ☛

the fringes. Most football coverage, by contrast, is frighteningly unnecessary – detailed reports of games we all saw on the telly last night, ghosted columns by retired footballers and recently-fired managers and all the endless arguments about the nascent Super League, which all supporters lost interest in as soon as they realised that it had nothing to do with football and an awful lot to do with suitcases full of money.

words isn't a sentence, it's a novel. But although the sportswriter knows we don't believe it, and we know he knows, and he knows we know he knows, everybody just lets it pass. (Although if Paul Gascoigne was quoted as saying 16 words in a row, perhaps a few eyebrows would be raised…)

It's when they report actual matches (that we all saw on telly last night) that football writers really come into their own. Games 'explode into life'. A team 'grabs' victory. One player 'notches' a hat-trick. (When he scores his first goal he 'opens his account'.) Goals are 'coolly slotted in', 'fired home', or scored with a 'bullet' header. Teams don't draw, they 'take home a hard-earned point'. And they don't win, they 'hit fellow strugglers Barnsley with a three-goal blast.' *Plus ça change, plus c'est la même chose.*

I WAS WELL AHEAD WITH MY MANSELL PIECE WHEN THE COMPUTER CRASHED

RACING

As anyone who has tried but failed to watch a whole episode of *Trainer* will bear out, the racing world is an arcane and enclosed little universe, whose physical laws bear little relation to the real world as we understand it. Look at racing correspondents. Unlike most other sportswriters, and indeed people, all racing correspondents have not one but two names, one fairly normal and one very silly indeed. There is no explanation for this. In the *Daily Mail*, for instance, Jack Millan is also known as 'Robin Goodfellow', or possibly vice versa – the real facts are lost in the mists of time. The *Telegraph*'s J A McGrath calls himself 'Hotspur', a *nom de plume* that is for some reason considered less silly than 'Crystal Palace' or 'Brighton and Hove Albion'. And the *Daily Express*'s John de Moraville, or 'Bendex', goes even further: he has no normal name at all, but two exceptionally silly names. Only in this way – and by wearing a hideous brown trilby – can you ever hope to be taken seriously as a racing expert. (My new tipster column, under the title

The Arsenal team of the Thirties looks on happily as George Graham sticks to his 'no entertainment' policy

Scotland's manager, Andy Roxburgh, used to be a school-teacher. It is therefore unlikely that he came across any of his current fans in days gone by

A Life of Brians: *10 managers speak out*

- 'You can play well for 89 minutes and then lose it in one minute'

  Graham Taylor, England

- 'Who would be a football manager? I feel as if I went through all 90 minutes out there'

  Andy Roxburgh, Scotland

- 'I thought it was a harsh sending off. I felt for Ian, it affects his career and his destiny'

  David Pleat, Luton

- 'Points are more important than performance'

  George Graham, Arsenal

- 'Rovers are my life and that has been taken away from me'

  Don Mackay, ex-Blackburn

- 'We won't win the league this month, it's all about what happens next month'

  Alex Ferguson, Manchester Utd

- 'He couldn't score in a brothel'

  Neil Warnock, Notts County, on striker Kevin Bartlett

- 'We deserved what we got, because we gave away two soft goals'

  Howard Wilkinson, Leeds Utd

- 'If someone brings me a Martian who can score 25 goals a season, I'll take him. If he only wants £400 a week, even better'

  Dave Bassett, Sheffield Utd

- 'I don't think we gave them a kick – apart from the two goals'

  Trevor Francis, Sheffield Wed

By CAPTAIN HEATH (Colin Mackenzie)

then he will be retired ... an bill of health on ...

By THE SCOUT (John Garnsey)

off-colour for most of ... again ...

By HOTSPUR (J A McGrath)

RICHARD HANNON ... in spect ...

NEWSBOY'S VERDICT

3.00

TOP SHOT

TELLY TIPS By TEMPLEGATE
ET smart and col-
't on Collide (3.5)
the Moss Bros ...
'takes at

MANDARIN

the Shadeed colt ran
ongly to get within a len ...
enry Cecil's
King

TRUSS
(2.20 at Worcester)
Three points win
One point place

INFORMATION

WINNING favourite
the last 10

Insufficiently inspired by the results of their infant christenings, a group of humble Kens, Jacks and Colins are transformed into mightily becolumned nagmeisters via the adoption of a ludicrous moniker

Naff Naps: *10 racing writers with silly pseudonyms*

- Bendex – John de Moraville, *Daily Express*
- The Scout – John Garnsey, *Daily Express*
- Mandarin – Michael Phillips, *Times*
- Robin Goodfellow – Jack Milan, *Daily Mail*
- Hotspur – J A McGrath, *Daily Telegraph*
- Captain Heath – Colin Mackenzie, *Daily Mail*
- Clockform – Ken Hussey, *Daily Star*
- Top Shot – *Today*
- Templegate – *Sun*
- Newsboy – *Daily Mirror*

'Trousersnake', begins in *Punch* next week.)

Once again, though, the language has its own precise rules, which, if broken, disallow you from prefixing Goodwood with the adjective 'glorious' ever again. Horses have 'runs' and 'outings' in good or bad 'company'. If good, horses are 'much vaunted' or 'warrant respect on home gallops'. Peter Scudamore is a 'jump giant', Lester Piggott 'the maestro'. Poor horses are 'disappointing in the face of a stiff task behind Bottle Top'. Jockeys 'take the mount', especially if they are one trainer's 'regular pilot'. Holding back for a late run, a jockey 'saves his powder' and if there are pots of money to be won, you'll find there are 'rich pickings on the hoof'.

The upshot of all this is that non-punters are completely confused, which is, of course, exactly what the racing world wants. So when 'Hotspur' writes knowingly, 'He reported that the girths were three holes longer than when he ran in the Irish Derby,' he does so in the safe and warming knowledge that most of us have not the vaguest idea what he is going on about.

CRICKET

Here we must pause and define our terms. Two sorts of journalists cover cricket – the cricket correspondents, who are interested primarily in whether the ball was moving off the seam or not and whether Pringle will be selected for the next Test, and the sports journalists sent to cover cricket, who like all non-cricket fans are interested in only two things: Botham and smut, and preferably both. As far as most tabloid newspapers are concerned, Botham is cricket.

The sport's other characters, though interesting in their own way (Gooch impassive, Gower airy-fairy public schoolboy, Gatting funny beard and high voice), simply haven't the same appeal. If Botham is playing in a Test match and does little but take a catch at slip, while someone else scores 150, the tabloids will usually concentrate on the catch. The fact that the great wobblebottom almost certainly 'pouched' the thing in his ☞

He's a brilliant sportswriter – his knowledge of clichés is unsurpassed

enormous spreading gut is, of course, entirely irrelevant.

Meanwhile, boundaries will have been 'hammered', quick 50s 'thundered' and centuries 'cracked'. An innings, in the tabloids, is a 'knock', a century a 'ton', while fast bowlers (especially those who 'bag wickets') soon become the 'spearhead of the attack'. Good teams 'build a mighty score', bad teams are 'skittled out' and the West Indies have 'a relentless pace battery'. No one, however, 'clobbers' runs – with the exception of Ian Botham.

THE HEAVIES

The serious newspapers naturally approach sport in a different way – often by writing about it in almost recognisable English – but even then there are interesting diversions from the norm. Football reports, especially those in the *Daily Telegraph*, often read like excerpts from old school stories: players 'unleash a confident shot' but are 'denied by the woodwork'. Players are not obstructed, their 'progress is blocked'. Teams are 'fleet of foot in attack'.

Cricket, by contrast, appears to be played for much higher stakes. Since Matthew Engel upped the ante in the *Guardian* a few years ago, all cricket writers are now humorists. It's no longer good enough merely to fill your copy with loads of choice cricketing phrases like 'deceived in the flight' – now jokes are required and sometimes (particularly in the *Independent*) reports are so full of them that it's hard to work out what actual cricket took place.

Nonetheless, that mandarin *Telegraph* style still survives: batsmen are still 'dislodged' (having been 'entrenched'), partners are still 'durable allies', and last innings remain 'valedictory'. Only in the *Telegraph* is a bad shot still 'injudicious' – long may that remain.

Owzat? *10 super-wordy penmen*

A loud, aggressive varlet, or an inspiring grand old man of sport? Either way, he's still the man they call 'Jimbo'

● 'When their (Middlesex's) turn came they also bowled like dogs, frequently exploiting virgin areas of the pitch, missed a couple of catches and generally conveyed the air of a side glad that September had come and the agony can end.'
Mike Selvey, *Guardian*

● 'Giggs swept past Hurlock before cleverly back-heeling for Kanchelskis to cross, Robson to head back and Hughes to drive home.'
Russell Thomas, *Guardian*

● 'The ball bounced a little waspishly at times and seamed about in a lively but not extravagant manner.'
Christopher Martin-Jenkins, *Daily Telegraph*

● 'He (David Gower) seemed well set for his first century of the season, when the Devil whipped his bottom hand through and deep leg gratefully accepted.'
Jeremy Allerton, *Daily Telegraph*

● 'Jimmy Connors is loud, aggressive and, with the face and hairstyle of a medieval varlet, he personifies a generation which tips its hat to no man.'
Ian Wooldrige, *Daily Mail*

● 'Derbyshire's hopes of securing a top three place were compromised by injuries and punctured by penetrative bowling, but nothing deflated them more than the feeble acquiescence of their own batting.'
Neil Hallam, *Daily Telegraph*

● 'It took them (Wales) 44 minutes to test Taffarel (Brazilian goalkeeper) and the examination was of the 11-plus variety.'
Joe Lovejoy, *Independent*

● 'A third wicket stand of 91 salvaged a modicum of pride after Barnett and Morris had perished to lamentably inappropriate wafts.'
Neil Hallam, *Daily Telegraph*

● 'Mattheus conducts midfield like a latter-day Sir Malcolm Sargent.'
Steve Curry, *Daily Express*

● 'The class act of the afternoon was Villa's goal, Atkinson bamboozling Ablett and Richardson striking nut-sweet.'
Stephen Bierley, *Guardian*

PAUL THOMAS

Who's harassing whom?

GREAT FIGURES IN HISTORY, AS SEEN BY BRITAIN'S SPORTSWRITERS

● **Jesus Christ:** the bearded carpenter's son from Bethlehem who gets onto the end of crosses

● **Dracula:** he's a biting striker but he spends too much time in his own box

● **Hitler:** Germany's firebrand right-winger, who failed to skipper his team to World Cup glory

● **John F Kennedy:** he's America's top target man but he goes to pieces on the big occasion

● **Winston Churchill:** the cigar-chomping England supremo who never knows when he's beaten

● **Joe Stalin:** he's a hard man, but fair, say team-mates of the man they call, 'Big Joe'

● **Marie Antoinette:** an elegant performer but she loses her head on the big occasion

● **Captain Scott:** normally ice-cool but freezes on the big occasion
(That's enough big occasions, Ed)

● **Attila the Hun:** he was the wild man of the mountains but he's still too soft for Wimbledon

● **Paul Gascoigne:** he's the man they call, 'A fat Geordie git'

'Brilliant – see how he controls the ball and at the same time obscures the defenders' logo'

'I blame Nigel Kennedy'

'He's sponsored by Mister Whippy'

'Nice top you've got there, Doreen'

'Talk about flaunting his wealth!'

'Serves me right for saying I wanted to work with animals'

This DESIGNER-TRACK-SUIT-clad individual wearing the HI-TECH TRAINERS is immediately recognised as...

LOOSE FIT DISGUISES BEER-BELLY AND ALLOWS UN-RESTRICTED MOVEMENT OF THE DRINKING-ARM

HIGH-TECH TRAINERS ADJUST FOR LONG PERIODS STANDING AT THE BAR OR FOR QUICK SPRINTS AT THE SIGNAL, "LAST ORDERS!"

Whether a SPECTATOR or a PLAYER, the **BOOZE FACTOR** in SPORT cannot be ignored...

...THE SPECTATOR

MATERIAL ALLOWS FOR HOURS OF SLUMPING IN FRONT OF T.V. WITHOUT UNSIGHTLY CREASING

The U.K. boasts two distinct categories of SPORTS ENTHUSIASTS. The SPECTATORS and The PLAYERS

The BOOZE FACTOR plays an important role in most sports...

ANGLING for instance

THE ANGLER'S REST

ANOTHER YARD OF ALE, BARMAN

Here, the object appears to be to DRINK more than...

... one's OPPONENT

RUGBY players, too, must consume vast quantities of beer as part of their training program

I'D BUY YOU A DRINK BUT IT MIGHT AFFECT YOUR AMATEUR STATUS

Currently, concern is being expressed about the effects of BOOZE on some SPORTSMEN. **SNOOKER** players in particular...

HE SPENDS MORE TIME UNDER THE TABLE THAN AT IT

SNOOKER

I NEED A REST, PLEASE

... and IAN BOTHAM's T.V. promotion of ALCOHOL-FREE-LAGER is hoped to counteract the past attempts of some of his team-mates to **DRIVE US TO DRINK**

TEST-MATCH SPECIAL

(GIN + WHISKY + VODKA + RUM)

SWIMMING, however, is one of the few sports in which the BOOZE FACTOR is irrelevant, since, usually...

CALL THIS A DRY SPORT?

... there is more liquid **OUTSIDE** the competitors than **INSIDE**

IF LANGER COULD SINK **PUTTS** THE WAY YOU SINK **LAGERS** WE'D STILL HOLD THE RYDER CUP

NO MORE FOR ME — THE BOSS HAS ORDERED ME TO GET TO BED EARLY — DO YOU THINK 3 A.M. IS EARLY ENOUGH?

HE'S OVERDOING THE SOCCER — HIS PERFORMANCE ON THE DANCE FLOOR TONIGHT WAS PATHETIC

DISCO BAR

The professional **FOOTBALLER**, also immediately recognised by his attire (*trendy disco-gear*), is well aware of the BOOZE FACTOR. For him, BOOZE and SPORT are incompatible

This is invaluable preparation for a game in which most of the time is spent...

... falling FLAT ON YOUR FACE

In the **DARTS** world, the BOOZE FACTOR is shortly expected to force a change in the RULES...

YOU CAN STAND AS CLOSE TO THE BOARD AS YOUR STOMACH ALLOWS

ONE HUNDRED AND **EIGHTY** AND THAT'S JUST HIS COLLAR SIZE

HE NEVER FINISHES ON A DOUBLE — HE PREFERS TO STICK TO PINTS

Finally, with 1992 almost upon us, we must all, **PLAYERS** and **SPECTATORS** alike, settle down to a STRICT TRAINING REGIME. Only then can we hope to PEAK just in time for THE OLYMPICS

BEER GLASS STAIN REMOVER

Booze boy

Booze is an eerie subject to face on a seedy October morning, the eyes poached in their own blood, teeth taken out and turned round as I slept, palpitations, numbness and deep ill-will. I shouted at the bad woman all night until she went to sleep on the floor; towards dawn she crept back and I bopped her on the nose. Forearm smash. You hardly have to roll over. Now everything smells of herring and spleen.

Once I would have sworn never to touch another drop but that's for cissies. Now I go for the regime instead. Look:

1. Beroccas. They sound like part of an Australian mating ritual ('Show us yer Beroccas, then') and taste like one too. In fact they are lethal-dose Vitamin B tablets which glow in the dark. Take four, in water. They will take your liver's mind off its problems by giving it an infinitely worse one to deal with.

2. Into the bog, taking a can of Lucozade, a packet of Walker's crisps, two Lucky Strikes (unfiltered) and a copy of *Weirdos from Another Planet*. Experience small stroke.

3. Violent coitus.

4. Hot bath.

5. Dispute with fat bailiff in cheap shoes.

6. Beans on toast with raw egg stirred in.

7. (2)

8. (3)

9. Small vodka and lime. Large vodka and lime. Large vodka, no lime. Two macaroons, condemned Cornish Pasty, pickled onion, large vodka and lime, cup of lukewarm tea with dog-end fallen into it, helium, one green chilli, bird seed, heroin, toast.

10. Strap bad woman spread-eagled on bed, achieve large erection, stare at it blankly for a while, go to sleep.

This regime does not work but it is so much worse, in so many ways, than the symptoms themselves that you will soon be champing at the bit, ready to go out and do it all over again.

Do what?

Get drunk, of course.

Have no truck with people who say 'Why do it?' or 'Since I stopped drinking I have felt fitter and clearer-headed than ever before.' They are bores and frauds. Worst of all are the Alcoholics Anonymous lot. They take themselves terribly seriously. You have to stand up and say 'I am Ken and I am an alcoholic,' and if you say 'I am Sir Florizel Bargepole and I am an alcoholic, mine's a large vodka-and-methadone, what are the rest of you having?' they all look incredibly solemn. It's all about God, really. The born-agains are taking it over, grisly little men with caring eyes. They mean well. They are genuine. They have found Jesus. They are so bloody awful sober that you can't even imagine what they are like drunk.

Except, of course, you can, all too well. *In vino veritas* does not refer to what people say, but what they become. I, in my cups, am rigorous, virile, seductive, multi-talented and, 70 per cent of the time, arrested. Others are not so fortunate. The dim bulb in brown trousers does not become more illuminated after a few Mackesons; he merely becomes more so, often involving snapshots. They may be snapshots of trains or snapshots of gloomy belfries containing blurred, wan turnip heads called There's Old Leonard Again. Sometimes they are snapshots of fish. If your man is a camera buff, they will be snapshots of cameras.

One Dim Bulb Drunk who used to infect my local bar in Brooklin Massachusetts, was an organ enthusiast. Once pissed, he would reach into his windcheater and pull out snapshots of organs. Every snapshot had an associated specification sheet, neatly typed out, flue stops in black, reeds in red, mixtures underlined. He would make you hold the snapshot while he read the specification. 'Great Organ,' he would drone, 'Double Diapason, 16 foot. Stopped Diapason, 16 foot. Open Diapason I, eight foot. Open Diapason II, eight foot. How about that, huh? Why, I'd give...hey, which photo've you got? Let's see? Well, hell. I read the wrong specification. Yup – this is the one. Listen...'

And it would all start again. *In vino veritas.*

It applies across the board. If you think that, by getting drunk, you are revealing new and hitherto-unexplored regions of profundity, forget it. You remain what you are. The executive berk in the grey suit does not, ever, ever become a poet, warrior or Real Man by getting drunk. He becomes more of an executive. He gets nastier and more frightened. His speech becomes more and more thickly-larded with grim nonsensical executive-speak. He becomes more frantically status-conscious and hungry for approval until finally he blacks out in a lurching horror of acronyms, brand-names and unaccommodated greed.

The brainless grebo, dispossessed, disenfranchised and turned by our educational system (prop Shirley Williams) into a *tabula rasa* for the drivellings of bureaucrats, does not reveal his soul when smashed. He does not reveal his soul because he has no

a naughty then?

BARGEPOLE faces up to liquidity problems and offers a philosophy: I drink, therefore I ram

soul. Where his soul should be is a copy of *TV Times* and a Stanley knife. Nor does he reveal a hunger for Culture, for he has none, not even a vestigial sort of arthropod desire to understand what Julie Burchill has to 'say'. He merely becomes more horrible and empty, and the only saving grace is that, when drunk enough, he may practise rudimentary carpentry on a pickled executive or organ bore.

Even the more grotesque manifestations of drunkenness are, if you have kept your wits about you, predictable. The middle-aged couple who suddenly start talking about 'swinging' were identifiable from the very beginning, if you had known the signs. Both were startlingly unattractive, weren't they? Did she not have mad eyes, a bad hair-do and big, unwholesome breasts? Was he not smaller than she, with wet hands and dry lips? There you are then. So when they start leaning over towards you and with stale breath, scented with half-metabolised booze (ketones, acetaldehydes, despair) and worse, you know what to do. Read Bargepole's Guide To Ten Commonly-Encountered Drink-Related Situations, which, curiously enough, follows directly.

● **What do I do if a couple of complete strangers start talking about wife-swapping?** You saw it coming, didn't you? (see the signs above). Right. You look them in the eye, say 'Fine. What do you want to swap her for? How about 20 Silk Cut and a Filofax Guide To London Late-Night Shopping?' If he agrees, hit him in the face (lack of chivalry). If he refuses, hit him in the face (parsimony). If, however, she is a slithery, snake-hipped sink of vice and corruption, agree, leave the bar with them and only then hit him in the face before making off with her.

● **What accessories should I carry when going out for a night's drinking in a singles bar?** A mobile telephone. You will end up in some woman's flat. In the morning, she will be bruised and nauseous, but will have no milk for your coffee. You will be unable to tolerate daylight. Note her telephone number. Go out to buy milk. Use the mobile telephone to ring her up and ask where she lives, because by the time you have bought the milk you will be completely sun-blinded and need to be talked back. Meanwhile, programme your telephone to give you an alarm call. When you get back, it will ring. Make your escape, leaving her to stew uneasily in the rank sweat of her enseamed bed.

● **People say you should never mix your drinks. Is this true?** Of course. That is the barman's job. Better still, why not drink *man's* drinks.

● **What are man's drinks?** Things drunk by people who look as though they might punch you in the face if you suggested wife-swapping. Essentially, man's drinks are a) brown or b) colourless. They must have no form of decoration in them at all, although in a few rare cases a slice of lemon is permissible; it should, however, be removed with a shout of 'Bloody poofter nonsense! I ordered a *drink*, not a f***ing Del Monte ad.'

● **What is a suitable drink for a woman on the first date?** You shouldn't be worrying about that, honey. If you are with the right kind of man, he will simply put you onto a bar-stool, call over the bartender, point at you with his thumb and say: 'Fill her up.' Then he will stand, saying nothing but watching you gradually deliquesce, whereupon he will take you home.

● **I went out with a guy like that and when we got home he couldn't crack a fat. What is correct behaviour in these circumstances?** Correct behaviour is not to talk about 'cracking a fat'. The correct term is 'temporary alcohol-induced erectile incompetence', and correct behaviour is to say 'There, there darling it really doesn't matter.' But who gives a fig for correct behaviour? The *right* thing to do is laugh, point, waggle it back and forth saying 'Oh God! Nothing's so silly as a little limp willy,' take Polaroids and ring all your friends. If you have artistic leanings, you may occupy the still watches of the night in making a sign to hang on his back as he leaves, saying 'I couldn't get it up last night!' This will gain him lots of attention at the office, which is what the pathetic, impotent wimp wants anyway.

● **I do not know anything about wine and am embarrassed when dining with business contacts. What should I do?** Take control. Demand to be the one who looks at the wine list. Scan it rapidly, sneer, and say 'If that's the best you can do, we'll have six cans of Red Stripe and an ounce of Chinese White. Each.'

● **I don't know whether it's my Scottish blood or what, but once I start drinking I can't stop. I get completely smashed and cry and talk about my soul and stuff, and people give me odd looks. What should I do?** Invent a secret but deadly disease – most people find cancer suitable – which you tell people you've got once you get to the crying stage. Within a few minutes, they'll all be crying too, and you can have a wonderful time. Alternatively, move to St Petersburg. They're all like that there anyway.

● **My boyfriend is from Finland. He drinks heavily and talks about suicide a lot. I fear that he may be an alcoholic. Or perhaps he is just a manic depressive. What do you think?** 'Or'? What do you mean 'or'? Of course he is an alcoholic. And of course he is a manic depressive. He's from Finland.

● **I'm, er, there's a bit of a, oh God I think I'm going to...sorry about that, it's just that last night I, oh Jesus there's blood everywhere, excuse me, oh no! Oh no! What happened to my eyes? Maybe I'm...aaah! Who's this woman? Who are you? Hello? Hello? Er...**What you need is a good stiff drink. 🦡

'People try to put us down...'

'He's supposed to chase sheep, he's the bloody sheepdog'

'And folklore has it they never forget!...'

CAT AEROBICS

'That's bloody cunning isn't it?
I'd never've guessed Nigel was away on holiday'

Don't fancy Eeyore's much..

How to be a has-been...
SPY

The hey day

You're master of the microfilm and doyen of the diplomatic bag. When everyone's shaken, you're not even stirred. You're the Mr Cool of the espionage world. But it's all downhill from here...

The slippery slope

1. The Soviet Union collapses and the KGB winds up. 'Does that mean I get my 00 number?' you ask M.
2. 'No,' he replies. 'You get the P45 number.' You travel to the States. 'My big CIA friends will look after me,' you tell *I Spy* magazine. Your big CIA friends...
3. Are now on welfare. You offer your services to a Middle East government.
4. 'Do you take IOUs?' asks Saddam Hussein. You apply for a job with Mossad. 'Join the back of the queue,' they answer.

The futile gesture

5. You open a spy school in Dorking. 'You could learn more from a Len Deighton novel,' sneers Chapman Pincher.
6. 'Who's Chapman Pincher?' you ask on the Oleg Gordievsky's LBC *Chat-Back Line*. You become an industrial spy...
7. For a builder's merchant. You open the Fifth Man pub. 'It's more like the Legless Publican,' suggests MP Rupert Allason (under privilege, in the House). You threaten to sue.
8. 'Have you got £400,000?' asks your lawyer. You go to Australia 'to live off my pension'. One problem...
9. You haven't got a pension. You claim Wilson, Macmillan and Mrs Thatcher were Russian spies. But disaster!

The killer blow

10. No one bans your book. You are forced into a uniformed position. In the Corps of Commissionaires.

The cruel twist

After your death, fooling around with an exploding cigarette packet, Rik Mayall plays you in the hit film *The Spies Who Loved Me*. It's banned in Britain, under the Official Secrets Act.

MIKE CONWAY

ILLUSTRATION: DAVID LYTTLETON

Review to a kill

MIKE CONWAY reports on the mystery critics who write attacks on book reviews not books

The only feedback a Fleet Street literary critic used to get was his book review being quoted on the cover of the paperback edition. Now the hapless hacks of Grub Street can't move for attention. The *Sunday Telegraph*, the *Sunday Times*, and *Bookseller*, which bills itself as 'the organ of the book trade', all cast pseudonymously critical eyes over other book reviews. This genre of reviewing the reviewers offers infinite extension; the logical step, which we boldly take here, is, of course, to review the reviews of the reviewers.

First off is *Bookseller* with its 'Critics Crowner' (sic), the crustiest of the three columns. Written under the ho-ho nom de hack of Quentin Oates (Q Oates, ie quotes), its primary aim is to summarise the coverage of new products for retailers. But a recriminating finger is often wagged by Oates, whose opinions can be stern. Reviewers are scolded for being 'pompous', 'over the top' and 'toffee-nosed'. The 'great names' of the past are nostalgically mourned, and invariably Auberon Waugh's writing about books 'is not a patch on what it was'. The constant regret is that 'Quite simply, there are no stars any more.'

Mr Oates's turn of phrase is equally antediluvian. One *Independent* reviewer's 'grim prose' is said to ensure 'this reader felt that he was being pinned in the corner by some elder of the kirk.'

Representative of the Oates tone is his review of Martin Amis's review of Bill Buford's soccer violence study, *Among The Thugs*. 'One does not expect football hooligans on the book pages,' avers Mr Oates, 'back-stabbing, venom and genteel mayhem, perhaps...' Then 'young Mr Buford' gets the kiss of death by being dubbed 'literary flavour of the month' by old Mr Oates who sternly announces that 'some may dispute Mr Amis's claim that Mr Buford was "one of the greatest literary middlemen of his time".' Indeed they may.

The *Sunday Times*'s round-up of reviews, 'On The Critical List', goes under the alias Harvey Porlock (after Coleridge's infamous interrupter and the fictional rabbit). By far the spikiest of the three, Porlock thrives on attacking the major players on the London literary scene. In response to the *Times Literary Supplement*'s 'leaden summary' of Margaret Drabble's *The Gates Of Ivory*, he says, 'If this is the novel of ideas, give me good old Hampstead adultery any time.' He also lets fly at the *Literary Review*'s Nicola Watson in her Drabble review for resorting to 'a bad case of the Bron syndrome', which is, apparently, 'a compulsion to include jokes and gossip in any review'.

The Bron in question is, of course, the aforementioned ailing talent Auberon Waugh, Britain's most overpaid journalist and editor of Ms Watson's magazine. It seems only natural that Ms Watson should nod in the direction of her master's style, despite the magazine's derisory £25 per review pay scheme. But in Porlock's private war against Bron, there are no prisoners. 'Serious work by serious novelists deserves better than this in an allegedly literary magazine,' he sniffs.

Intriguingly, Porlock rarely fails to include a couple of jokes and the odd bit of gossip in his own column. 'Boy what a party. There's Mark Lawson, Tom Shone, David Sexton and James Sayno...James Wood, Mick Imlah, Adam Mars-Jones, Michael Vermeulen...What else but the new Martin Amis could pull in a

Those literary Rottweilers who criticise the critics

● **Nom de plume:** William Startle.

● **Column:** 'Review of Reviews' in the *Sunday Telegraph*.

● **Typical Quote:** *(On Brian Master's biography of E F Benson)* 'E F (Fred) Benson, son of a much reviled Archbishop of Canterbury, and more to the point, the creator of the delightful *Mapp and Lucia*...'

● **Pet Phrases:** 'Olympian uncertainty'; 'quibble'; 'revived by a cup of tea'.

● **Nom de plume:** Harvey Porlock.

● **Column:** 'On the Critical List' in the *Sunday Times*.

● **Typical Quote:** *(On Auberon Waugh)* 'Build your career on bile, persecuting and mocking your enemies...you will...become a much revered sacred cow. Like Bron himself or his most slavish imitator Julie Burchill.'

● **Pet Phrases:** 'An odd piece'; 'slimily unpleasant'; 'Can we have the review now?'

● **Nom de plume:** Quentin Oates.

● **Column:** 'Critics Crowner' in *Bookseller* magazine.

● **Typical Quote:** '"The Anthony Burgess Review": I cannot imagine anyone buying a Friday *Independent* just to read that one piece. It is quite some time since I have read anything really startling by Mr Burgess, who if not in his dotage, is heavily into his anecdotage.'

● **Pet Phrases:** 'A mild wigging'; 'a worthy novel'; 'a real telling off'.

EB

Porlock, on the other hand, went straight for the jugular. He made fun of the *Sunday Telegraph*'s odd choice of reviewer, the right-wing, why-oh-why scribe Professor Kenneth Minogue – 'like picking Albert Einstein to review P G Wodehouse because they both disliked the Nazis.' And he took a swing at the *Observer*'s John Sweeney, quoting from his grovelling interview. 'To stereotype [O'Rourke] as simply a humorist is to do him an injustice. He is a *penseur* too.' The Porlock verdict? 'Lachrymose, self-important tosh.'

This is all good knockabout stuff but how fearless are the writers behind the ho-ho false names? And why do they need false names? Is it that the writers so lack integrity they can't criticise their fellow hacks? Or is it that unmasking themselves would prohibit their joining in the literary scene?

First off, we rang the *Sunday Telegraph*'s book pages to see if its Mr Startle would stand up and be counted. A literary lackey was very protective, not to say disingenuous: 'I...I...*believe* it is a pseudonym...er...I'm afraid I can't tell you who it is. I just *can't*.'

Next we tried *Bookseller* to see if its geriatric critic would discard his Zimmer frame and let the real Mr Oates stand up. Not a hope. 'His or her identity is *very* closely guarded here,' said a staffer as if it were the Coca-Cola formula.

Finally we turned to the books section of the *Sunday Times* in an effort to find the true identity of Harvey Porlock. A laughing female told us, 'Yes, that one is a pseudonym, and no, I am not allowed tell you his name. It's easier with a pseudonym

because he knows the people he reviews and he's often rather critical. He does get the odd letter of complaint.'

Further inquiries revealed that there are, in fact, two Harvey Porlocks. We can exclusively reveal that though one Harry Ritchie occasionally writes it, the man who usually wields the poison pen of Porlock is...is...step forward Terence Blacker. Mr Blacker has an impressive literary pedigree which includes giving 'editorial advice' to ex-jockey John Francome about his 'racing thrillers'. Despite his professed disgust with salon life, Mr Blacker is a natural literati *boulevardier*. He once got vinously robust with the airport book novelist Sally Beauman on a trip back from Spain. 'We drank ourselves silly,' bragged a buoyant Ms Beauman afterwards. This is dramatically at odds with Porlock's demands for a 'serious' approach to literature. For any aggrieved novelists who are victims of 'Porlocking' there is a photograph of Mr Blacker reprinted below – suitably masked. One doesn't want to totally ruin Mr Blacker's future enjoyment of literary ligs and publishing parties.

Unmasked! Here is the first ever picture of acidic *Sunday Times* book critic Harvey Porlock (real identity: novelist Terence Blacker). He has been disguised for his own safety.

crowd like this?' he asks. The glib, chatty style is often employed to patronising effect: 'Wood had some difficulty in conveying the narrative technique employed in *Times's Arrow*. "Think about it. If everything goes backward, so do we – we absorb it." Thanks, James, I think we get the picture.'

The *Sunday Telegraph* has produced what they no doubt consider an antidote to such combativeness. Somehow, though, William Startle's 'Review Of Reviews' is not quite the killer blow (Startle is a character in Johnson's *Idler*). For a start he reads too much like an exile from the *Spectator* or, perhaps more likely, a hopeful emigrant, slavishly following the 'scones and tea' eccentricities of that magazine's ex-editor Charles Moore.

The clash of styles was amply summed up when both Porlock and Startle reviewed the reviews of P J O'Rourke's *Parliament Of Whores*, recently serialised in these pages. Startle started off by saying that P J's 'humorous assault on the American political system did not please many.' He noted two dry and miserable reviews from those paragons of self-righteousness, the *Independent* and the *Independent On Sunday*. The former, by Scott Bradfield, felt the book left 'a bad taste in the mouth', while the latter, by David Rieff, thought with 'indignation' that it was 'scarcely worth noticing'. All fine, so far. Startle ably showed the *Independent* men's immunity to humour. Then disaster! He blew it with his own stuffed-shirt attempt at wisecracking. 'If it can provoke such *priggish* outbursts as this,' he concluded like a good young fogey, 'the book can't be all bad.'

Contacts is Thames TV's late-night lonely hearts show with a cult following. **JOHN HIND** and **STEPHEN MOSCO** went undercover to see just how weird a would-be suitor could be and still get on air

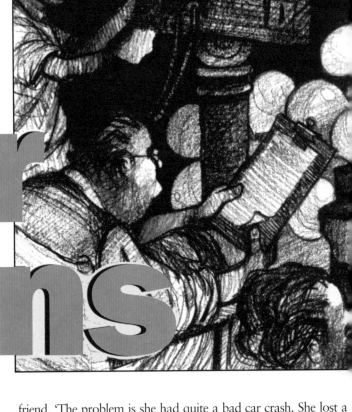

Utter swains

It is now through television – and not the traditional post-bag – that the modern true romantic searches for a soul-mate. Take *Contacts*, Thames TV's late-night show which recently finished its seventh series of matchmaking. Unlike *Blind Date*, this show prides itself on having genuinely offbeat and eccentric guests. Characters such as Jacky, a topless policewomanogram from Loughton, and Kevin, a Whitney Houston-loving car-sales rep, whose legs were once run over by a lorry. Most – if not all – of human life is there. From Nurse Betty, who wants to meet 'a sugar-daddy with an elephant I can wash down' to wife-seeking, tomato-coloured Barry, who dresses as super-hero 'Captain Beany'.

Inspired and invigorated by such love luminaries, we embarked on our own campaign of phone calls to try to get on *Contacts*. We wanted to find out just how far-out a suitor could be before they said no. But we also wondered if we would find a long-term serious romance, plus wedlock and nippers, or just get palmed off with some rapacious vamp who was only after our bodies.

Our man 'James Fishburn' (architect, 35) was first to call the *Contacts* hotline. 'I'm interested in meeting female twins,' he informed the researcher. 'I'd like to develop a relationship with attractive identical twins. Would this be possible?'

'I don't see why not,' declared the lady. She laughed only after Fishburn added, 'I'm not insisting on a *ménage à trois*. I could develop a close relationship with only one at first.

Does that sound perverse to you?'

'Noooo…!' the researcher replied. 'It sounds perfectly reasonable.' But sadly Mr Fishburn did not hear from her again.

Next up was 'Colin Cocker' (meat-packer, 32), who phoned to ask whether *Contacts* could put him in touch with an ex-girl-

friend. 'The problem is she had quite a bad car crash. She lost a leg and both arms, and then we lost touch, so to speak. It's a long story, but I was responsible. The last I heard she was living in Penge in 1980.'

'I see,' sympathised a *Contacts* researcher. 'Can you tell me more?'

'Obviously given the horrific nature of the accident she must be on crutches,' explained Mr Campbell. 'And I have a press photograph of the accident which you could put on screen.' For some reason, Mr Campbell was not invited on air.

Then 'Peregrine Arkwright' (hairdresser, 29) received ten seconds of silence on first announcing effeminately, 'Hello, *Contacts*? I'd be really, really, really interested in coming on the shoooow…I'm looking for a nice man. Do you do gay contacts?'

'Ummm, I'm not sure,' replied the nervous researcher. 'I'll take your details and then hopefully someone might call you back. But obviously we do have many, many people who want to come on – so it can be a very slow process. I'll write "Looking for a male friend". Anything else you want to tell me?'

'Well, I don't mind cross-dressing. Have you had many effems on before?'

'I'm not sure,' responded the researcher. 'Hold on…I've just asked the producer and she said, "Tell him we have no discriminatory policy and anyone can come on the show." So leave it with us, and we'll get back.' But they didn't.

As any request to star romantically on the box was still not forthcoming, we doubled our efforts. Our 'Mike Snail' (filing-clerk, 34) called in search of a female ferret-collector to share his 'passion for ferrets…and more' but mystifyingly he received lack-lustre interest. 'Dave Bullock' (bouncer, 26) asked *Contacts* to

find him 'some hard mates to be sporty with – weights, kick-boxing, fist-fighting, wet-towel-flicking, things like that…and can I just ask, when I come on the show, will you let me arm-wrestle with the presenter, Michael McNally?'

'I don't see why not,' warmed the researcher. 'As long as you don't damage him. I suppose it could be fun!' Nevertheless the TV contact-makers did not make further contact.

One *Contacts* researcher, Karen Walsh, sounded particularly flustered on picking up the phone to 'Jack Norton' (car mechanic, 27). "Ello gal!' Norton announced cheerfully. Karen put down the receiver. Later, Norton phoned again. "Ello doll, I tried to ring on Friday. Your phone was as busy as a Dubrovnik bricklayer. I'm after romance, doll! I'd like a woman to ride on back o' me bike. I work at Rogers, the car mechanics in Norwood and I got a Kawasaki 840i – a really big bastard. I'd like a road-bitch into bikes.'

'OK, anything else you can tell me?' asked Miss Walsh.

'She must be a Christian,' said Mr Norton.

Miss Walsh had the following let-down: 'There are far too many romantics than we have room for, to be honest. Sorry about that!'

Adopting a gentler approach, 'Alan Poole' responded to presenter Michael McNally's request for folk with unusual hobbies to come on the show. Mr Poole announced himself as a collector of grit and gravel.

'Mmmmm…are they semi-precious stones?' asked a researcher. 'No? Well, it's certainly a very unusual request, I'll pass it on immediately.' The next morning, Karen Walsh called our Mr Poole. He told her he was a gardener with a collection of over 2,000 varieties of grit and gravel. And he asked if there was anyone (female or even male) out there with a similar passion?

'What's the fascination?' asked Miss Walsh. 'Ummm, errr, is it because…err, do grits look different? Different colours and textures? I wonder if there's an association of gravel collectors who could help you better?' Mr Poole said he knew of no such society; that was why he desperately wanted to go on the telly.

'We've only got a few progs to go,' said Miss Walsh laconically. 'And I'm very sorry to say this looks like the last series. We've lots and lots of people to get on. So leave it with me!' Yet just two days later she phoned again, urgently inviting Alan to come for a 'prelim'.

Our man Poole prepared thoroughly for the interview by painstakingly affixing gravel picked from his garden that morning on to cards, and labelling them with odd names. At the *Contacts* office, Miss Walsh was so impressed that she summoned producer Liz Neeson into the room.

'Aah! This is really quite impressive, isn't it?' said Ms Neeson. 'I thought you were going to come in and just tip a big bucket of gravel on the table. Do you plan to keep them in glass cases eventually?'

Mr Poole's efforts were rewarded when they left the room for a 'consultation', during which he overheard many barely-suppressed guffaws. But a grinning Miss Walsh returned to exclaim, 'Can you come on next week? Sort out some particularly interesting samples, and avoid wearing white, black, or small checks.'

On the day of the recording, at the exact moment when he was due at the studio, instead of turning up, Mr Poole decided instead to phone.

'Green Room, hello!' answered Miss Walsh. In a tearful voice he spluttered out his amorous tragedy, 'There's been a catastrophe, Karen. When I came home this lunchtime to get ready ☞

for the show my girlfriend went bloody berserk with PMT and threw away all my gravel.'

'Ahhhhhh…' commiserated Miss Walsh.

'Six years work down the drain,' he sobbed. 'And now she says she's leaving me. I don't know what's bloody going on here. I don't believe she's done this to me. She's thrown the whole bloody lot in the dustbin.'

'Ahhhhh…Don't get upset. I know it's a terrible thing to happen, but calm down,' soothed Miss Walsh, before getting alarmed. 'Why did she do that? So you wouldn't go on telly?'

'She says I'm not romantic – that I care more about gravel than her. She hates grit too.'

'Aaaaaahhhhhh…Errr, we can't really expect you to come along now, so don't worry about us here. It's worse for you than it is for us, actually. I mean, we're only a television programme. It's relationships that are more important. What can I say? Don't worry – we can cope.'

One of our suitors, however, did keep his appointment to appear on *Contacts* the following Monday, namely 'Nigel Eddington' (writer, 31). Mr Eddington had earlier phoned for 'an attractive female travelling companion, Girl Friday, nurse, mother-daughter-lover and female motor-mechanic, with whom to travel through Central and South America.' He'd told our old friend Karen Walsh, 'Obviously we'd have to, um, get to know each other beforehand. I desire someone who enjoys both washing out an Elsan and nude sunbathing amidst wonderful Mayan scenery.'

In the Green Room of Thames's studios Mr Eddington was greeted by Karen (who confessed to being a 'great fan of Sooty and Sweep'). He was placed with half-a-dozen fellow romantic hopefuls and introduced to presenters Susy (who also works on a beauty mag) and Michael (who'd just bought a £600 suit). They were then informed, rather dramatically, 'This is a very sad and yet very special day – this is the last ever *Contacts*.'

Nigel and the other small-screen newcomers sat silently watching a monitor screen showing the presenters rehearsing their patter for two hours. Yet not even Geordie presenter McNally's camera-kissing antics and mid-show rendition of 'All You Need Is Love' (rehearsed nine times with his brother) could stifle their love spirit.

The other suitors on the show were:

● Karen, 36, a divorced single-parent and 'children's 'telegram' entrepreneur. She desired a rugged Australian.

● Lyn, '40 plus', twice-married, twice-divorced, into Stephen King novels and marriage. She craved a Sean Connery look-alike who was 'good at electrics'.

● Simon, 33, a civil servant into badminton, who desired 'an emotionally-stable high-achieving woman like Jane Seymour'. He stressed that, 'To me marriage is a life-long commitment.' 'You've been married twice, Simon,' said co-presenter Susy dur-

ing the show. 'Once actually,' he replied. And then there was:

● Damon, 25, from St Lucia via Surrey, a long-haul flight attendant into water-sports. He had chronic flu and had lost his voice in the Green Room minutes before going on air. 'Probably because of all this smoke in here,' said Ms Walsh, lighting up a fag. 'You'll have to try the best you can – croak or something.'

And then there was our own Nigel Eddington, who wanted an exquisite lady companion for travel through Mexico, Honduras, Nicaragua, Costa Rica, Colombia, Peru and the Amazon – and back – in his dad's Land Rover V8i with reclining seats.

In the Green Room, mid-rehearsal, Mr Eddington began entertaining the others with his theories on old-style masculinity. 'It's not the Australians' fault that they've got hairy backs,' he said loudly. 'Men are the way they are for a reason. Why d'you think cavemen went out to hunt and the women stayed home knitting and picking berries?' He was swiftly ostracised by the others. One woman came over to say, 'If you're going to be offensive then we're not going to talk to you.'

All the other guests needed retakes for their appearances, but our man Eddington did it in one take – because he thought it was just a rehearsal.

'Why are you looking specifically for a woman?' asked presenter Susy, before the viewing public.

'Because I couldn't bear spending five months with a man, sharing a small mosquito net…I'm looking for an Amazon-esque woman.'

Within moments the show was ending. This took the form of a bizarre celebration of *Contacts'* seven series on air, which have resulted in 'at least eight weddings and several engagements'. After a request for romancers to write or phone immediately, the presenters and the final show's love-seekers gathered on a long couch to sing the Everly Brothers' 'Bye Bye Love'. The production crew dropped a hundred balloons on stage, Mr McNally's brother strummed a guitar, the presenters grinned, canned audience applause was over-dubbed, the guests sang nervously but eagerly. Meanwhile Nigel Eddington, our spy in the house of love, remained firmly on the sofa amid all the jubilation. He had decided to weep uncontrollably into a ragged old hanky as the cameras rolled. The woman next to him, 40-year-old Lyn, was snootily upset by this display of emotion. But Mr Eddington sobbed on, dabbing his eyes melodramatically and honking his nose inconsolably.

'What on earth did you think you were doing?' asked the production assistant afterwards, visibly aghast at Mr Eddington for spoiling all the fun. 'It looked like you were weeping all through our credits!' As Mr Eddington made his exit a cameraman came over to sympathise: 'I tell you, mate, I wish I had the guts to go off to Brazil with a bird, like you. But I've left it too late. I'm stuck in television now.' ✎

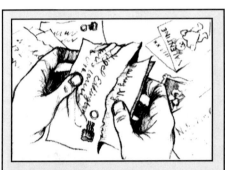

The fruits of love

CONTACTS YIELDED EXACTLY seven envelopes for Nigel, five if you deducted the £30 appearance fee and a personalised thank-you from the producer. Letter A began with epic enthusiasm for the love-trip, but at the end of sheet two said, 'I'm not seeking love. However, if you find someone who is, would you mind me tagging along? I am in limbo – not knowing which way to jump.'

Letter B came from a lady with the endearing surname Valentine. She was under the impression that Nigel was going 'climbing through South America'. 'I would be very happy to do it with you,' she said. Letter C came from a Maureen who, 'having done quite a bit of reading about what happens to women in South America,' felt that 'I would have a lot more protection if I was with you.' She mentioned 'love' three times.

Letter D came from deepest Pimlico and simply stated, 'I would very much like to come.' And finally, Letter E, equally brief, exclaimed, 'You seemed OK. We both have the itch, I suppose. So why not?' Now who says romance is dead?

Tony Reeve

'There I was, up at the front…The spit was flying…Suddenly a microphone stand flew over my head…'

'White riot – I wanna riot…'

'And can you put "Piss off, you obnoxious bastard"?'

'Well, son – love is a very special thing which happens between a drummer and six or seven groupies'

'Not this year – I've got a headache'

'Well, if you're sure it wouldn't be sexist of me'

'Ah yes – they don't write lyrics like that any more...'

Basildon blonde

Essex and its girls are as cheap and tasteless as a bag of soggy chips, says modern mythology. Ugly lies, says STEPHEN PILE as he spends some time there with the current Miss Essex (above)

It is an article of faith on this rain-soaked island that the county of Essex has no art, no taste, no hills, no charm, no style and no young women of sufficient chastity to keep their undergarments fully hoisted throughout two consecutive evenings.

Let us start with the hills. All right, so the highest point is 500 feet above sea level. All right, so you don't need crampons. And, yes, it is a pathetic pimple in the mountainous panoply. But it is an outright lie to claim that this fine county, the home of Tiptree Jam and three vineyards, is flat. It is nothing of the sort. The landscape is rolling. Look at Essex long enough and you could feel seasick.

God created this exquisite county and the laughter started almost immediately. Even in the Victorian age, Matthew Arnold was saying 'How unjust the world is to Essex.'

As early as 1902 the Essex patriot, Frances G Burmester, was driven to despair: 'It has been given a bad name as a flat county, an uninteresting county, an aguish county, a county without society, a hopelessly unresidential county, in fact so many bad names have been bestowed upon it that it has been hanged over and over again and may be reckoned as a dead county.'

The public relations department of Essex County Council was busy in the Eighties trying to dispel the previous bad image (as a boring commuter suburb) when they were knocked asunder by new and foul libels.

First, *Brewer's Dictionary of Phrase and Fable* included a definition of 'Essex Man' as 'a wealthy but poorly-educated male who typically lives in Essex, supports right-wing Thatcherite policies, shows conspicuous bad taste and has few if any cultural interests. The implication is that Essex Man is a throwback to a less civilised form of hominid.'

And then from nowhere came this tidal wave of jokes about 'Essex Girl'. Although they are unfounded and distasteful, m'lud, I am, as counsel for the defence, forced to repeat these vile calumnies to show that they are Essexist.

Question: 'How do you know, m'lud, when an Essex girl is having an orgasm?' Reply: 'Because she drops her bag of chips.' Supplementary question: 'Why does an Essex girl wear knick-ers?' Riposte, m'lud: 'To keep her ankles warm.'

In suing for libel with damages, we are concerned that you look at the evidence. All right, so streakers at rugby matches always come from Harlow. All right, so Epping Forest is arguably the world capital for burying chopped-up bodies in suitcases. All right, so a doctor, a farmer and an antiques dealer in the village of Coggeshall were all suspected of murdering their wives.

However, these are minor blemishes on an otherwise faultless record. But I cannot defend this country until the besmirched reputation of its womenfolk is cleared.

I have here, m'lud, a dossier on the women of the region which I compiled during a night out with the reigning Miss Essex, Josephine Jocelyn. Not Sharon or Tracey, you see, but Josephine Jocelyn. (She came with her chaperone, Mike, who is deputy manager of Raquels discotheque in Basildon.)

First of all, reports that her crowning ceremony was greeted with cries of 'What a moose!' from the audience are totally unfounded. Mike has written a full rebuttal of this disgraceful claim which has now been printed in the *London Evening Standard*.

Second, when the new Miss Essex walked into Strings Piano Bar prior to our evening at a local Chinese restaurant, she did not slouch, limp, bounce or wobble. Far from it. She glided in a serene, almost unearthly manner. From the ankles up all was classical composure. If you had pulled her along on a trolley she could not have had better deportment.

This smart young woman could not be more different from the prevailing jokes. She is a student of graphic art in Southend where her most recent college project was to design a stamp. 'Mine had a bumble bee on a daisy and a tortoise.' I call for the immediate withdrawal of all stamps throughout the known world so that this attractive motif may gain a wider and richly deserved currency.

With great modesty, she told me that she was keeping her feet on the ground during this heady period and hopes to break into modelling once her brace has been removed. Already she has advertised paint, fireplaces and Mazda cars.

She lives in Canvey Island and is so wholly satisfied with the place that she 'only leaves it for art college and shopping,' which I understand is a passion with her, as with her boyfriend, Spencer. 'He is 18 and drives an Orion,' that does not contain a single, dangling furry dice.

'These "Essex Girl" jokes don't bother me,' she said, 'because I know I'm not like that.' Nonetheless, they have made her the most interviewed beauty queen ever crowned in Basildon. In spite of this sudden fame she is keeping her feet on the ground, her head on her shoulders, her nose to the grindstone and her chin up.

Apparently, Raquels decided against having a wet T-shirt competition. They wanted something a bit more up-market despite a sign outside advertising 'Sensational hen night: hunky fellas welcome.' They found the Miss Essex title was in abeyance and went for it. One judge said they were looking for 'class'.

When the fine Jocelyn woman arrived at Strings she was wearing an all-in-one, button-through silk, floral trouser suit and a black waistcoat-style jacket with padded shoulders and full blouson sleeves. But her interest in fashion does not stop at clothes. Her boyfriend, Spencer, is an 18 year-old insurance broker who shops at Next and 'spent all summer riding his mountain bike'. Surprisingly, these were the height of fashion in Essex, even though it is first equal with Lincolnshire as our flattest county.

As for Josephine's hobbies: she likes 'to relax and go for saunas'. She also plays badminton with her brother, Wayne, who has his own gym in the garage and hopes to sign apprentice terms with West Ham at 16. 'And then there's my art. I like drawing models: Jerry Hall, Madonna. I usually give art away as presents. I did Madonna for my gran.'

I asked her to identify the best of Essex and she said the Lakeside indoor shopping centre at Thurrock where there is a big McDonalds. She was also keen on a local swimming pool with 'lots of tubes and different activities.'

Both Mike and Miss Essex have relatives in Bournemouth, a town which compares unfavourably to Essex in all matters of fashion. Essex is first with any trend. Mike, for example, saw people with windsurfing equipment nailed on to skateboards at Leigh on Sea promenade recently. He stopped his car to observe and when he got home telephoned his friend Graham to see if they had this development yet in Bournemouth. Needless to say they had not.

What is more, Raquels in Basildon was the first to pioneer 'the human velcro fly trap.' You dress up in a velcro boiler suit, run, bounce off a trampoline and the one who sticks highest up a 16-foot inflatable wall wins. 'They had this in the north of England, but it was dangerous,' said Mike. 'They had a wooden wall. We had a special one made like a bouncy castle. This was pioneered in Essex and is now touring 150 nightclubs all round Britain.'

Miss Essex denied that local women are loose. 'They are friendly and start conversations. Perhaps they are being misunderstood.' She also denied that men of the county spend their entire time driving brainlessly up and down the same road in Ford Cortinas. 'That only happens on Southend seafront and at Canvey Island. And they are not Ford Cortinas. They are BMWs, Porsches and Cabriolet XR3i convertibles.'

She spoke so highly of the Roller World skating facility at Colchester and showed such love for her county that I was inspired to travel round it. This, m'lud, has produced a second dossier from which I now quote.

First, it is wholly unfair to speak of 'Essex Man' when what you actually mean is 'London Overspill Man'. Essex was a blameless agricultural county until 1830 when the railway encouraged East End migration. In the Thirties, 'champagne trains' brought Londoners out to buy holiday plots from local speculators who got them tipsy on the bubbly. Furthermore, in 1951 the population of Essex was 830,500. By 1990 it had grown to 1.53 million.

The result is that today, Essex is two counties: north and south. Away from East End influences, the northern half continues on its own quiet, rural, beamed, rather pretty and heritage-packed way. Frinton is a resort of such gentility that by-laws ban all pubs, chip shops, coaches, changing on the beach and ice cream without wrappers.

Furthermore, this county has a famous cultural history. Holst wrote his famous and popular suite, *The Planets*, at Thaxted. Tennyson wrote *In Memoriam* at High Beech. Anthony Trollope hunted in the county and said that 'few had investigated more closely than I have done the depth and breadth and water-holding capacities of an Essex ditch.' And Dickens wrote in a letter that 'Chigwell, my dear fellow, is the greatest place in the world.'

John Clare, the nature poet, was inspired by Epping Forest and William Morris wrote 'I come not from heaven, but from Essex.' Dick Turpin was a local boy, but they tend to brush over that and point out that for almost a week in 1381 Chelmsford was Britain's seat of government. Richard II was there for six days quashing a peasants' revolt. Sadly, he was too busy passing edicts to appreciate fully the charm of this attractive town.

Colchester is the oldest recorded town in Britain. Boadicea lived there and for all I know still does. It is said to be the home of Old King Cole who was a merry old soul and a merry old soul was he. It is one of the less dramatic British legends but at least Colchester has its own nursery rhyme, which is more than you can say about Harpenden, for example.

Of course, Suffolk makes a great fuss about Constable, but when he painted Flatford Mill he was almost certainly standing in Essex. (Most of *The Haywain* behind the cart in the river is definitely Essex.) Marconi invented the radio there and the first ever broadcast sent the voice of Dame Nellie Melba across the world from Chelmsford.

The county was good enough for John Locke, the philosopher, Thomas Barnardo, the philanthropist, and the ancestors of George Bush, the president, who lived near Tiptree. It was also the home of R A Butler, former Conservative MP for Saffron Walden and founder of modern education until Shirley Williams. Mr Butler, described as 'the best prime minister we never had' personifies the generous, friendly, intelligent solidity that is the true picture of your actual Essex man. M'lud, I rest my case. ✍

Six nice things about Essex (we couldn't find ten)

1. The cricket team won this year's county championship.

2. Sir Winston Churchill was an Essex MP during his finest hour.

3. Sade's mum runs the maternity unit in Clacton Hospital.

4. World champion train spotter Bill Curtis lives in Clacton.

5. And world champion bricklayer Tony Gregory lives in Horndon on the Hill

6. It's got a village called Ugley.

🐭 *Simon Fanshawe*

Winter of content

Oh for a raindrop, a ship's biscuit and a nice glass of mineral water

Thank God it's January. The last month has been a nightmare. I have eaten my own body weight in brandy butter, drunk the EC wine lake and discovered that I have yet another nephew. It is now clear to me that there is little about my family that is nuclear, apart from its tendency to proliferate. And during the festive season, that just means more presents. As a result of being an uncle at Christmas, I now have less money than the Maxwells. I do like giving presents – I just don't like giving them 23 at a time. Never, in the field of human generosity was so much spent this year, on so few, for such little reason.

No amount of 'thank you' letters will make up for the fact that I have had it up to here with indulging children 'because of the time of the year'. In fact, I would like to take this opportunity to say, without any kind of possibility that I shall be accused of ruining the spirit of the holiday, that I now hate children. They should be neither seen nor heard and definitely not bought anything from Nintendo.

But, despite getting as near as possible to a Chernobyl-like nuclear family meltdown, the relatives and the presents were the best bit of the season. The worst was the parties.

This may come as a shock but, unlike 97 per cent of the population, I am quite able to enjoy myself at any time of the year. I neither need three wise men nor the seasonal rush at Harrods as an excuse. I would eat and drink out at the slightest opportunity, even if the news had just come through that my hamster had committed suicide, my savings were deposited with BCCI and my lover had run off with the postman.

This is apparently not the case for huge numbers of other people. I assume that they go out once a year and then only when there's a star in the east and the prospect of a virgin birth. Otherwise they wouldn't behave as they do. Practice would make them better, if not

perfect. They clearly have no real idea how to do it properly. Their behaviour is simply not conducive to the Theory of Evolution. Mooning in front of every passing car, wearing tinsel round the reproductive capacity and singing 'Good King Wenceslas' on a karaoke machine do nothing to separate humankind from the apes. But, apparently, these very exploits are the male and female British office worker's idea of the Very Best Time In All The World. And all month I hated it. Like the Big Birthday Boy Himself, for 40 days and 40 nights I was relegated to a social wilderness. It was impossible to go out anywhere without encountering this unrestrained wave of testosterone and oestrogen coursing through the streets.

And the only thing that was worse than having one's favourite restaurants full of these social Scud missiles, wreaking indiscriminate damage wherever they went, was being invited into their own territory

'I shouldn't get too involved with the clients if I were you, Jobshaw'

for the office do. This was the worst kind of living hell. Not even my relief at it finally being the New Year and time for the January sales, can make up for them. It is one of those ironic facts of human nature that 12 months is long enough to bring about a form of selective amnesia. Consequently, when one is asked to the office do the following year, one actually goes. It was not enough that last year one of the creepier specimens from BBC Accounts told you that having sex on the photocopier didn't guarantee a multiple orgasm, or that you spent what seemed like the half life of a tonne of uranium talking to people whose IQ recently dropped below the price of shares in Polly Peck. All office parties should be banned.

There was a kind of very noisy desperation that infused the ones that I went to. There was a definite sense that if people didn't get either hitched or unhitched, or at least experience some kind of change in their conjugal circumstances, before you could say safe sex, then their limbs would drop off. All around their temporarily converted offices, with holly patterned table cloths draped over their word processors, people spent the month doing more damage to their job prospects than John Major claims the EC Social Chapter will do. I cannot imagine the benefit of making Kennedyesque suggestions to your seniors. Then again…

Even so, I trooped along to a series of dreary events and these have left me panting for meaningful social intercourse with people to whom I can be nice without either effort or mounting self-loathing.

Now it is January. Today it is drizzling. The fires aren't burning and there is no sign of good cheer anywhere. I have shouted at a young person just for being young. I have given no one a present and I have eaten only an oatcake and drunk just a glass of mineral water. I love January. It comes like the long awaited breaking of wind after a bad Mexican meal. 🐭

Luis Zypher

When Robert Maxwell said that he would leave his children nothing, he was, for once, telling the truth. But the Maxwell clan is not the only family to have problems with its inheritance, as ANTHONY LEE discovers

Where there's a will there's a war

It is always with a profound sadness that one considers the poverty of the Princess of Wales. As 1991 seeps expensively into 1992, one can only wish her a more prosperous New Year than it seems her father and step-mother are likely to offer.

As Fleet Street *[and Punch – Ed]* gleefully revealed last year, Raine Spencer's refurbishing skills at Althorp are not appreciated by her husband's children. The Earl's publicised policy of flogging a reported £2m worth of family knick-knacks to finance la Raine's DIY has transformed the filial reaction from that of the displeased to the dispossessed.

Lord Spencer's heir, the incandescent broadcaster Viscount Althorp, has seemed particularly perturbed, perhaps with good cause. His erstwhile employer, America's NBC is tightening its ☞

ILLUSTRATION: DAVID LYTTLETON

McLACHLAN

'Remember the Bay City Rollers?'

own belt, and who can say it will not tighten it around His Lordship's neck? While some people, however, may feel that the British aristocracy is walking evidence of intellectual liposuction, it must be said that Earl and Countess Spencer are a couple whose discernment is worshipped the world over. That mere profit has been far from their minds is demonstrated by their sale some years ago of a painting by Salvator Rosa for £50,000, which was sold on to the National Gallery two years later for seven times that amount.

Lord Spencer has reportedly invoked the ingratitude of children, mindful perhaps of the unhoused King Lear: 'How sharper than a serpent's tooth it is/To have a thankless child.'

But what can the Earl do about his snakelike progeny? Well, he might care to pull his serpent's teeth right out; out of his will that is, as has a disgruntled parent in America, whom, for the sake of his privacy, we shall simply refer to as 'Ron'.

Ron, a retired elected official with past Hollywood connections has a daughter, 'Patti'. Ron's wife, whom for the sake of anonymity we shall call 'Nan', has called her own relationship with said daughter: 'one of the most painful and disappointing aspects of my life.' As evidence of Patti's anti-social tendencies, Nan has testified that when she was two years old, she held string beans in her mouth but refused to swallow them.

Now any two-year-old who refuses to eat string beans deserves every evil which is coming to her. What she does not have coming to her, however, are any of Daddy's dollars, for Ron has cut Patti from his will. Not because of the string beans, one must add. Her final act of filial perfidy was to accuse her father's ecologically-oblivious administration of allowing thousands of dolphins to be slaughtered.

Nan's reported account of Ron's reaction to this horrendous charge is restrained to the point of hernia. 'As he wiped a tear from his eye he asked me: "Mommy, why is Patti doing this to me?"' Mommy proposed a solution to their daughter's infamy: Patti is thus deprived of £1.2m, but it is only fair to warn Mr and Mrs Reag – oops, almost gave the game away – and the Spencers, that inheritance can be as great a source of aggravation within families as interior design has been within Althorp.

In 1984, Sol Goldman was the biggest private landlord in New York City. But Sol was undergoing a divorce. Wife Lillian said Sol was cruel. Sol said Lillian was crazy. Three of their four children apparently agreed, since they filed an affidavit saying their mother needed psychiatric care. Sol and Lillian attempted an agreement regarding the homes in New York (but not those in Long Island and Palm Beach); the two Rolls-Royces; the customised Cadillac; the Mercedes; and the $1m worth of jewellery. Three years later, still married, Sol had the bad luck to die.

Lillian considered her own luck only marginally less malodorous, since the will gave her substantially less than the proposed agreement. Her children challenged her attempt to stick to the former deal, going so far as to suggest that since a divorce was pending, their mother could not be considered their father's wife. This complex imbroglio continues. But if children can get extremely nasty, so too can siblings.

Exercising will power: 'Ron' and 'Nan', Henry Ford II, his wife Kathleen, Robert Maxwell. Opposite page: Earl Spencer and Raine

A certain Mary Bonfils displeased her father, the *Denver Post* newspaper magnate Frederick, by eloping with a piano salesman. Frederick reacted in a way that Lord Spencer might bear in mind: he halved Mary's inheritance in favour of her sister Helen. Not caring too much for her elder sister, Helen instructed the newspaper's editors that Mary's name should never appear unless it was to her detriment.

Mary's response was equally sulphurous. Selling her stock on condition that it was not resold to Helen, she precipitated a fully-fledged takeover bid. Helen fought back successfully but the dispute destroyed constructive management and together the squabbling geese scrambled their golden egg, the paper being sold in 1980. Helen's sanity was never called into question, though her alternative career as a Broadway producer might have given some pause for psychiatric thought.

Lord Spencer could, of course, confound the family critics and favour the grandchildren. After all, one of them, the future William V might well need an extra bob or two should his grandmother ever be gracious enough to pay income tax, and grandchildren are good allies.

Nieces, however are not. Hardly was oil and art tycoon Armand Hammer laid in his grave than his family started fighting over the spillage. Hammer's only son, Julian, has sued his son Michael to have him removed as Daddy's executor. Michael himself was arguing with Joan Weiss, niece of Hammer's third (and last) wife on the very night that grandfather's own pump packed up, and only the timely arrival of the Los Angeles police force prevented a squabble over the deceased's suitcases.

Joan is suing the whole family for misrepresentation and fraud, charges old Armand had already levelled against the Weisses just before he died. Accusations that Hammer had used Frances's money to build up a fortune he happened to call his own have propelled the problem into a dilemma of Maxwellian dimensions.

Still in search of a ruse to rebuke his heirs, Lord Spencer might imitate Rebekah Harkness, the Standard Oil heiress who died in 1982, leaving a rash of expensive properties spread across the world. Not caring too much for her own son and daughter, Rebekah took to making wills the way other mothers make cookies, her creations proving just as crumbly. Her greatest jest was disposing of property she did not actually possess.

This is a great wheeze and puts all your beneficiaries in their (duly diminished) place. Rebekah's son was already in his place, courtesy of a jail sentence for manslaughter, so it was left to daughter Terry to ask: was Rebekah belligerent or simply bewildered? Terry averred that Rebekah had long been under heavy medication and noted that the doctor doing the medicating had also become the beneficiary of Rebekah's boodle, a coincidence of some remarkability.

To avoid uncertainty or engage in a final, two-fingered farewell, Lord Spencer might do as did Henry Ford II. Before time took its toll on bodily functions, Henry faced the cameras and committed his testament to video. This inventive wave from the grave was of much use to his widow Kathleen when Henry's 55-page will was deemed insufficient evidence of his wishes by the disinherited family.

From the children's point-of-view, I hope that both Viscount Althorp and Princess Diana will be mature enough to ignore the case of Mr Geoff Stanbridge. He spent 40 low-wage years managing his millionaire father's Buckinghamshire farm, only to learn that the family fortune was to be divided equally between himself and his four siblings. Somewhat unsympathetic to such generosity, Mr Stanbridge drove a five-ton tractor through his living father's living room.

Now, we know that, being an urban girl at heart, HRH is probably not the sort to straddle the Massey-Ferguson and air-condition the west wing of Althorp, but we know little of sisters Sarah and Jane. Best for Lord Spencer to keep his own counsel, for exciting suspicion that your offspring have incurred your financial displeasure can inspire a degree of disaffection even more discommodious than that of Mr Stanbridge.

When, in 1985, Steve Benson was short of a little cash, he extracted some from the bank account of his mother, Pennsylvania tobacco heiress Margaret. Fearing that Mummy's response might cut him out of her will, Steven took a precaution. It was called a pipe bomb and ripped her apart at her Florida home. Alas, for Steven, Mother knew her son, and had changed her will just days before her (untimely) death.

Of course, no one is suggesting that a whiff of cordite might ameliorate the artworks of Althorp. Nor is there the faintest suggestion that one of the Maxwells was standing behind *père* Robert when he took that final, fateful plunge into the briny. But when you're an elderly gentleman with a substantial fortune, it's always wise to take precautions. After all, your last will and testament can always be your last laugh, too. And you know what they say about he who laughs last. ✎

'When he's in training he finds a balanced diet essential – left and right ears!'

'And that's for getting a bigger male modelling contract than m

'Good grief! Somebody have a word with them!'

'If you ask me, it's becoming all too commercialised'

'It's an orphan I'm trying to get adopted'

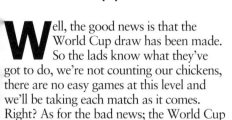

No American do!

How can we stage the World Cup in a country that doesn't appreciate the game?

Well, the good news is that the World Cup draw has been made. So the lads know what they've got to do, we're not counting our chickens, there are no easy games at this level and we'll be taking each match as it comes. Right? As for the bad news; the World Cup will definitely be played in the United States. Sorry.

Now those of us who have spent our best years writing about children's games are not easily surprised by cynicism, hypocrisy or simple greed. Decades of dealing with boxing promoters, football directors and the International Olympic Committee have rendered us ethically shock-proof. But this is the Big One, the epic scam, the manoeuvre which puts the rest in the shade.

Since its birth in 1930, the World Cup has been staged in the following countries: Uruguay, Italy, France, Brazil, Switzerland, Sweden, Chile, England, Mexico, Germany, Argentina and Spain. Some are shamelessly rich, others grindingly poor, while the England of 1966 (prop. H Wilson) hovered between those two extremes. But all have one thing in common: the overwhelming majority of male citizens over the age of 12 possesses a working knowledge of the off-side law.

True, they may not be able to articulate it in terms which would satisfy the Attorney-General but all their instincts tell them that when a ball is played through the back four and a forward finds himself in two yards of space, it is the defender's sacred duty to raise his right arm and scream at the linesman.

Those instincts may be shared by perhaps one American in a hundred thousand but no more. They neither know, nor do they care about the game which most of them still call Soccer Football. Yet it is in this uncomprehending republic that the World Cup finals of 1994 will take place. It is as if Oslo were being asked to host a Test series.

Over the next few months, the PR men will slip into overdrive. We shall be told that this is a missionary venture, a concentrated effort to convert the heathen Yankee to the joys of this great game of ours. Do not believe them. For this is a brazen commercial exercise, carried out at the behest of sponsors and television, with the simple aim of grabbing a slice of the richest market in the world.

Time was, a decade or more ago, when it seemed that the game might be making a little headway in the States. It was the era when ageing stars like Pele and Beckenbauer would finish their careers at the New York Cosmos, much as pre-war European aristocrats would end their days in Biarritz.

The enterprising sports hack would use the occasion of the American Cup Final – or SoccerBowl, as they called it – as the excuse for a five-day thrash around Manhattan. Sadly, the game itself was usually the low point of the trip.

The match came complete with commentary and musical sound effects:

'Cosmos throw-in. Hey, great throw! Cosmos attack. Helluva kick!' And the crowd would bounce up and down to the kind of organ music which once accompanied John Wayne into battle with the Sioux. It was magnificent, in its way. But it wasn't football.

The American media tried earnestly to fulfil their mission to inform. I remember Dennis Tueart, who once played the real game for the likes of Sunderland and Manchester City, winning a SoccerBowl with a dramatic head-high volley which screamed in from 20 yards. After the match, 50 journalists cornered him in the locker room. 'Tell me, Dennis,' began one Stateside sportscaster, 'was that the easiest goal you've ever scored? I mean, just kinda kicking it in like that?'

The game fell away with the decline of Cosmos. The large crowds which watched football at the Los Angeles Olympics were there to support the Games rather than the games. FIFA, world football's governing body, successfully ensured an American presence at Italia '90, and the collection of willing college boys and functional pros did not disgrace themselves. But, in truth, they made no greater impression upon the competition than, say, Wycombe Wanderers make upon the FA Cup.

And yet this is the nation which has been entrusted with the game's ultimate tournament. Already, the PR men are busy. No, we won't try to simplify the rules; well, not much. Yes, we will play some games indoors; hell, it might rain! And did you know that the USA have just won the Women's World Cup? Wow!

I recall meeting an old friend at the opening of the 1986 World Cup in Mexico. He was an Italian journalist, with all the splendid cynicism of the breed. 'We should always hold the World Cup in a Latin country,' he said. 'The Latins are broad-minded. They don't worry about a little stealing.' I told him of the rumour that FIFA were contemplating a World Cup in America. He shook his head. 'They wouldn't dare,' he said. 'Stealing is one thing. But grand larceny...'

Lowry

'What I really miss is that huge ball of fluff that used to accumulate on the stylus…'

'It was many, many years ago – Elvis was still the King'

'Bad news, I'm afraid. Our artistic licence has expired!'

'The Man In Black? Are you trying to tell me you're Johnny Cash?'

'Bin listening to the peace talks'

'Miss Bradshaw – I want you to send in my rocking shoes 'cause tonight I'm going to rock away all my blues…'

'Thank you. I just thought I'd try running that one up the flagpole to see if anyone would salute'

Rock Stars' kids anonymous..

'Hi, my name's Moonbuggy Dweezil'

'The hype's brilliant but I think you should do some more development of the product'

'New Country night. They all stand around crying into their Perrier water!'

'The limousine in the pool really dates you, Simon'

Bennett's *Madness* boggles the mind

BEFORE THE CURTAIN rises, **The Madness of George III** arouses dubiousness with its very title – it is based on historical fact, and it describes a state rather than an action. How will Alan Bennett manage to make an original drama out of this? Three hours later, we have watched the distressing and affecting spectacle of a man losing his wits and finding them again, and we have seen a parade of engaging characters chatter in a quaint and robust fashion. Yet the doubt aroused by the title has not been laid to rest. Though there is a great deal of movement, its only purpose is to distract us from the unswervable progress of history: the king becomes ill, the king gets better. Not much plot there; certainly no suspense.

Disappointment, however, doesn't set in for quite some time, what with Nicholas Hytner's brisk, forceful production, Mark Thompson's bold set of glowing palaces and inky chambers, and some sharp performances, notably Nigel Hawthorne's as George. Given to punctuating his remarks with 'Eh, eh, what, what?', George at the outset is a genial monarch, calling his wife, in the privacy of their bedroom, 'Mrs King'. We then see him degenerate into rambling nonsense, incontinent sexual fantasies, and outbreaks of violence – including an attack on the unbeloved Prince of Wales (played like a petulant pig in britches by Michael Fitzgerald).

In all these moods, Hawthorne is agonisingly believable – so much so that one may want to avert one's eyes from the painful sight, and one may feel a bit queasy about the Act I climax, in which the king, in his shirt and smallclothes, is strapped into a chair, and sits howling, like some tormented Bacon portrait, while a Handel choir blasts away. The contrast seems overly calculated for effect, as does a scene of George being stuffed into a straitjacket followed by one of Prinny squealing at the 'torture' of having his corset laced. The technique is that of an earnest documentary that juxtaposes shots of beggars with those of

THE MADNESS OF GEORGE III
MICHAEL FITZGERALD as The Prince of Wales
NIGEL HAWTHORNE as King George III

the rich at a buffet table, except that Bennett doesn't have even an elementary point to make.

While the king suffers, and his doctors disagree, the Whigs and Tories battle for supremacy. Prime Minister William Pitt – enacted with Arctic mystery by Julian Wadham – speaks in favour of 'the elimination of waste'. Pitt is talking about the economy but he also enunciates one of the play's major motifs – the king's filled chamber pots are waved about, discussed constantly, and peered into by eager disease detectives. The Whig leader, Charles James

Fox, refers to the king as 'an anal fistula,' and others discuss his lack of bowel control. I'm not denying the period rightness of this subject and talk but all the botty jokes and bondage methods get rather sordid and edge perilously close to campery.

Anyway, praise also to Mark Lockyer, for his Bertie Wooster-ish Fred, Duke of York, and Richenda Carey's large and frightening Lady Pembroke.

IN HIS THREE-HOUR long **The Strange Case of Doctor Jekyll and Mr Hyde,** David Edgar has added an arch Scottish sister for Dr Jekyll ('Were ye never tempted to have a wee wife and some bairns?') and a lot of psychologising but has subtracted the story's basic ingredients, atmosphere and terror. Roger Allam, as Dr J, seems to be playing at 33 when everyone else is at 45, and, as his alter ego, Simon Russell Beale gives the only dull performance of his I've ever seen – a nodding, cringing Mr Hyde about as frightening as a film buff.

Rhoda Koenig

'Let's face it. Blow Sumo is pretty boring'

Don't touch that dhal

All the hot news on those curry TV dinners

EVER SINCE I WAS TAKEN through the round window by Brian Cant on *Play School*, and subsequently exposed to the fascinating machinations of a sweet factory (I think it was Liquorice Allsorts), I have wanted to visit one first hand. Last week I had the opportunity finally to fulfil this ambition – with a slight modification. I was invited on a tour of a production line making not Mr Bassett's incomparable Allsorts, or indeed any type of confectionery, but another type of food close to my heart. I went to visit a curry factory.

You've probably never heard of Noon Products plc. But you may well have tasted their curry. Noon make frozen and chilled Indian dishes for a number of brands, including Birds Eye, Wall's, Sainsbury, and Waitrose. As you can imagine, that's a lot of curry. Hence I expected to see a lot of heavy machinery, huge quantities of raw ingredients, and large numbers of extremely clever robots. But it wasn't like that at all.

The fun began with a dressing-up game, as we all had to wear white rubber galoshes, white coats, and distinctly unflattering Ena Sharples-style hairnets. This was all part of the elaborate and rather impressive hygiene ritual, which also involved – the reason for the galoshes – wading

'He says he won't eat it without tomato sauce'

through pools of disinfectant between each section of the factory.

To my surprise the main cooking areas were entirely bereft of hydraulics and robots. Instead there were real people, busying themselves with remarkably authentic kitchen tasks. I watched one of the chefs – a title he certainly deserved – preparing a dish of Bombay potatoes. In went the sliced onions – admittedly tens of kilos of them – on to a hot plate spitting with soya oil. When these were soft and well-browned, having been regularly and lovingly turned with a ten foot spatula, the garlic and ginger (puréed but fresh, around a pound of each) were added. Next came the spices – coriander, cumin, turmeric, chilli to name but a few – added in a very specific order, seeds first, then powders. Then the potatoes, which had been par-boiled and vacuum packed, but not frozen. Lastly a shoe-box size pile of finely chopped fresh coriander leaves hit the heat, releasing a fine nose-filling aroma, as of the best Indian restaurants.

If the child in me was a little disappointed by the lack of crunching, grinding, gleaming or noisy machinery, the gourmet was most impressed, not to say peckish, after witnessing this demonstration. Apart from differing in scale, the preparation of this dish was true to time-honoured techniques.

Inspection of the store cupboards revealed a dedication to freshness and quality of produce, from the chickens to the chillis. One of the more alarming discoveries was a dozen or so ten-kilo tubs of peeled garlic cloves – enough, I calculated, to contaminate the breath of the entire population of, say, Cheltenham. Though all in a good cause, of course.

Naturally the morning ended in a tasting of dishes. These were all hot – or at least chilled and reheated, as intended – off the production line. Interestingly, it turns out that the different brands which Noon supply have different policies on heat – as in spice, I mean. Those who like their curries to force steam out of their ears should head for Waitrose, and the chicken vindaloo in particular. Here you will also find the Bombay potatoes, which fulfil all their early promise. Sainsbury's chicken korma is an excellent mild dish, and their channa dhal (yellow lentils in spicy tomato sauce) fragrant with fresh coriander. Birds Eye's dishes are unlikely to make your eyes water, but their lamb passanda with lemon basmati rice has a good authentic ring about it.

So that's my TV dinners sorted out for the next couple of weeks. You know where to send them, Mr Noon.

Hugh Fearnley-Whittingstall

'He's my taster'

Oldies aren't such goldies on little silver discs

They call it 'catalogue' in the business but we know it better as old stuff. The business doesn't pop champagne corks over slow, steady sales, which is why it's not interested in catalogue-worthiness. Yet it's catalogue which can cover many an exposed posterior when quarterly accounts are drawn up.

The advent of CD was the best thing to happen to catalogue since albums were invented. Here was a new medium designed to bid disenchanted listeners to replace their battered vinyl with deathless silver. Since we're still in the short-term of CD, that boom continues to endure. It never shows up in charts but you can spot indicators by looking at something called the 'certification list', published monthly in America, which tabulates new sales records achieved by big-selling albums. Steve Miller, who hasn't had a new hit for years, fea-

tured twice in last month's certifications. His dog-eared *Fly Like An Eagle* album and *Greatest Hits* set chalked up their fourth and fifth million respectively. Amazingly, a fair percentage of those sales have been racked up over the last few years, a grain-by-grain momentum that builds inexorably to a mountain.

Nice for such old codgers. But there are two problems which are beginning to spell trouble for catalogue. An acquaintance of mine has always sworn by Van Morrison's *His Band And Street Choir* as a personal talisman, and since he's never been too

careful with his records, he's had to replace it several times over the years. Since it came out on CD, the scuffs and thumb-prints which have blemished his vinyl have become a thing of the past. Provided that CDs really do last forever, so will his present copy of *His Band And Street Choir*. When collections have been rebuilt, a lot of unsold classics are going to be left behind.

Unless they don't get into the shops in the first place, which is the other difficulty that's needling the industry. Catalogue may be extensively represented on CD by now but that doesn't mean you can go straight

Clear as a *Belle*

Rivette's shortened masterpiece is small but perfectly formed

THE MINEMA IN KNIGHTSBRIDGE makes a welcome reopening with **La Belle Noiseuse: Divertimento** (15), the shorter version of Jacques Rivette's splendid *La Belle Noiseuse* which runs for four hours and which we were

'I expect he's their warm-up man'

shown the other day. Shorter (the film at the Minema runs just over two hours) but not minor. *Divertimento* still tells the story of the French painter (Michel Piccoli) who is distracted by the appearance of a young artist and his girlfriend (Emmanuelle Béart) from his determination to leave a portrait unfinished and live quietly with his wife in the country. Now with the beautiful girl as naked model he works again – and disrupts his life.

I admit that I prefer the longer film, but that may be because I saw it first. Possibly the emphasis in *Divertimento* on the actual act of painting (the hand of Bernard Dufour supplies the work on the canvas) is stronger. Possibly the feeling for the hot French south is less marked; there may be a shade less

stress on the role of the model in a work of art. But nothing vital is missed. The miracle of sharing, as the audience of both versions shares, in the devotion of the artist to his work and in his emotional involvement is always the motivating force. *Divertimento* gives you a chance of looking a second time, without much delay, from a slightly different point of view. At any rate I am grateful.

At the ICA cinemas **Scorsese x 4**, a 75-minute programme of short, early and sometimes student films by America's distinguished Martin Scorsese. An interview with the director's parents (memories of the past from the father, instructions on sauce-making from the mother) is dated 1974; it has reminiscent, out and buy it. The irony attending the new medium is that while shops ought to be able to stock more CDs than vinyl, they're often delivering fewer different titles.

The current charts display some of the symptoms: they're dominated by a handful of releases – Dire Straits, Bryan Adams, Simply Red, Bryan Adams, Guns 'N' Roses, Bryan Adams – which are pushed so mercilessly by their patrons that retailers are compelled to pile their storerooms with the same few records.

In America, catalogue sales are in terrible shape. Desperate to latch on to big hit records to generate a way out of the moribund state of the business, managers have elbowed venerable old stuff out of access.

Over here catalogue is being squeezed still further. Artists with a dozen or 15 albums to their credit could once look back on a fine body of work in the public domain, but most are lucky if their admirers can actually find half of it still available.

Yet catalogue is indispensable. The most enduring thing about records has always been their ability to reproduce a music just as it was when it was first released. If it was fresh then, there's no real reason why it can't be fresh now. The fact is, catalogue isn't old; it's just not new. Besides, when you're beachcoming on your desert island the eight records you're most going to want washed up at your feet will be catalogue, won't they?

Richard Cook

personal touches. The two earliest pieces come from the Sixties: a sketch looks at obsession with a painting, another hints at an interest in criminal society, and a rather later sketch (*The Big Shave,* 1967) has suggestions of future edgy jokes. I am afraid I personally see not much of a guide towards, say, the brilliant *Cape Fear*. **Kuffs** (15) MGM (Trocadero and Various Cannons) is about the San Francisco Patrol Specials, a body privately run to police some areas of the city with, apparently, considerable licence in the use of firearms. The rather likeable hero is played by Christian Slater; Bruce A Evans directs.

Dilys Powell

East side story

The Russians may not be coming but their wines certainly are

POLITICIANS MAY BE squabbling over who owns the bombs and ordinary Russians and Ukranians may be queueing for three hours for a sausage, then three more for a potato, but some good news is coming out of what was once the Soviet Union.

In 1988, some time before the USSR began to crumble, Martyn Assirati set up the Russian Wine Company in London and travelled east to see what he could find. At the time, the CCCP was considered to be the third, fourth or fifth largest wine producing country in the world; any reliable figures were buried in bureaucratic tangle. Nobody else was importing much beyond a few bottles of sweet red sparkling stuff from Crimea, so he had the field to himself.

But there were a few hurdles to jump first. Everything from wine to paperwork had to go via Moscow. What started out as fresh, clean white wine made from Aligoté or Rkatziteli grapes in Georgia or Moldavia had to be tankered up to the capital for bottling. It lost all fruit along the way and by the time it received an export licence it was beyond drinking. It wasn't until last autumn that the producers were able to say 'Forget Moscow; deal directly with us.'

It will take a while to install the proper temperature-controlled and sterile treatment facilities that fresh white wines demand, so they are not in the portfolio just yet. Nor strangely – in view of the company's name – is any Russian wine. At the moment it's all from three wineries in Moldavia.

Kodru 1987 (from the Krikova winery) is a ripe, juicy wine with bags of fruit, a blend of Cabernet Sauvignon and Merlot (£4.49 from Grog Blossom). Krikova's Krasny Reserve 1983 (£6.95 from Butlers Wine Cellar in Brighton) combines Pinot Noir with Merlot and Malbec in a rich wine that tastes like chocolate dipped in tar; a drink to satisfy those who still hanker after old-style beefed-up Burgundies.

Occasionally, some bottles from a particularly fine vintage were put to one side. There was, of course, no commercial motive for this; the wines were kept for curiosity, party bosses or state functions. But the value of old stock is beginning to be realised.

One of the best of these 'Collection Wines' is a 1969 Negru de Purkar (£8.95 from Butlers Wine Cellar) that blends Cabernet Sauvignon with native Saperavi and Rara Niagre grapes. What other drinkable 22-year old wine would you find for under a tenner? And this is more than just drinkable, it is an enormous, fruit-packed wine, smelling sublimely of ripe blackcurrants. Form an orderly queue please.

Jim Ainsworth

Christmas and how to escape it

Are there are any places in the universe where you can get away from the festive season? ROLAND WHITE investigates

It's the time of year when, by tradition, the Queen shows us pictures of her family and calls for reconciliation and peace. It's the time of year when, by tradition, a small African country that nobody has heard of invades a small African country that nobody can pronounce. And it's the time of year when, by tradition, police will surround a flat in west London where a man, driven to fury by the *Blind Date Christmas Special*, the *Beadle's About Christmas Special*, and the *Darling Buds Of May Christmas Special*, will be holding his family at knifepoint.

Carol singers will have been round every night for the past six weeks, singing the well-loved favourites:

Good King Wenceslas looked out
On the feast of Stephen
Answer the door and give us some cash you tight bastards
Deep and crisp and even

It's the season of goodwill, the time of good cheer. Aaarrgggggh! God how I hate it!

Now that department stores offer trips around Santa's grotto in October, we spend around one-fifth of our lives preparing for or celebrating Christmas. There is almost no place on the planet where you can be certain of avoiding mistletoe, Santa Claus or tinsel. We asked Alfred Marx, the employment agency, to find us a job on 25 December where we could avoid Christmas. 'Sorry,' they said. We tried to book a holiday in the Gobi desert. 'Sorry,' said Bales Tours. 'We are a responsible travel agent and would not send anybody into the Gobi over Christmas – it's far too cold.'

The Middle East seemed the ideal place but all Middle Eastern countries seem to have strong ex-pat communities where Christmas is celebrated even more vigorously than in the Home Counties.

But don't lose hope. Here are ten ways to avoid tinsel, turkey, and any Faithful who might be coming towards you looking sickeningly joyful and triumphant.

Sleeping in an igloo on Baffin Island

For people who really, really hate Christmas – a Thomas Cook tour to the Canadian Arctic. The Iqaluit Hotel, Baffin Island offers dog sledding by day, and the chance to sleep in igloos or tents in temperatures of around -28C by night. You will see polar bears, caribou, and seals; you won't see turkeys, crackers,

and *The Wizard Of Oz*. Julie Morgan, of Thomas Cook, says: 'You are as likely to see a polar bear as another human being, but we recommend that you take plenty of thermal gear.' The resident population of Baffin Island is some 3,000, mostly Indian but with some Canadian. If you are unlucky, you might stumble upon a makeshift Canadian Christmas in the hotel, so stick to the igloo.

● *A week at the Iqaluit Hotel and return flight from Air Canada costs from £1,200 a week from Thomas Cook (061-832 9474).*

Visiting the VAT office in Norwich

The Hotel Nelson, Norwich (three star, riverside location) offers Scrooge Breaks on which guests can bring Christmas decorations to be burned in a ritual fire in the hotel garden. Unfortunately, they don't offer this service on Christmas Day. General manager Peter Mackness says 'We're very busy over Christmas but we do run a week afterwards, mainly for people who've been working over Christmas. There are normally 30 – 40 people: shop people, tradespeople.' The guests, who are given their own Wee Willie Winkie candles, are guaranteed absolutely no carols, turkey, or Christmas puddings. But they do get the opportunity to see Norwich prison, City Hall, and the VAT office. There isn't actually much to see in the VAT office – desks, chairs, a few bits of paper – but as Peter Mackness so rightly says 'it's a bit different'.

● *Three nights (available 28 December – 4 January) on the Scrooge Weekend cost £52 b & b. Contact Hotel Nelson (0603-760260).* ☞

Tinsel-free in Ulan Bator

Christmas trimmings are so difficult to come by in Mongolia that seven years ago, the *Times* hired a Rolls-Royce to drive a Marks & Spencer pudding from London to the British Embassy in Ulan Bator. The ambassador, who opened the embassy door, was overcome with emotion at the gift. 'There's a gentleman from the *Times* at the door, dear,' he shouted back to his wife.

Being a bit miserable at home

Watching television is out on Christmas Day. Channel 4 is showing *Pavarotti In The Park* (8pm) and Status Quo's *Rock Til You Drop* (7pm), but unless you nip out for a cup of tea as soon as the credits roll, you won't escape the continuity announcers with Christmas trees and Santa outfits. You will only escape Santa be-bearded continuity announcers on radio. Here are four programmes on Radio 4 that are guaranteed Christmas-free:

● 11am – noon: *The Hobbit*. First part of the Tolkein story.

● 12 – 12.25pm: *Namesakes*. As recommended by Big Ears (see page 64). Famous people (David Owen, Steve Davis, Victoria Wood) meet their not-so-famous counterparts and fail to discuss Christmas.

● 5 – 5.30pm: *The Tingle Factor* Sir Anthony Jay, who co-wrote *Yes Minister*, discusses his favourite words and music with Robin Ray. No *Jingle Bells*.

● 10.05 – 10.45pm: *A Search For DNA*. A dramatised feature in which a microscopic Dr Alan Maryon Davis is injected into the bloodstream of a pregnant woman to discover the origins of life.

A trip through the Indian Desert

Sloanie tour operator Abercrombie & Kent (071-730 9600) will arrange a trip through the Jaisalmer Desert in north-western India, riding a camel in temperatures of around 20C by day and sleeping in a tent by night. The tour will be tailor-made to your requirements (those requirements being no readings of *A Christmas Carol*, no pulling crackers etc) and arranged by the company's Delhi office.

Be a Buddhist

The London Buddhist Centre is running a meditation course over the Christmas week (21 – 29 December). Around 70 people will be paying £200 (£108 for the 'unwaged') to stay in Oxfordshire to learn meditation techniques and chanting. You will also be instructed in confessions and resolutions – writing down on a piece of paper everything you have done but regretted and burning the piece of paper, then writing down everything that you would like to do on a piece of paper which you then keep. In the evenings there are entertaining talks, one entitled 'Why I Am A Buddhist'.

● *Sign up with the London Buddhist Centre (081-981 1225).*

No Christmas on Christmas Island

There are no hotels, there is no public transport, and – most important of all – there is no Christmas on Christmas Island, just 200 miles south of Indonesia. The population (approx 1500) is mostly Chinese, so there are temples and a mosque, but no Christian churches. (Australians, who make up 15 per cent of the population, could hold makeshift Christmas celebrations, but they are easily avoided.) The island's rainforest houses plenty of fascinating wildlife, none of it remotely resembling turkey.

Hark the herald angels sing? Not round here, matey

Three of the bird species are rare and unique to the island – the Abbott's Booby, Christmas Frigatebird and Golden Bosunbird. Christmas visitors might also be able to watch thousands of red crabs shuffling along the beach in the annual spawning migration that marks the beginning of the wet season.

● *Book up Christmas on Christmas Island through Island Holidays, Comrie, Perthshire (0764-70958). Cost – £1,720 per person for an 11-day trip, leaving London on 18 December.*

Caribbean Christmas

There is a carnival every December on the Caribbean island of Monserrat, but it has nothing to do with Christmas. 'It's just an excuse to have some fun,' says John Renton, an architect who built some plantation-style houses on the island. By renting one of his villas, you can swim, play golf and tennis, windsurf, peer into the craters of extinct volcanoes without any prospect of being dismayed by any merry gentlemen. One word of warning, though: the Monserrat Festival opens with carol singing on 22 December at 7pm. So stay in that night.

● *Prices start at £1,042 per person (self-catering). The price includes a return flight from Gatwick via Antigua. Details from Montpelier Travel (071-584 1050).*

A mile high, club class

Japan Air has two flights on Christmas Eve (7pm, 8.35pm) and one flight on Christmas Day (7pm) leaving from Heathrow's Terminal Three. It takes just over 11 hours to fly to Tokyo. 'We won't be serving any special meals,' said a spokesman. Nor will staff be wearing paper hats and pulling crackers. The economy fare is £1,420 (first class, £2,644).

Party time in Pyongyang

It's always party time in the North Korean capital Pyongyang, where the great halls of the people will not be decked with boughs of holly but pictures of the country's Scrooge-like leader Kim Il Sung, secretary of the Korean Workers Party and president of the country for absolutely ages. 'We do not celebrate Christmas,' said a North Korean. Non-communist visitors were not allowed to visit North Korea until 1986; they are now permitted into the country only if accompanied by an official guide-interpreter. On Christmas Day you and your guide can visit the city sights – Kim Il Sung's birthplace, a bronze statue of Kim Il Sung commemorating the anti-Japanese struggle, a monument to celebrate the 70th birthday of Kim Il Sung. Aeroflot (071-491 1764) flies from London via Moscow for £510 return.
Research by Juliet Benjamin.

Toupee or not toupee?

Since Terry Wogan announced the end of his BBC chat-show, two vital questions remain: who keeps the fabled hairpiece? And is it a wig at all? STEVE SMETHURST investigates

The Rug-o-matic guide to Terry's incredible non-shrinking hair

1970: the young Terry in well-groomed and luxuriantly beside-burned shock

1977: Punk Rock has no impact on a wildly coiffured, not to say windswept, Wogan

1991: the present day and Tonsured Tel is still a perfectly pompad-oured presenter. Father Time has been very kind...

When BBC1's Celtic chatsmith Terry Wogan said last week that he is to quit his thrice-weekly talk show, the response was swift. Mac, the *Daily Mail* cartoonist, depicted a props man explaining to a smooth-skulled Terry that the teeth, the suit and the wig were the property of the Beeb. But is Wogan really a betoupeed blarnymeister? And will he be pulled from under his rug by the make-up people next year? To solve the mystery we contacted some veteran syrup-spotters.

 First off we rang the BBC who promptly handed us to **Gaynor Vanity**, the PR officer for Mr Wogan. When quizzed if Mr Wogan sported a toupee, she said emphatically: 'No he does not – absolute *rubbish*! Goodbye.'

 Thus rebuked we sought informed opinion from the *Daily Mail* showbiz watcher **Baz Bamigboye**. 'I have noticed that you Caucasian men do lose it rather easily,' he observed. 'And the top of his head has a certain rug-like quality.'

 None the wiser, we turned to one of Terry's brothers in armchair, Channel 4's pate-laden **Clive Anderson**: 'Of course, I have in fact been wearing a bald toupee for some years now and I do in fact have a full head of hair. Yes, you have successfully 'outed' me, but I have no comment on Terry Wogan...'

 Frustrated by this diplomacy we turned to former Bitch on the Box, **Nina Myskow**: 'I believe it's a hair-weave, not so much Terry Wig-on as Terry Weave-on. It's not a proper wig like Tony Blackburn's – his wig curls up at the back like a British Rail sandwich.

But it's common knowledge around the BBC about Terry, he does have some hair of his own but it's supplemented.'

 Supplemented? Trichologist **Glenn Lyons** explained, 'It is definitely not a full wig. It is either a piece or a weave but I really couldn't say.' What is a weave? 'It's just a case of interlacing sections of the real hair with a false piece which is more secure than an ordinary toupee.'

 Armed with this new word 'weave,' we set off to re-quiz **Ms Vanity**. While strenuous, her reply was encouragingly not a full denial. 'I *really* do have *nothing* to say. Look, I know you are only doing your job. But I have absolutely no comment,' she said.

 But **Carol Walker**, trichologist and hair-piece expert, added a new element when she told us: 'The only way to accurately tell the difference between a toupee and a weave is from above; a toupee has a supple base whereas a weave looks like the edges of a grass skirt. Did you know there is a weft, which is strings of hair woven across the bald patch?'

 A weft? We returned again to the patient **Ms Vanity** with our new theory that 'it's not a wig, it's not a weave, it's actually a *weft*!' She finally cracked...up laughing: '*Look*...I know you have to do this, but I have *nothing* to say. I really *cannot* comment...'

So alas the Wogan mystery persists. Perhaps one of his BBC chauffeurs could accidentally leave the sunroof open and see if the fur flies... 🐱

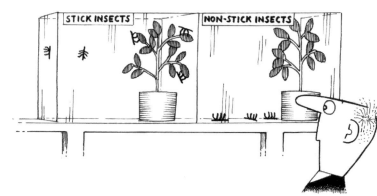

'You've been feeding him steroids again'

'Sheer emotional blackmail, if you ask me'

'Let the other buggers find their own formula, I say'

'I wish he'd go out and take drugs like normal teenagers'

'Ignore Harold, he only does it to get attention'

'It's a serial killer, Sarge – he wants Mr Bun the baker for the set'

'Hush, hush, whisper who dare, Christopher Robin's been put into care'

The annual
Guttersnipe index

Guided by the motto 'A civilised guide to an uncivilised world', Guttersnipe has combed the tabloid demi-monde for grimy gossip and prurient peccadilloes. Now Mr Mitchell Symons and his man, Smethurst, proudly present their annual alphabetised reference guide

ASHBY, Miss Delicious 'Debee' (*the Page Three personage*)
20 February: renouncement of love-making. **27 February:** discovery of 'live-in lover' *à deux* with other man.
BASINGER, Ms Kimberley 'Kim' (*the cinematic vamp, the pouting thespienne*)

See under Hall of Shame

27 February: realisation she's 'above God'. **27 March:** ostracisation of her by boys at school. **15 May:** nude equestrian sortie, informs policemen, 'I bet you haven't seen melons like these in a while, boys.' **22 May:** her beau attends 'Love Addiction' meetings. **25 September:** pays £75 a day to have an umbrella over her head.
BEADLE, Mr Jeremy (*the pariah*)
17 April: recognition failure by a 'victim'. **29 May:** ownership of electric bed with 101 positions. **9 October:** rift with mother-in-law.
BEATTY, Mr Warren 'Bunny' (*the libidinous thespian, the male escort*)
17 April: purchase of land in Wyoming. **4 September:** fainting during childbirth video.

Guttersnipe Hall of Fame

Best Man of the Year:
Mr Oliver Reed for his boisterous appearance on *After Dark* which proved that the last of the hellraisers will fight the evil spectre of Political correctness to the bitter end – as long as there's a well-stocked hospitality suite. What a prince.

Best Woman of the Year:
Miss Gorgeous 'Gayner' Goodman for being, and indeed showing, her natural self the whole year round. What a trouper. (Jeremy Beadle's mother-in-law gets a commendation for saying of the barbigerous prankster: 'Low? He should be 30ft under with a block of flats on him.')

BLACK, Ms Priscilla (*the nasally-amended televisioniste*)
24 April: her children can't stand her on TV. **30 October:** wearing of a hat to a wedding.
BRUNO, Mr Frank (*the guest appearance, the erstwhile pugilist*)
20 March: avowal that carnal relations are 'the most natural thing in the world'.
31 July: yearning to be 'Britain's answer to Eddie Murphy'.
DE CADENET, Miss Amanda (*the one time 'wild child'*)
1 May: unveiling of torso. **5 July:** donning of white socks. **18 September:** delight at being 'with child'.
CHER, Ms, aka Mrs Cherilyn Bono (*the spare parts, the thespienne and diva*)
26 June: bitter feud with mother. **31 July:** surrounded by satanists. **14 August:** moving house to escape satanists. **18 September:** dislike of tattoo on her behind.
CICCONE, Signorina Madonna (*the outrage, the libido, the Sicilian chanteuse and tragedienne, the Catholic chanteuse*)
16 January: cast as lead in *Evita*. **30 January:** proposal that prophylactics be distributed free to schoolchildren. **13 February:** alleged bullying of lovers. **3 April:** protection of cone-shaped chests. **29 May:** posing for 'bizarre' photographs for *Rolling Stone*. **3 July:** cinematic project *Truth Or Dare* watched by Saddam Hussein. **7 August:** enjoyment of repast with Mr Michael Rourke. **16 October:** arrangement of numerous dates. **20 November:** M. Jean-Paul Gaultier proposes three times.
COLLINS, Ms Joan (*the shoulder pad*)
17 April: view that 'men are not necessary anymore'. **8 May:** transformation to a 'raddled old hag'.
CONNOLLY, Mr William 'Billy' (*the Caledonian court jester*)
9 January: instruction to *Sun* photographer: 'Take any more f****** pictures and I'll stick that f****** camera up your f****** a***, you ****.' **10 April:** his mother's frugal existence. **19 June:** claim that 'ruining' the night for Mrs Thatcher's daughter ensures 'life is worth living'.

See under Donovan

COSTNER, Mr Kevin (*the straight man*)
23 January: desperation 'to bury the ghost of his porn film past'. 6 March: lachrymose outburst during carnal activity. 8 May: search for employment in a bank.

CRUISE, Mr Thomas Mapover (*the diminutive thespian*)
19 June: addiction to love potion. 3 July: request to wife for 'a date'.

DEPARDIEU, Monsieur Gérard
20 March: allegations of infant career as a ravisher of maidens (subsequently denied).

DONOVAN, Mr Jason 'King' (*the all round entertainer, the twinkling star in the firmament that is showbusiness, the all-round entertainer, the out-and-out all-*

See under De Cadenet

round antipodean entertainer, the confirmed heterosexualist)
9 January: statement of desire for fatherhood. 13 February: insistence by Donovan Snr of his son's red-bloodedness. 27 February: announcement of dedication to carnal matters. 6 March: denouncement of homophobes as 'w******'. 5 June: unrequested assertion of red-bloodedness. 7 August: squiring of a 'tom-boy heiress' about town. 14 August: suing of the *Face* over 'gay' slurs. 4 September: bicycling through Notting Hill. 13 November: his children's TV presenter 'chum' to take over his slot as Joseph (see under Mr Philip Schofield).

EASTWOOD, Mr Clinton 'Clint' (*the make-my-day*)
20 March: payment of £2.5m to Ms Sondra Locke after marital rift. 28 August: imbibation of Newcastle Brown Ale.

FOX, Miss Samantha (*the embonpoint and vocal stylist*)
20 February: renouncement of copulation. 17 April: perusal of literature during aeronautical flights. 1 May: gramophone release entitled 'Hurt Me, Hurt Me (But The Pants Stay On)'. 5 June: dubbed the 'new Madonna'. 19 June: is to play a princess in a new film. 10 July: considers herself to be 'working class'. 31 July: continuation of celibacy. 28 August: doesn't fake orgasms like Madonna.

FRENCH, Ms Daybreak 'Dawn', (Mrs Leonard Henry) (*the comely comedienne*)
20 February: refusal to wear miniskirt. 13 November: nascent sexual experiences.

GASCOIGNE, Mr Paul aka Gazza (*the commodity, the publicity stunt*)
23 January: unveiling of new coiffure. 6 February: photographed with Sindy doll. 3 July: composition of poems that rhyme.

GOODMAN, Miss Gorgeous 'Gayner' (*the Page Three dignitary, the pulchritude*)
9 January: wishes her fans a 'happy nude year'. 27 February: learned conjuring from her 'dad'. 17 April: intention to purchase automobile. 8 May: addiction to scuba diving. 22 May: inability to steer her dinghy. 29 May: deportment of a brooch on her lingerie. 5 June: takes up golf. 25 September: desertion at air terminal.

Hawkes, Chesney (*the block off the old Chip*)
24 April: vanquished in a 'talent contest'. 19 June: discombobulation of Mr Roger Daltrey, a troubadour.

HIGGINS, Mr Alexander aka 'Hurricane' (*the snooker professional*)
9 October: ingurgitation of Mrs Oliver Reed's *parfum*. 27 November: murmuration of four-letter filth.

HOUSTON, Miss Whitney (*the single songstress*)
22 May: denial of 'torrid lesbian affair'.

ICKE, His Holiness David, (*erstwhile custodian of the posts with Hereford Utd and snooker commentator, the saviour*)
27 March: confabulation with Socrates. 3 April: intimacy with the Angel of God and

the Daughter of God,

IDOL, Mr William 'Billy' (*the vocal stylist*)
9 January: sending of *inamorata* into audience to recruit more 'willing' female. 30 January: announcement that it's a 'new girl every night'. 6 March: predilection for youthful female company.

JACKSON, Mr Michael (*the beige chanteur, the tinted diva*)
12 June: self image is that of 'a freak in many ways'. 14 August: the father of the bride (Liz Taylor). 6 November: plan to stage mock wedding. 27 November: orders destruction of old photographs.

JONES, Mr Thomas 'Tom' (*the lungs, the pelvic thrust, the voice*)
9 January: infatuation with attractive student 'young enough to be his daughter'. 13 March: squiring of a 'stunning 21-year-old girlfriend'. 30 October: use of Listerine to ease abrasions on manhood after robust bouts of carnal exercise.

See under Goodman

LLOYD, Miss Kathy (*the Page Three personage*)
26 June: renouncement of equestrian betting after inevitable losses. 28 August: avowal of arachnophobia.

LUSARDI, Miss Linda (*the erstwhile Page Three personage*)
10 July: difficulty of singing and dancing simultaneously.

MICHAEL, Gorgeous 'George' (*the diva, the bubble with the stubble*)
6 February: unveils new pompadour. 13 March: supposed three-month fling with one Miss Amy Swan. 27 March: allergy to facial growth.

MINOGUE, Miss Dannii (*the sister*)
29 May: fear of going out. 3 July: intention to compose songs with her sibling. 30 October: wearing of a 'sexy' blonde wig.

MINOGUE, Miss Kylene 'Kylie' (*the moppet, the diminutive diva*)
1 March: has a new *inamoratum* in her life. 6 May: no longer has a new *inamoratum* in her life. 19 June: cancellation of journey to Yorkshire. 3 July: intention to compose *lieder* with her sibling. 18 September: possession of 'kinky' manacles in customs hall.

MIRREN, Ms Helen, (*the thespienne*)
10 April: pledge to carry on stripping until she's 90.

MURPHY, Mr Edward 'Eddie' (*the joke,* ☞

Guttersnipe Hall of Shame

Worst Woman of the Year:
Ms Kimberly Basinger for suggesting her lover Mr Alec Baldwin go to Love Addiction meetings to ease his 'sex drive'.

Worst Man of the Year:
Mr Alec Baldwin for actually going.

See under Nielson

the foul-mouthed American humorist)
20 March: allegation that the tinted thespian 'isn't choosy'. **9 October:** claim that Robin Givens was his 'worst lay'.
NAVRATILOVA, Miss Martina (the tennis player beaten by a girl half her age)
10 July: intimate details of her sapphic relationship with Ms Judy Nelson.
NICHOLSON, Mr Jackson 'Jack' (the leer, the libidinous thespian)
17 April: purchase of 'lots' of Wyoming. **31 July:** indulgence in 'sordid sex games'. **27**

See under Minogue

November: fatherhood before films.
NIELSON, Ms Brigitte (the implant, the uplifted thespian, the tragedienne famous for her gravity-defying embonpoint)
27 February: possession of tattoos of previous 'lovers' over her body. **5 June:** spotted openly 'kissing and canoodling'. **10 July:** desertion of third husband. **7 August:** donning of 'figure-hugging mini-dress'.
O'CONNOR, Ms Sinead (the unsolicited opinion, the scalp, the scantily-coiffured Hibernian chanteuse)
20 March: her son thinks she's 'a piece of s***'. **26 June:** subjection to unsolicited attack from Madonna. **25 September:** refusal to be presented to Princess Stephanie. **20 November:** troubled marriage is 'over'.
PACINO, Signor Alastair 'Al' (the height-challenged Latin thespian)
30 January: agreement to marry Miss Diane Keaton (later reneged on). **6 March:** revelations that 'women turn him on, girls don't. A woman can be 14 and a girl 63.'
RANTZEN, Ms Esther (the so-I-said, the busybody, the so-he-said)
13 March: forced three kids to smoke.

19 June: says hostelries should be converted into 'family centres'. **21 August:** campaign against women drinking. **28 August:** opposition to 'weird rituals'.
REED, Mr Oliver 'Ollie' (the thirst, the full-time thirst, the Guernsey boulevardier)
6 February: 'F***, b*******, let's get p*****' – unscripted jollity on television series *After Dark*. **29 May:** return to a hotel while intoxicated after being instructed to 'get out'. **14 August:** embarkation on heroic 'pub-crawl' while on prison visit. **18 September:** comical consumption of carrots disguised as goldfish. **9 October:** provision of perfume for Alex Higgins to drink.
ROBERTS, Miss Julia (the pretty woman, the wide-mouthed thespienne, the siren)
10 April: eternal accompaniment by the ghost of her father. **15 May:** was 'two-timed' by Mr Kiefer Sutherland. **19 June:** postponement of her nuptials. **3 July:** cancellation of her nuptials. **10 July:** ordered to renounce tobacco consumption. **14 August:** employment of a 'stand-in' for her posterior. **18 September:** performance in a 'raunchy video'. **16 October:** attachment of a homing 'bleeper' on her body to foil kidnappers.
ROSS, Mr Jonathan (the diminishing ratings phenomenon, the cheeky chappie)
7 August: tears a ligament in birth celebrations. **27 November:** buys a matching pram and dress.
SCHWARZENEGGER, Herr Arnold (the marketing opportunity, the Austrian)
24 April: once read a magazine out loud on an aeroplane. **22 May:** guarded by eight bodyguards. **21 August:** appreciation of popular music group Jesus Jones. **4 August:** loves doing the washing-up. **20 November:** voted top of a posterior appreciation poll.
SCHOFIELD, Mr Philip (the not-boring-televisioniste and phonograph equestrian)
6 November: attack by an 'unstoppable sex machine'. **13 November:** slipping into the slot vacated by his 'Ocker pal' as Joseph (see under Mr Jason Donovan).
SEYMOUR, Jane 'Jane'
30 January: said to be 'shattered' by

revelations of her husband's narcotics consumption. **27 March:** provision of comfort by Mr Peter Cetera.
SHIELDS, Brooke
29 May: announcement of long overdue loss of her maidenhood.
SMITH, Ms Mandy (the erstwhile wife)
1 May: romance with the Association professional, 'Pat' Van Den Hauwe.
STALLONE, Signor Sylvester 'Sly' (the diminishing return, the grunt, the speech impediment, the Hollywood thespian)
23 January: proposal of marriage to Miss Jennifer Flavin. **13 February:** payment to have his *inamorata*'s embonpoint enlarged. **25 September:** knocked out by Fergie's charms. **13 November:** loss of 50 balls while playing golf. **27 November:** allegedly achieves penile erection by means of 'air-powered machine'.
STEWART, Mr Rodlington 'Rod' (the role model, the troubadour, the grave-digger-turned-crooner, the Caledonian vocal stylist, the tartan amour)
New Year edition: embrace of his wife. **23 January:** is quoted as saying 'Anne-Marie can call on me any time'. **13 February:** claim to be more beautiful on the inside. **13 March:** passion for raw onions. **3 April:** a blonde's claim that she had carnal knowledge of Mr Stewart just weeks before his marriage. **21 August:** payment of £3,000 for a pompadour. **30 October:** avowal that he would rather face castration than be sexually infidelious.

See under Seymour

WRIGHT, Miss Fionula 'Fiona' (of the banana marketing council, the erstwhile executive courtesan)
6 March: used to be a £500-a-time hooker. **8 May:** has plastic surgery on her 'boobs'.
WYMAN, Mr William 'Bill' (the schoolgirls' friend, the lover and occasional musician)
30 January: opening of restaurant. **13 March:** failure to turn up for a 'video shoot'. **21 August:** acquisition of 30-year-old lady companion.
YARWOOD, Mr Michael 'Mike' (the someone else)
16 January: sad endurance of celibacy for five years. ✎

Open the pod doors, Hal

...and Terry the Tortoise is guaranteed a future, thanks to the efforts of Princess Di.

CREAK

Meanwhile, the savage attack from the Red Planet continues to provoke interplanetary outcry

Lucky no-one's spotted our secret hideout

International Cockup are even now launching intercept rockets from an unknown location

Take that, puppets of imperialism

...and if these cuts continue, the Government soon won't have a leg to stand on

VAT + CON / EMU = FAB

What the £@?!! do you think you're doing, Brains?

The main computer seems to be up the spout, your Ladyship

Praise the Great Tharg in the sky! Torybirds are Gone!

Not so fast - here comes Captain Scarlet!

I'd like you to meet my new assistant

That was the

Glass in hand, glint in eye, girl in shock, BARGEPOLE looks at the '91 that should have been

This week I will review 1991. Next week I shall offer you my predictions for the forthcoming...no. Bugger it. A mug's game, in my opinion, and this is my column so it's my opinions which count.

Why the hell should I review 1991? Neither you nor I have the remotest idea what happened in it, and we do not care. What is the use of pretending? We have no interest in politics and world events, except as stuff to drivel about at dinner parties to excite the admiration of women with big breasts and the rage of men called things like Norman Dogdeath from Internal Audit, and Dr Bendigo, and Shirley's friend Adrian Whitgift, you must remember Adrian, you know, he writes for *Railway World*, works in valves or possibly siphons, anyway I think you'll like him and for God's sake don't get carried away about Vic Reeves, you know what happened last time.

Which is a pointless exercise. Dogdeath, Whitgift and Bendigo are no more interested in politics than you are. What they really want to talk about is:
(1) Money.
(2) Their operation.
(3) Their relationships.
(4) Their feelings.

Your best bet is to operate the California Gambit, and immediately launch into an earnest recital about how you had to have this incredibly expensive operation which broke up your relationship and now you are trying to come to terms with your feelings. Be sure to remember that it all goes back to your relationship with your mother, who made you feel that you were only acceptable as long as you continued to come top of the class and scored goals and always had a clean face and shiny shoes and pulled your tassel back every time you had a bath. It is advisable at this point to quote Philip Larkin. You may use a Northern accent if you wish, but be sure to remember that the important line is 'They fuck you up, your mum and dad,' contrary to all human experience which suggests the second line is the one which counts, the one which goes 'They may not mean to but they do.'

Bendigo, Dogdeath and Whitgift will now be thoroughly irritated, and the skinny blonde with the tic and the hot, toffee-coloured eyes will be feeling enough pity to be convertible into an empathy poke later...but how are you going to get through the next three hours? There is the meat to come ('Yes, not bad, is it? I got it at Smithfield this morning, Mariella won't countenance Safeways and I must say Smithfield is fascinating, all those Brueghel faces, have you read that book *Meat* by that French woman, it's about this girl who works in a boucherie') and then the pudding ('It's Perdita's grandmama's recipe! The secret's the fresh orange peel!' 'Great!') and then the Drambuie ('Have you seen their commercial?' 'With the actor from – is it *The Terminator*, I think – that one...' 'And then the butler drops it!' 'God yes!') and then the coffee by the fire ('It's actually not a coffee pot actually, Alistair brought it back from the Hindu Kush, they make this infusion of rock samphire and cardamom but they don't do rock samphire at Safeway.' 'Or Smithfield ha ha!' 'Ha ha or Smithfield!')

But you have to get through it, so you might as well reminisce about the sort of year you have had. Given that you cannot remember a thing, as aforesaid, about your actual year, I am prepared, as a gesture of seasonal ill-will, to provide you with a year to look back on. Cut it out and take it with you. If you get stuck, you can slip off and read it on the lavatory. No worries, eh?

January You first started to have some worries about that man John Major. You couldn't sell your house. A pair of Dutch lesbians shunned you on the bus. You believed something you read in *GQ* magazine but on the other hand your verruca came back. On Wednesday 9th you were going to have lunch with someone but she cancelled. Later in the month you thought the Wigmore Hall was in Kensington, and on the 24th Anthony rang you to say he'd seen a laser.

Oh, darling..... you remembered...

...Your Valentine's Day message to me in the paper.... 'Elephant Ears loves his little Piggy Nose'....

Thank you, darling.

year that wasn't

February Well, frankly, you had been thinking about it and you were glad that miserable mad old bitch was thrown out. You realised she was single-handedly responsible for the mess the country is in, all those estate agents and barrow boys. On the 6th you asked Mr Curtis what the stuff the Chinese call 'seaweed' really is. He didn't know, but did you ever try that Japanese food? Sandy found your briefcase but your Ribena Berry Bunch Musical Money Box still didn't arrive. You couldn't work up much excitement about the Gulf War but frankly anyone with any sense could have seen that Saddam was up to no good. And what about that supergun, eh?

'And you shall be taken from this court and hung by the neck until you develop a nice, gamey flavour'

March You read something about shirts in *GQ*, but didn't agree with it. The verucca lotion seemed to do the trick until the 5th. Perhaps it was the Hush Puppies you bought in Ventnor the summer when you were going out with that Joanna, the one with the wall eye. The gas-filled height extender column on your desk chair went wonky but there was nothing Len could do about it. Funny, you'd forgotten about the wall eye. Abigail Rostrand mentioned a book about Palestrina over coffee. Mr Cassell queried your chitties. Say what you like, Mrs Thatcher was firm, more than could be said of the hooting, wet-lipped so-called 'Government' she left behind. Your house didn't sell.

April Your verrucas went away but your cold sore came back. Some actors and stuff were banging on about Aids and safe sex. You abjured that Melissa from Corporate Communications, even though she was gasping for it. On the 15th you could not recall whether you had told Geoff that you'd had her or not. On the 22nd, somebody rang in tears from the Notre Dame Hotel, Jerusalem, at three in the morning, wanting to speak to Terry Foulkes. You never did find out who Terry Foulkes was.

May A woman from St Lucia told you that your lucky furniture was the coffee-table. On the 12th, you wondered who, if anyone, wore Dunhill clothes. Mrs Fellowes had three nose-bleeds in one day. You had a nightmare about Mr Mepstead. On the 28th you decided not to take up Tai Chi Chu'an because you couldn't remember where the apostrophe went.

June A tall, big-nosed man with a red face in Gordes told you he knew how to get to Peter Mayle's house, but you lost your nerve. A clown followed you to Avignon. Your Barclaycard expired in the middle of dinner. On the way home again you shared your *couchette* with a mysterious stranger who crept into bed in the middle of the night with an alluring rustle of silk. In the morning he turned out to be a computer programmer from Maastricht. On the 18th you awoke with what looked like an erection, recession or no recession. Nobody came to view your house while you were away.

July Nobody came to view your house, though you were here the whole time. You were going to have dinner with Annelise but she had diarrhoea instead. Someone rang to ask if you'd like to address the IBM Sales Conference in Juan-les-Pins, but it turned out they thought you were Terry Foulkes. You felt it was too early to judge Mr Major's performance, but on the other hand that Francis Maude gave you the willies. Thingummy, what's-his-name, that Mr Cracknell from Reconciliations, he said that Francis Maude gave him the willies, too.

August Somebody came to view your house but you were in bed with a bug and didn't hear the doorbell. You got a fertilised egg on the 20th. You thought that sort of thing didn't happen any more, what with battery farms and everything. On the 22nd you remembered about the little lion, but couldn't remember whether it was before your time or not. American Express cancelled your card.

September You wondered if you were going to be made redundant. Dicky Greenstone said it was all the bankers' fault. You said, what about the accountants, then? He agreed. Mr Furtt said he thought those NatWest people had a cheek, they called you in and shouted at you while all the time it was all their fault the country was going down the plug. Thirty quid to bounce a cheque? A bloody liberty. You agreed it was a bloody liberty. Dicky Greenstone agreed it was a bloody liberty. On the 30th, Mr Twiss of NatWest called you in for a chat. You said it was a bloody liberty. He asked you to make alternative banking arrangements.

October You had the dog's abscess dealt with. Mrs Stoney's tree finally fell down. On the 17th you had your tooth done. If you had died in the dentist's chair that would have given her something to think about. You read an article in *Cosmopolitan* about how horrible men were. You said, what about women, then? Alan Horowitz from Data Processing agreed.

November They didn't make Jumping Jacks any more. Hadn't for years. Bloody women.

December You decide that the recession was well set in. On the 10th you went to Hamleys for your god-daughter's present. You wondered about children. Bloody women. Nobody came to see your house. You were made redundant after all. You told Naomi Bender that things could only get better. She said she should bloody cocoa. Bloody women. 🖎

old
Guttersnipe's
almanac

JANUARY

Mr Richard Branson, the self-publicist, is created a knight in the New Year's Honours List and celebrates by dressing up as Sir Walter Raleigh and proffering his cape for the **Duchess of York** to walk over. The Duchess and her family later jet off to Sir Richard's holiday island in the Caribbean in order to open a new leisure centre. **Paul 'Gazza' Gascoigne**, the one-time Association football professional, fractures his big toe while attempting to kick a medicine ball for the edification of watching newspaper men. 'Ahm reet sore, but a'll be playin' fer Lazio by September,' he says. **Miss Madonna Ciccone**, the sleaze, announces the forthcoming release of her latest promotional motion picture, *Doin' It The Hard Way With Madonna*. **Miss Esther Rantzen**, the televisioniste, summons the gentlemen of the press to the launch of Broadline, a telephone helpline for broadcasters who have been the objects of attacks by the press. 'I think it's very important,' she trills, 'for those of us in a privileged position to do things for those who aren't.'

FEBRUARY

Mr Dennis Waterman, the Londoner, and **Miss Roulade 'Rula' Lenska**, the photo-opportunity, reveal exclusively (to every tabloid journal) that they will be having a 'secret dinner to discuss a possible reconciliation'. When a journalist asks Mr Waterman whether this isn't just a publicity stunt, Mr Waterman fixes him with a steely glance and replies, 'Do what?' **Miss Kim Basinger**, the Hollywood tragedian, enters the *Guinness Book of Records* for the Lengthiest Stay In A Trailer On A Motion Picture Set. **Miss Kylene 'Kylie' Minogue**, the thespian turned diva, announces the forthcoming release of her latest promotional motion picture, *Doin' It The Hard Way With Kylie*. **Miss Brigitte Nielsen**, the

Miss Lenska: what does she see in him?

ex-wife, goes into hospital to have her breasts reduced in size. 'I am determined to be a great actress,' she says, 'rather than just a pin-up who was once married to Sylvester Stallone.'

MARCH

Mr Rodney 'Rod' Stewart, the chanteur, becomes a father for the fourth time and declares himself to be 'over the moon'. Trough the press, he apologises publicly to **Mrs Rachel Stewart** for missing the birth of the child but

'Cowdenbeath Reserves were playing away and my private plane just couldn't get me back in time.' **Miss Jane Seymour**, the doyenne of the televisual miniature series, invites *Hello!* magazine into her 'sumptuous mansion and talks frankly about her new-found romantic happiness.' **Paul 'Gazza' Gascoigne** shatters his leg in three places as a result of jumping out of a nightclub lavatory window in an attempt to escape 'them reet frightenin' pink elephants what was chasin' me, mon. But a'll be playin' fer Lazio by Christmas.' **Miss Ivana Trump**, the divorcee, launches a new scent entitled L'Air d'Alimonie. It is, she claims, 'a real attempt to synthesise my experiences of the past three years.' **The Prince of Wales** makes a plea for parents to 'stop sending children to private schools as this is the only way that the state system will be improved.'

APRIL

Mr and Mrs Lawrence Fortensky celebrate their six-month anniversary. Unfortunately, they are not together at the time as, according to Mrs Fortensky, 'We are having a trial separation although I'm sure it will work out.' **Miss Julia Roberts**, the wide-mouthed tragedian, is selected as Joan of Arc in **Steven Spielberg**'s controversial reworking of the story of the legendary French heroine. **Mr Robin Williams** is cast as the Dauphin. **Miss Cher**, the miracle, defends her decision to appear at last month's Oscar ceremony wearing nothing but a G-string as 'the right of women everywhere to flaunt their bodies – and flout men's rules.' **Miss Amanda de Cadenet**, the erstwhile wild-child, gives birth to her first child and tells *Hello!* magazine that 'my first priority is to get my figure back.' Kensington Palace announces that **Prince William** will be sitting the entrance exam for Eton in June 1995. **Miss Madonna Ciccone** announces her intention to make a sequel to her last motion picture to be entitled *Hittin' The G-spot With Madonna*.

I was hoping to become a lollipop lady

MAY

Mr William Wyman, the bass (sic) musician, publishes a collection of 'genuine reproductions of bus and train tickets collected by members of The Rolling Stones in the Fifties.' The *Sunday Mirror* purchases the serialisation rights. **Miss Kim Basinger** emerges from her trailer to announce that she and her co-star have not been enjoying carnal relations for the past six months but had merely been 'essaying penetrative character assessments of one another.' **Prince Philip** goes to the United Nations and delivers a lecture on global poverty. 'It is bloody ridiculous,' he avers, 'that some people have two homes while others have none.' **Miss Kylie Minogue** announces her intention to release a sequel to her last motion picture to be entitled *Hittin' The G-spot With Kylie*. **Sir James Savile**, the-uurghh-how's-about-that-then-guys-an'-gals, smokes a cigar while competing in the London marathon. Cigar sales in the UK plummet. **Paul 'Gazza' Gascoigne** releases his FA Cup Final single in company with Jive Bunny, a reworking of the Jackie Wilson classic, 'Reet Petite'.

The beknighted Jim

JUNE

Miss Amanda de Cadenet publishes her eagerly anticipated tome, *How To Get Your Figure Back After Pregnancy*. It is serialised in *Today* newspaper which is unable to publish pictures of Miss de Cadenet as she is reportedly at a 'secret hideaway health farm trying to slim down to a size 16.' **Mr Jason Donovan**, the out-and-out all-round entertainer, rushes into

print to defend himself against the 'charge' of being a 'ballet-lover'. 'Unfair dinkum!' he storms. 'I'm as red-blooded as the next man and I hate ballet. Just give me Aussie rules football any day of the week. So long as there's a really beautiful sheila to go home to at the end of the day. Know what I mean?' **Miss Esther Rantzen** summons the gentlemen of the press to the launch of Fruitline, a telephone helpline for members of the public who are distressed at being overcharged by greengrocers. 'I think it's very important,' she trills, 'for those of us in a privileged position to do things for those who aren't.' **The Duchess of York** returns from her royal visit to the Côte d'Azur to perform her regal duties at the Wimbledon Lawn Tennis Championships.

JULY

On the nine-month anniversary of their wedding, **Miss Elizabeth Taylor** announces that her marriage to **Mr Lawrence Fortensky** is over: 'I gave it my best shot but it just didn't work out. I'll always be very fond of Larry.' **Mr Oliver Reed**, the one-too-many, is detained by the local constabulary for publicly dipping his manhood in a gin and tonic in a public house and challenging the publican to 'come outside' when asked to desist. **Miss Jane Seymour** invites *Hello!* magazine

Mr Oliver Reed, the sage of Guernsey

into her 'stunning holiday villa and allows them to share the secret of her latest love.' **Mr Thomas 'Tom' Jones**, the voice, reveals an unfulfilled ambition to play Shakespeare's Hamlet. 'I've always felt this great affinity with Hamlet, see,' he says. 'It's true that he didn't wear tight trousers and commit adultery all the time but he was a prince and I've recorded a song by Prince so I feel we have plenty in common.'

Mr Thomas Jones: born to wear black tights

AUGUST

Miss Madonna Ciccone announces her intention to make a follow-up to her sequel to her last motion picture entitled *Keepin' It Up With Madonna*. **Miss Cher** defends her decision to attend the Democratic Party Convention wearing only a badge by saying, 'I don't think that politics and nudity are mutually exclusive. When you're hearing a message it's important not to be confused by the messenger.' **Miss Amanda de Cadenet** reveals her plan to emigrate to the United States where 'they, like, really know how to treat the larger-than-average woman.' **Paul 'Gazza' Gascoigne** ruptures his bladder after taking part in a contest to find out who can drink the most Newcastle Brown Ale without going to the lavatory. 'I'm reet mad about it like,' declares the sporting hero. 'I canna believe tha' I didn't win but a still intend to be playin' fer Lazio by the beginnin' of next season.' ☞

Miss Joan Collins, amuses her admirers by painting two baby skunks on her face

Sly Stallone: his ego   isn't all that's inflated

SEPTEMBER

Miss Brigitte Nielsen goes into hospital to have her bust enlarged. 'It's all very well being a great actress,' she says, 'but it is so important to be a woman, too, as my ex-husband S y l v e s t e r Stallone always used to say.' The handcuff- wielding **Miss Kylie Minogue** announces her intention to make a follow-up to her sequel to her last motion picture

This is not Madonna

entitled *Keepin' It Up With Kylie*. **Miss Joan Collins** purchases the film rights to Martin Amis's *Time's Arrow* and promises to turn it into 'the best TV mini-series ever.' 'I shall be playing the leading role,' she enthuses, 'even though it was written for a man but I just can't wait to go back through my menopause, loss of virginity and puberty to childhood.' **The Prince of Wales** makes a heartfelt plea to Britain's bosses to be more flexible and understanding with their workers as 'without them we're stymied'.

OCTOBER

Miss Esther Rantzen summons the press to the launch of Aqualine, a telephone helpline which Miss Rantzen urges is for anyone who feels that their life has been unreasonably worsened by not having access to a private swimming-pool. 'I think it's very important,' she trills, 'for those of us in a privileged position to do things for those who aren't.' **Mr J a c k s o n Nicholson**, the leer, turns down

Jack-the-dad

a reported $410m to star as **Edward Kennedy** in the motion picture putatively entitled *You Don't Need To Wear A Safety Belt For Such A Short Journey*. On what would have been the first anniversary of her marriage to **Mr Lawrence Fortensky**, **Miss Elizabeth Taylor** announces her engagement to **Bubbles**, a chimp owned by **Mr Michael Jackson**, the beige diva. 'I know that Bubbles and I come from different backgrounds,' she declares, 'but I love him and this is the last time I'm ever going to get married.' **Mr Rodney 'Rod' Stewart** denies that the blonde lady with whom he was caught embracing in a London nightclub establishment poses a threat to his marriage. 'Rachel is the mother of my child,' he says, 'and I'd be crazy to jeopardise our future just for the sake of a bit of fun.' Kensington Palace announces that four employees have been summarily dismissed for failing to stand up the second the **Prince of Wales** entered the room.

NOVEMBER

Mr Sylvester Stallone, the grunt, is spotted partaking of a repast with **Miss Cher** at his Planet Hollywood restaurant. 'Uh,' he retorts when questioned. 'I have a lot of respect for Cher and, who knows, if she has her breasts enlarged, anything can happen.' **Miss Madonna Ciccone** announces her intention to make a sequel to the follow-up to her sequel enti- t l e d *Tuckin' It A w a y For A

Rainy Day In Madonna. After the United States presidential election, **President Mario Cuomo** declares that he could never have done it without his running mate **Mr Warren 'Bunny' Beatty**. 'Once I put Warren on the ticket, it was a cinch,' he tells *Hello!* magazine as he shows them round his 'palatial' home. 'I figured we'd only need the votes of half his ex-girlfriends to swing California our way.'

DECEMBER

Paul 'Gazza' Gascoigne suffers a compound fracture of the skull after attempting to 'nut' his own reflection in a mirror. 'I'm reet gutted,' he says, 'but I wasn't gonna let that bastard gerraway from us again an' I hope to be playin' at Lazio by the start of the season after next.' **Miss Amanda de Cadenet** announces her intention to become a full-time thespian but is passsed over for the eponymous role in *The Life And Times Of Roseanne Barr* on the grounds that there isn't time for her to get down to her target weight. **Miss Kylie Minogue** announces her intention to make a much-anticipated sequel to the follow-up to her sequel entitled *Tuckin' It Away For A Rainy Day In Kylie*. **Mr L a w r e n c e Fortensky** is reported to be 'working c o n s t r u c - tion'. 🐉

Madonna: a clean living, home-loving, sweet kinda gal who likes to wear pointy bras

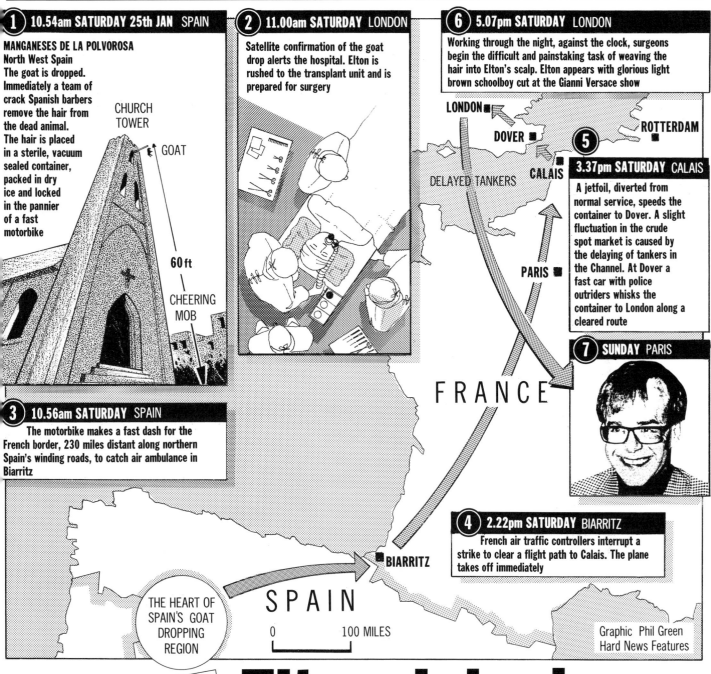

① 10.54am SATURDAY 25th JAN SPAIN

MANGANESES DE LA POLVOROSA
North West Spain
The goat is dropped. Immediately a team of crack Spanish barbers remove the hair from the dead animal. The hair is placed in a sterile, vacuum sealed container, packed in dry ice and locked in the pannier of a fast motorbike

CHURCH TOWER

GOAT

60 ft

CHEERING MOB

② 11.00am SATURDAY LONDON

Satellite confirmation of the goat drop alerts the hospital. Elton is rushed to the transplant unit and is prepared for surgery

⑥ 5.07pm SATURDAY LONDON

Working through the night, against the clock, surgeons begin the difficult and painstaking task of weaving the hair into Elton's scalp. Elton appears with glorious light brown schoolboy cut at the Gianni Versace show

LONDON

DOVER

ROTTERDAM

CALAIS

DELAYED TANKERS

⑤

3.37pm SATURDAY CALAIS

A jetfoil, diverted from normal service, speeds the container to Dover. A slight fluctuation in the crude spot market is caused by the delaying of tankers in the Channel. At Dover a fast car with police outriders whisks the container to London along a cleared route

PARIS

③ 10.56am SATURDAY SPAIN

The motorbike makes a fast dash for the French border, 230 miles distant along northern Spain's winding roads, to catch air ambulance in Biarritz

F R A N C E

⑦ SUNDAY PARIS

④ 2.22pm SATURDAY BIARRITZ

French air traffic controllers interrupt a strike to clear a flight path to Calais. The plane takes off immediately

BIARRITZ

THE HEART OF SPAIN'S GOAT DROPPING REGION

S P A I N

0   100 MILES

Graphic Phil Green
Hard News Features

Elton John in new 'rug' shock

On Monday 27 January, the popular press carried two major stories. One concerned the tragic slaughter of a Spanish goat, hurled from a 60-ft church tower as part of a bizarre religious ceremony. The other tale featured balding pop superstar Elton John, who amazed spectators at last

Left: The Star (27.1.92) tells the world about That Goat

week's Paris fashions with his lush head of light brown hair.

Until now, these two events were believed to be entirely separate. But *Punch* can exclusively reveal that Elton's hair-weave was composed of goat-hairs, shaved from the dead beast and rushed to a surgery in England. Our diagram shows the extraordinary, military-style manoeuvres that enabled the handsomely-berugged tunesmith to wear his wig last week.

171

Inside image (speech/signs): I WAS MOUNTED BY THE PRESIDENT ON MOUNT RUSHMORE · THE PRESIDENT LOVES YOU ~ TWICE A NIGHT · SAY, HAVE YOU SEEN 'ALL THE PRESIDENT'S WOMEN'? · WASHINGTON NEVER TOLD MANY LIES · MAKE ABE HAPPY ~ VOTE LINCOLN IN · MR PRESIDENT TOOK A LIBERTY WITH ME UP THE STATUE OF LIBERTY... · HAVE A NICE LAY, MR PRESIDENT! · TRICKY DICKY LIQUOR STORE · READ MY LIPS, BABY · STEAM COMING FROM UNDERGROUND PRESIDENTIAL LOVENEST

All the presidents' women

Given the current moral climate, just how many of the great American presidents would have made it into the White House today?

MARSHA DUBROW opens the Oval Office's can of worms

'We know of no spectacle so ridiculous as the British public in one of its periodic fits of morality.' – Thomas Macaulay

Macaulay was certainly right except for one detail. He forgot to include the American public during election year. Their quadriennial stampede for the moral high ground is more fervent than ever, as Democrat Bill Clinton and Gary Hart before him can testify.

The scrutiny of a presidential candidate's private life never used to be so intense. But during the Eighties, when materialism and malfeasance predominated, the electorate suffered guilt pains. If anyone was going to give Mother Teresa a run for her money, they thought, it had better be the president. By 1988, one campaign button admonished that 'You Can't Run For President With Your Fly Open'. The result of such stringency is a vetting of would-be candidates that makes the post of Pope look like slumming. The interesting question is, under today's restrictions, just how many of America's great leaders of the past would still have made it to the White House.

This issue of a candidate's personal integrity is known as the 'Zipper Test' (often euphemised as the 'Character Question') but in Britain adultery or promiscuity is now only a terminal problem if the politician lies about his exploits (since Lucrezia Borgia women have rarely figured as dissipated politicians). Tory minister Cecil Parkinson survived the impregnation of his then secretary, Sara Keays. And Liberal leader Paddy Ashdown's popularity actually increased after the revelation that he'd dipped more than just a toe into the typing pool.

But these are humdrum mid-life crises when compared with America's presidential wannabes and has-beens. To start with the martyr of the moment, take pilloried candidate Bill Clinton, who is now lumbered with the nicknames 'Slick Willie' and 'Mr Beef'. Mr Clinton's only crime so far is to have been accused by an ageing cabaret artiste of infidelity. The charge has not even been proved but it left him 12 per cent behind Paul Tsongas in the New Hampshire primary. This is rather cruel when set against the examples of his predecessors.

Take the charmed prince John F Kennedy, the Casanova of the Casa Blanca, whose paramours included a mafia moll. Or Ike who more than liked his wartime driver and mistress, Kay Summersby. Franklin D Roosevelt found that happy days were here again for 30 years with his lover Lucy Mercer Rutherfurd.

Presidential scandal is often lipsmackingly venal, in both a financial and sexual sense. No polls are necessary to reveal a trend of scandal: Democrats do to mistresses what the Republicans do to slush funds. But several administrations have combined both. The original sin began in the first cabinet when treasury secretary Alexander Hamilton was said to have misused a married woman and government funds. A family man himself, Hamilton paid blackmail money for two years to the cuckolded James Reynolds and his wife Maria. After this shockeroo was leaked, Hamilton saved himself by writing his own version which became a best-seller in American and in Britain.

Thomas Jefferson became the third president in 1801 despite published accusations of his seducing two married women and keeping a slave mistress. The opposition press also said he'd pupped at least five children. Jefferson made no public denial, preferring, as he told a friend, to trust his countrymen 'to judge me by what they see of my conduct on the stage where they have placed me.' Hear ye, hear ye, candidates.

Andrew Jackson won the presidency in 1828 in spite of his pipe-smoking wife Rachel being branded 'adulteress' and 'whore' for purportedly marrying before she was divorced. The rumours killed Rachel Jackson before hubby took office, just as they had killed his 1824 presidential bid.

Grover Cleveland had the last laugh about reports of siring a bastard son a decade before his 1884 campaign. Republicans chanted, 'Ma, Ma, Where's My Pa?' to which Cleveland's supporters later retorted, 'Gone To The White House, Ha, Ha, Ha.' A role model for damage control if not birth control, Grover acknowledged the son and cabled his party leaders: 'Above all, tell the truth.'

President Warren G Harding's affair with Nan Britton was a minor tempest compared with his administration's many scandals, which included the case of the Teapot Dome oil reserves. This was a bribe-riddled deal which resulted in the first imprisonment of a former cabinet official. It also provides a useful example to journalists bored with adding the suffix '-gate' to the names they give to all political scandals, regardless of whether they have anything to do with break-ins in Washington: by adding '-dome' hacks can bring a new sense of variety to their reports, regardless of whether they have anything to do with teapots. Harding had a wilder sense of fun than Nixon, too. In-between excusing his notorious 'Ohio Gang' cronies, he had a literal tunnel of love carved to his mistress's boudoir. The legendary mole hole was exposed 30 years later when a startled construction crew smashed into it.

In *Incredible Era*, a book on the corruption of the Harding years in the Twenties, historian Samuel Adams wrote, 'A president is measured, weighed and catalogued by the character of his chosen intimates.' It's not known if Nixon or Reagan ever read this passage.

It was Vietnam wrongs and civil rights more than scandals that rained down on Lyndon Johnson 'like a Longhorn steer pissing on a rock', as less delicate Texans were wont to put it.

Asked about LBJ's reputed roaming from his home on the range, his wife Lady Bird chirped, 'My husband loved all people, and half the world's people are women.'

When critics accused Richard Nixon of 'indecent exposure,' they weren't revealing the origin of his nickname Tricky Dicky; they were referring to his 1952 TV speech where he was broadcast cuddling his cocker spaniel 'Checkers' in an attempt to clear his name (with dog lovers at least) in the first cock-up regarding a slush fund. This presaged by 20 years that apt acronym CREEP (Committee to Re-Elect the President), whose coffers financed the Watergate scandal which led to jail for ten aides and to Nixon's resignation in 1974 to avoid impeachment.

Numerous key Reagan administration figures were indicted for, and some convicted of, major offences ranging from violating federal ethics laws to perjury. Among those who had brushes with the law were former Attorney General Ed Meese, White House chief of staff Michael Deaver, the Housing and Urban

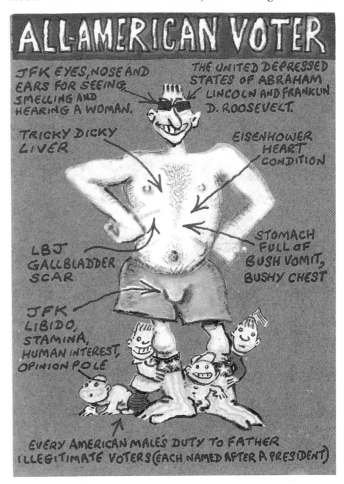

Development Secretary (the 'Dud from HUD') Samuel Pierce and aide Lyn Nofziger. That's aside from Iran-Contra which miraculously left Ron-bo and 'Poppy' Bush unscathed.

The only other printed hint of tarnish was George Bush Jr's denial of his father's rumoured affair: 'The answer to the Big A question is n-o.' Less cryptic was Barbara Bush, who once fumed at me after I made a similar inquiry: 'It's none of your business and absolutely not…It's a ridiculous question. It's outrageous to ask it…appalling…demeaning.' Popping that question was the nadir of my career. I agree with this lady and with the dictum of Jennie Churchill, Winston's American mum who dallied a bit herself: 'Just don't do it on the street and frighten the horses.' But if her advice were heeded, America's brain-dead presidential campaigns would be even more stultifyingly boring.

Not to worry. Suzanne Garment writes in her recent ☞

book *Scandal*: 'The great American scandal machine that we have built for ourselves is up and running with ferocious momentum.'

This machine does not just feed off 'peckerdillos'. There is also the fertile hunting ground of health. Will Bush's Graves' disease affect his candidacy? What about Democratic hopeful Paul Tsongas's lymphoma cancer which has not recurred for over five years? Did the fact that he is accompanied by a doctor on the campaign trail help to lose him last week's TV showdown with Clinton? Only the coming months will tell.

Elections, and history, might have been quite different had people known about the depressions of previous presidents like George Washington, who suffered terribly during the Revolution. Abraham Lincoln, too, had many well-documented major depressions. One forced him to stand up his fiancée Mary Todd at their first planned wedding in 1841. The worst of many

FDR's Splendid Deception by Hugh Gregory Gallagher: 'I seems undeniable that depressive neurosis – a state of reactiv depression – was a condition of the last year and a half of hi life.' This poses the worrying possibility that when the big thre Allied leaders got together, a dying depressive, an alcoholi manic depressive (Churchill, as diagnosed by one prominent psy chiatrist) and a murderous sociopath (Stalin, as diagnosed b almost anyone) were getting together to plot the downfall of genocidal maniac. And we wonder why the world has problems

FDR also suffered from paralysis and tried to deceive the public that he could still walk. He had ramps built for publi appearances and used his sons as virtual crutches. In the worst o three public falls, he 'crashed over like a tree' at the 193 Democratic convention, but aides rushed to hide him and picl him up. Then he wowed 100,000 cheering fans with hi 'Rendevous With Destiny' speech.

Most damaging to the action man myth of JFK was his seriou adrenaline disorder, Addison's dis ease, which gave him acute back pain During the 1960 campaign, the Kennedy entourage dodged the oppo sition's charges about the disease which was diagnosed two decade earlier by a London doctor who com mented, 'He hasn't got a year to live. At the White House, a medic whom JFK called 'Dr Feelgood' regularly gave him shots containing amphetamines.

Nixon's drug of choice wa liquor. Watergate co-star John Ehrlichman was quoted a saying that Nixon got 'pie-eyed' a least once. *One Of Us* by *New York Times* columnist Tom Wicker is les pithy: 'Physiologically, this fellow ha a disability. One drink can knock him galley west if he is tired.'

Alexander 'I Am In Control' Haig Nixon's last national security assis tant, was quoted as saying that he sometimes had to act as presiden when 'Nixon was drunk.' To be fai to Nixon, other aides question the famous account of a drunken presi dent in Bob Woodward and Carl Bernstein's *The Final Days*.

Although mild in comparison to Lyndon Johnson and Dwight Eisenhower's heart attacks, President Bush's arrhythmia threw the country into its own heart attack. Not least because J Danforth Quayle was grin ning inanely in the wings. Bush wins

We chart the grounds on which America's past presidents would be disqualified from the White House if they were running today...

	Jefferson	Lincoln	FDR	JFK	Nixon	Carter	Reagan
Sexual Peccadillos	'Lusty!'			'Insatiable'		Only in his heart	None, but what about Nancy?
Corruption				Mafia	Watergate		Irangate
Physical Infirmity			Elected with less than a year to live		Collapsed when jogging	Old but spry
Mental Infirmity	I'm going to kill myself	I'm so depressed			They all hate me!		Bibble-bobble
Medicinal Remedies					Booze	No, but Billy was a fish	
Media Relations	X	X	♥♥	♥♥	XXX	XX	♥

'uncontrollable depressions' during his first 18 months in the White House came when his son Willie died. 'Lincoln, by today's standards, would be disqualified hands down,' states Dr Ronald Fieve, author of *Moodswing*, citing dumped 1972 vice-presidential candidate Senator Thomas Eagleton after his depressions and electric shock therapy became known.

During World War II, President Franklin D Roosevelt showed 'classic signs of depression' including indecision, loss of appetite, weight, sleep, and staring into space. According to

in the most repulsive photo-op stakes for his much exposed Japanese upchuck. Bush's ingesting Halcyon has been partly blamed for the 'vomit thing'. But what substance makes him produce answers such as this to a question about extending unemployment benefits: 'If a frog had wings, he wouldn't hit his tail on the ground – too hypothetical.'

All of a sudden, it becomes frighteningly clear why over 40 per cent of the New Hampshire electorate were keen to see Pat Buchanan in the White House.

FERGIE

Aaaaaarrrghh!! The dogs!! Poor old Fergie.
After years of naff clothes, desperate diets and over-
publicised skiing holidays, she finally cracked. But
as she made her escape bid, the Queen let loose
wild packs of killer corgis, loosely disguised as
Palace press officers. Of course, the press office
did not mean to criticise the Duchess.
Oh, yeah, absolutely.

PUNCH

8 APRIL 1992
£1.30
US $2.95 DM 8.50

HOLTE

THE END

Dr No? It's about the vacancy

Oddjob club

Bored with commuting? A job with James Bond's villains promises plenty of adventure – but the penalty for failure is death. All the same, **MIKE CONWAY** drummed up 200 eager applicants

Dr No: is he your idea of a hands on employer?

Where do Bond villains get the staff? Wherever 007 goes, he can be sure of encountering megalomaniacs set on world domination. And every one of those evil hoodlums comes equipped with a horde of underlings, clad in silly uniforms and ready to die at a moment's notice. Take, for example, *Diamonds Are Forever*. The setting is Ernst Stavro Blofeld's oil rig, somewhere in the Gulf of Mexico. The villainous head of Spectre is under attack from the US Air Force, MI6 and the Florida Coastguard. An eminent scientist, duped by Blofeld into working for world peace, tells his Mao-suited boss that the game's up. Get back to your post or I'll have you shot! snaps back Blofeld. Then, gliding slyly over to a nearby telephone, he sends new orders to a quivering goon with the immortal Bond film catchphrase: Prepare my battle-sub immediately.

Blofeld is not alone when it comes to the Josef Stalin Caring Employer Award. In *Goldfinger*, when the plan to nuke Fort Knox goes awry, the glitter-loving head of Auric Industries machine-guns his own men. In *Moonraker*, beautiful specimens queue to join Sir Hugo Drax's space stud farm, unconcerned that he plans to blow up the world. Even Nick-Nack, the dwarf assistant of triple-nippled assassin Scaramanga in *The Man With The Golden Gun*, shows loyalty beyond the call of duty.

How can one acquire such loyal employees? If housewives can't get the help, how do megalomaniacs manage? We decided to find out. Working under the name of Professor Dent (a minor henchman in *Dr No*) we contacted newspapers and magazines to see if they would take the following advertisements:

DOMESTIC STAFF VACANCY
Our client is an international gun collector and specialist precious metal firearm manufacturer. After the sudden retirement of the previous postholder, we require a valet for duties at his

Oddjob from Goldfinger: who'd want his job?

home on a private island in the South China Sea. Our client operates an equal opportunities policy and positively welcomes applications from ethnic minorities, Hispanics, the disabled, and persons of restricted height. Please apply in writing to: Scaramanga Ltd, Fantasy Island, Hong Kong.

MAJOR EXPANSION DRIVE
We require central command staff to work at Crab Key, our magnificent Caribbean headquarters just outside Kingston, Jamaica. Our military personnel structure combines the high standards and severe sanctions against personal failure you would expect with a more-than-generous salary. Benefits include free uniform, seven weeks annual holiday (subject to Crab Key's alert status) and the opportunity to work with one of the world's finest scientific minds. Definitely not a hands-on employer!

No experience necessary. Hurry, hurry, hurry. Interviews to take place as soon as possible. Apply to: Dr Julius No, Bauxite Mine, Crab Key, PO Box etc.

INTERNATIONAL APPOINTMENTS
When the boss disappears, would you work on or wimp out? The first is the kind of trainee we require at the Special Executive, a world-wide expert in breaking up and re-assembling old bonds. We are now involved in even bigger projects, and the successful candidates could work for such companies as Ernst Oil, Stavro Construction and Blofeld Engineering.

Most trainees enjoy privileged access to top executives. These may be tough in their ☛

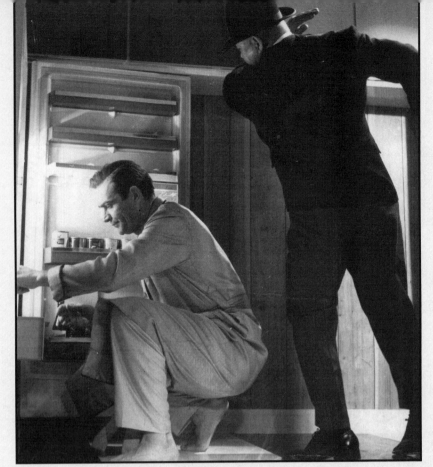

James Bond gets it in the neck from Korean goon Oddjob

methods, but if you survive, as we hope you do, the world will be your oyster. You may even meet the chief executive himself, as he travels from site to site in his corporate battle-sub.

If you have what it takes, send CV and covering letter to: Klebb Memorial Suite, Smersh, PO Box etc.

STELLAR OPPORTUNITY

'We at Drax Industries are experts at making the impossible happen. Now, under the patronage of our founder, and employing equipment surplus to the Soviet space programme, we are working to see if humans really can live in space.

If you want to become a trainee 'Master of the Universe', simply write to: Hugo Drax Esq, SPECTRE, Dept, 'Moon', Sinistre, Switzerland, PO Box etc.

Reaction was mixed. Those canny Scots at the *Glasgow Herald* rejected Dr No's craven appeals. I'm afraid we don t take adverts for foreign work, explained a tele-sales executive. *Ms London* immediately smelled a rat. Similarly, the *Birmingham Post* spurned the Scaramanga shilling. Poor old Professor Dent had to be part of a company, or else it was no-go. On his next outing, the Prof got smart.

The *South London Press* was faxed an advertisement on business notepa-per, Spectre Associates decorating the letter head, and listing a board of directors including ES Blofeld, Dr J No and V Stromberg CBE. A reply was received but again no luck.

One office sent a covert fax to Professor Dent saying, Keep this a secret but I m very interested in the position. Remember, you hold the key to my dreams in the palm of your hand. When phoned, the office told us that no

such girl worked there. Spooky

Switching to a smaller scale, we placed advertise-ments in South London newsagents. The response was terrible. Only one letter came for Sir Hugo Drax, asking for more details. And only one for Blofeld, saying, It's people like you who are ruining the eco-logical balance of our very planet.

The last resort was the *Manchester Evening News*, which finally ran our Goldfinger advert. The response was impressive: more than 200 replies. Of these, only four spotted the 007 connection. A Mr Smith of Manchester, writing on notepaper emblazoned with an eagle and the legend, TALON said, I am a mem-ber of Mensa, before adding, sagely, Your company name looks familiar. Mr Whitehead of Withington wrote. I must point out the startling resemblance between your advert and the basic storyline of the James Bond film *Goldfinger*. Even more intrigued was Mr Ryan of Bolton, who quipped, I have golf caddying experience and look good in a bowler hat.

From Levenshulme came Mr Higgins, who was a bit of a Bond expert. He said, I have never heard of Auric Industries before, although I have heard of Auric Enterprises. This concern was also based in Switzerland and Kentucky and made moves to expand in the Fort Knox area until the intervention of James of Universal Export.

Of those applicants who were oblivious of Bond, most were, like the geriatric security officers and weedy office workers, sadly wide of the mark. The 20-stone fork-lift truck operator was much more suitable, as was a private detective.

One former member of the Royal Corps of Signals had been to Hong Kong preventing the illegal entry of persons, which would have come in handy for protecting intruders at Goldfinger s headquarters. Another was a chauffeur to a lord — just perfect for Herr Goldfinger s gentrified lifestyle of plus-fours, horses and mint juleps in the afternoon.

Many letters came from ex-army personnel, all of whom stressed their loyalty. While not explicit, many implied that they would indeed fight to the death for their managing director. Others were RAF or Navy veterans — a must for villains equipped with the latest hardware. Their applications came complete with cur-ricula vitae and official Discharge Certificates and Conduct Assessments.

Our ad to recruit henchman

Had we kept the scheme going, we could soon have accumulated a size-able fighting force, ready to do battle on land, sea or air and happy to seize the controls of any passing battle-sub. More to the point, we had proved that a Blofeld or No need never be short of hired hands. All those who scoff at Ian Fleming's spy fantasies should think again. There are more Oddjobs than you think. 🐾

Auric Goldfinger: a firm but fair boss

'You know, Mother, one day I'd like to try some cereal other than Kelloggs Fruit 'n' Fibre'

Love and

The Haitian economy's gone to hell, the army's in revolt and the Tontons Macoutes are on the rampage. Just the right time, then, for the radical Reverend Al Sharpton to pay a visit. **ANDY KERSHAW** was with the portly preacher in Port-au-Prince

Total disinterest gripped the troubled island of Haiti. Gia[...] waves of indifference swept though Port-au-Prince. Foreig[...] journalists grumpily skipped breakfast. The Reverend A[...] Sharpton was in town. And no one had even the faintest ide[...] who he was.

The crisis of the Haitian boat people had spurred the rotun[...] New York radical into action. Fourteen thousand refugees hav[...] fled the country since a military coup last September overthre[...] the democratically elected president, Jean-Bertrand Aristide. H[...] had been in power for only nine months, breaking a 200-yea[...] tradition of violent dictatorships.

The refugees landed at Guant namo, an American naval bas[...] in Cuba. But the United States is now ferrying them all back t[...]

Haiti

speak to her? He handed me the phone. It was answered with a grunt. What time, I asked the drowsy preacher, was this press-conference?

8.30, he rasped.

Er it is 8.30.

A taxi-load of glum foreign hacks filed in. A dreadlocked spokesman for Big Al appeared.

Rev Sharpton will be with you when the *New York Times* finishes breakfast.

Suddenly he was among us, reeking of after-shave, swaying across the foyer like an unsteady Barry White on wheels. Behind him came his entourage, five activists, clergymen and attorneys, though you and I would have mistaken them for a rap group. An American reporter, seized with a rare attack of wit wondered: Haven t they got enough Macoutes in this country?

Not one Haitian reporter bothered to show. A couple of curious taxi drivers and a souvenir salesman sidled over. Was this everybody? I m afraid it was. Rev Al addressed the assembled, all ten of us, from the steps of the hotel.

We are here today to deliver this letter to the Presidential Palace Copies were passed round.

Al was angry and, I think, a little confused. Haiti is not a clear cut black/white problem. The goodies in Haiti are black but so are the baddies: a tricky place, this, for Sharpton to play the racist card. Nonetheless, he gave it his best:

This is the beginning of a battle, erm, to try and help from an African-American perspective our people here this type of environment is inhuman for the United States to sit idly by and ignore what s going on right beneath its borders is a sin and a shame and outright racism and we must challenge it from inside this country and we must co-operate on an international level with people of colour to end this abuse.

That said, we set off to meet the people of colour illegally occupying the National Palace. Our numbers were swelled by a straggle of beggars. The traffic on Rue Capois forced us to divide into sub-committees. Gardeners on the Champ De Mars put down their machetes to gaze upon the progress of this ridiculous man through a ridiculous city.

Is he someone important from America? a woman asked, mesmerised by Big Al s fluorescent-panelled shellsuit, blow-wave and swinging medallion.

I scanned the letter. On yesterday [*sic*], it began, we arrived in Port au Prince to seek facts on the reported abuses and murders that takes [*sic*] place here Time dictates your demise You will not quietly kill our people without the response of the world community You may have temporarily gained power but you risk permanently the loss of your soul Yours In Progress, The Reverend Al Sharpton.

Who, I asked, was the Reverend hoping to see at the palace?

No one. I m just dropping a letter. I m the mail man.

We all laughed, but Al Sharpton s face didn t crack once all morning.

Should Aristide (the deposed president) return?

I think that any nation should be run by the democratic☞

an uncertain future in lawless Haiti. Many face intimidation, possibly murder, at the hands of the Tontons Macoutes and a military out of control. Sharpton was here to let the goons know the world was watching.

I think I got him out of bed. A press conference had been called for 8.30am at the Sharpton billet, the Port-au-Prince Holiday Inn. This would be followed by a march on the National Palace.

By 8.27 the receptionist and I were the only ones there. Perhaps I d got this wrong.

Do you have a Rev Sharpton staying here? I asked. The front desk checked his guest-list.

Yes, he confirmed. She checked in last night. You want to

government that it elects. It's hypocritical to have a Persian Gulf affair claiming you're protecting democracy and then ignore the overthrow of a democracy right here under your borders. Either you're for democracy or you're not.'

What's your general impression of Haiti so far?

'I'm straight outta Brooklyn but this place is straight outta hell. Last night was the first time I remember sleeping that tense, hearing all that gunfire.'

Had he visited the slums of Port-au-Prince?

'The whole city's a slum. I've never seen such poverty.'

Was the impact of his visit undermined by the fact that nobody in Haiti seemed to have heard of Al Sharpton?

'I ain't here to get elected. I'm here to get those who were elected back in.'

Did anyone up at the palace know he was coming?

'No.'

Did he expect to be let in?

'I dunno. I just wanna drop this letter.'

The teenage soldiers on the palace gate received the Sharpton circus with complete bewilderment. Rev Al, shuffling on the pavement, couldn't disguise his humiliation – compounded, no doubt, by negotiations for his entry to the palace being conducted by French-speaking journalists in the group.

'Shall I have a word with them for you?' asked the Reuters man.

'Er...OK.'

'This is a very important man from the United States,' said Reuters to the guards. They looked at Rev Al and at each other. They said nothing.

Inwardly, Sharpton must have been squirming.

'Give me one dollar,' said a street urchin.

A small crowd gathered. An ice-cream salesman parked his barrow and began to work the throng.

'Will you let him go in to deliver a letter?' asked the *Guardian*.

Before we could block the street, the guards, eager to pass the buck, let the ample activist and his Muppet show through.

In the guardroom Sharpton produced his letter for the president and a pen.

'Now, what's the name of this guy?' he asked the Reuters man.

One Haitian official apologised for the confusion at the gate. 'If we'd known you were coming we'd have arranged a reception appropriate for a man of your size.'

Would the Rev Sharpton, the official wanted to know, be seeing Mr Honorat (the Prime Minister)?

'Who's Honorat?' said Al.

Al Sharpton was in Haiti for admirable reasons. The treatment of the refugees is appalling. There is little prestige to be gained back in the States by his striding around Port-au-Prince. American blacks tend to despise Haitians. He was here out of genuine concern for the plight of the refugees and, I sensed, some embarrassment, at the way 'people of colour' are treating his 'brothers' Sharpton, buffoon though he is, is the only international figure who's had the bottle, since the September coup to bang on the door of the Haitian regime and say this is a disgrace.

'We arrived in Port au Prince to seek facts on the reported abuses and murders that take place here ... You may have temporarily gained power but you risk permanently the loss of your soul ... Yours in Progress, the Reverend Al Sharpton'

Sharpton is regarded as a twerp largely because he looks like one. He likes to evoke Martin Luther King but MLK did not march on Washington or Selma, Alabama dressed for the beach.

I admire what Sharpton did in Port-au-Prince but we laughed at him for the way he did it. We'd take him more seriously if he took himself a little less seriously. The man has no sense of humour. And he could have done a bit more homework.

The last I saw of him, he was being driven away from the Holiday Inn in a pick-up for a tour of the capital. From the passenger window he unfurled a fat roll of dollar bills and began to hand them out to the urchins. It was like hell unchained: fights; men screaming; traffic swerving and honking; poor Haitians grappling in the gutter for torn banknotes; Big Al's truck hidden under ragged bodies who swarmed it like ants on a picnic left-over; the lower half of a Haitian sticking horizontal from Sharpton's window. The driver, although he couldn't see, tried to move off but the chaos, the downtown traffic, and the pot-holed streets meant escape at snail-pace. An old man with a stick hobbled after them. Only in Port-au-Prince could this mobile mayhem be caught by a one-legged beggar.

One Haitian, watching Sharpton's departure, turned to me and smiled:

'Well, if he's brought enough dollars along he could be president tomorrow.'

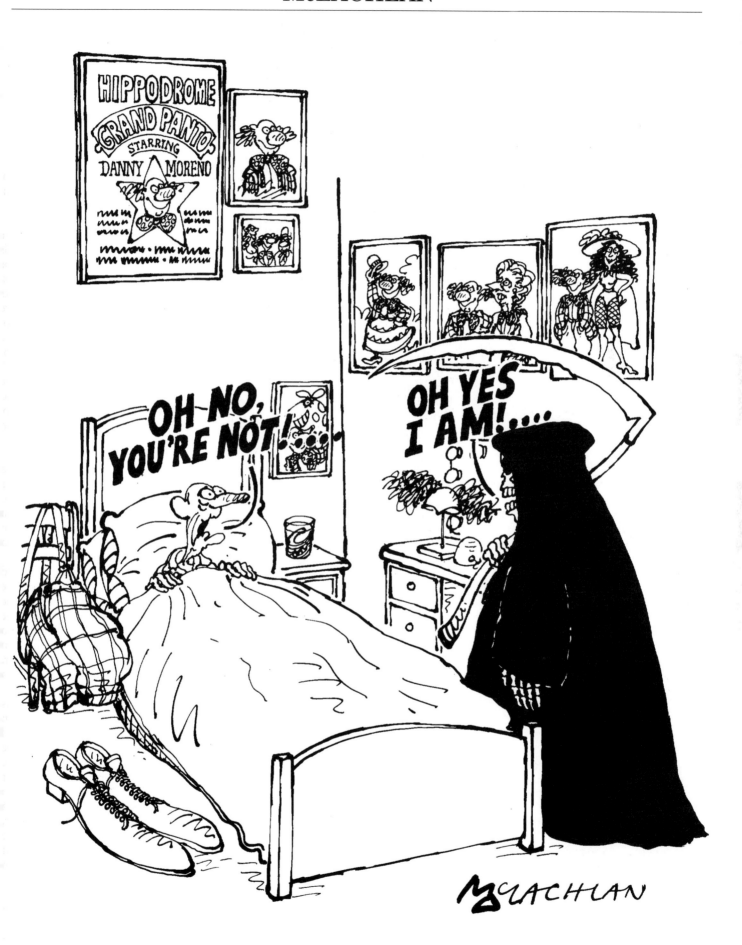

WORLD EXCLUSIVE! FERGIE'S PHOTO ALBUM

Me and Ted. He's got such a dishy nephew!!!

Warren - so that's why they call him Dick Tracy!!!

John Paul - I hope he believes in birth control!!!

Bragg

Melvyn Bragg's new TV mini series *A Time To Dance* is this year's *Blackeyes* – a high-brow sex romp. But is it really erotic art or simply good old-fashioned smut?

Spot the difference: which one of the following is the Melvyn love scene and which are by blockbusting smutmeisters like Jackie Collins and Harold Robbins?*

a) 'The deeper your passion…the better, the finer for me. And so I would f*** you gently and then more strongly and finally thrust in hard and suddenly and let everything go. "Slam into me," you used to say, "how you just slam into me!"'

b) 'You put your arms around my neck and pressed your body against me. I sought your lips but you turned your face away and buried it in my shoulder. I felt you take a deep, shuddering breath. You moaned softly and the heat came out of your body like steam from an oven. Your eyes were still closed as you leaped up on me like a monkey climbing a coconut tree.'

c) 'And then I drove down hard, plunging through your slick wet walls. Your body arched with the impact as I reached your deepest recesses in that one, long-awaited drive…"Don't slow down! Please…" you whispered.'

d) 'You moaned, a stifled sound, for I liked you to remain passive until I indicated otherwise. Your breasts strained to escape the confines of your bra. But I teased some more, playing with your swollen nipples through the material, tracing intricate patterns of intent.
'"Oh God!" Your face was flushed, I tortured you with the waiting, and yet it was sweet torture and you were addicted to every wonderful moment of it.'

e) 'You said words which made me so confident and insatiable that our love-making could go on for more than an hour and then, quite soon, begin again, this time for longer…And you said, three times, jab, jab, jab, as you went slack-thighed for the second time, you said (it was like booms of dynamite), "F*** me, f*** me, f*** me!'

ANSWERS ON OPPOSITE PAGE

*Technical note: in an attempt to introduce a level playing-field, all the extracts have been given the same epistolary format that Bragg uses in A Time To Dance. The actual content of the extracts, however, is entirely unchanged.

# of tricks

M elvyn Bragg is, without question, one of the foremost novelists of the age. At least he is if you believe the literary critics. His latest *magnum opus*, *A Time To Dance*, currently running as a Sunday night mini-series on BBC1, was hailed by the *Observer* as his best novel to date . The distinguished critic Alan Massie praised its direct and powerful impact . And even Booker Prize-winner Thomas Keneally couldn t refrain from saluting this great, tragic, raunchy novel .

Sexual frankness is the creative right of any literary genius. But television appears to be a more censorious medium and its critics have been less eager to praise Bragg's tale of obsessive romance between an ageing bank manager and a teenage gypsy. Jill Parkin in the *Daily Express* suggested Mr Bragg pack in his word-processor and hang up his dirty mac. And when he appeared for a chat on Radio 4 s *Woman s Hour*, poor Melvyn was verbally assaulted by feminist Gloria Steinem and presenter Jenni Murray, who claimed he had suggested that a young girl's rape trauma could be cured by, to use a distasteful expression, a good rogering.

Bragg has long been loth to admit that his work is the least bit prurient. Clive James once teased him about his novel *The Maid Of Buttermere* by reading out a passage about the heroine's caverns of longing on a chat-show. James impishly suggested that Bragg give tips to fellow guest Joan Collins on writing a block-bluster. Bragg was suitably amused by so far-fetched a notion. But looking at Bragg's latest bodice-ripper, is it so ridiculous?

How different is Bragg's eroticism from the extravagant sentimentalities of Mills & Boon or the brazenly upfront sex 'n' smut of that other Collins sister, Jackie? Is it genuinely brave and searingly honest (*Sunday Express*) or is it just the standard drivel one expects from a man in a mid-life crisis using fiction as wish-fulfilment?

The answer is provided on the opposite page. A selection of the dirty bits, sorry, erotic scenes, from *A Time To Dance*, is intermingled with excerpts from some trashy, airport lounge fiction — the sort of stuff that would never get an *Observer* review. But can you tell which is which?

Of course it's not autobiographical

Bragg denies that *A Time To Dance* is based on his own experiences and yet there are ten uncanny similarities between him and his fictional love-crazed oldster

Melvyn Bragg

1. Comes from Cumbria
2. Married (first wife died)
3. Lives in Hampstead, a middle-class segment *par excellence*
4. Drinks white wine at L'Escargot (upstairs), but doesn't smoke
5. Chairman of Literary Panel of Arts Council
6. Member of Garrick Club
7. Romantic interest in local history
8. Publishes articles in *Daily Mail*, *Evening Standard*
9. Dapper, wears pinstriped suits (with a Seventies Simon Templar feel) or rustic chic, full head of dark hair, clean-shaven
10. Is fittish (he jogs) but very springy (wears his belt a notch too tight according to Lynn Barber). Alarmingly effeminate hands

Andrew Powell

1. Comes from Cumbria
2. Married (wife dies)
3. Lives in 'middle-class segment of town'
4. Drinks whisky, Chablis, St Julien but doesn't smoke
5. Awards a writing prize to Lolita-esque lovely
6. Member of Rotary Club
7. Romantic interest in local history
8. Publishes his writing in *Cumbrian News*
9. 'Clean and neat', wears pin-striped suits or rustic chic, full head of dark hair, clean-shaven when not depressed
10. Is 'fit' and 'wiry' ('Never have the results of fell-walking been put to such good use!' he claims modestly of his love-making.)

a) & e) MELVYN BRAGG, A Time To Dance; b) HAROLD ROBBINS, The Carpetbaggers; c) JUDITH GOULD, Sins; d) JACKIE COLLINS, Rock Star

David Haldane

'Strewth! Worst case of heatstroke I've ever seen!'

'Who's the bastard in the trilby hat, white coat and 11 jumpers?'

'Looks like we're going to be in for some pretty flamboyant fielding from the West Indies'

'I see the TV cameramen are wearing protective helmets for the World Cup'

'Well, Fred, it looks like we've got a slight delay as a pitbull strays on to the pitch'

'Quite frankly, I don't think he knows how to handle fast bowlers'

'Of course, the cricket World Cup attracts the more knowledgeable streaker'

'And as the light fades, we watch the last urine sample of the day being taken slowly back to the laboratory'

How to be a has-been...
MEN'S MAGAZINE EDITOR

The hey day

You're the brand new editor of *British Tuxedo*, 'the magazine for the Britside man with the Stateside look'. With your cowboy boots, diamond-studded watch, Brooks Brothers' suits, and Old Etonian tie, you plan to 'kick a little ass in London medialand'. But it's all downhill from here...

The slippery slope

1. You 'straighten out' the magazine with more 'red-blooded' features. '*British Tuxedo*?' jokes *GQ*. 'It's more like Brutish Jockstrap.'
2. You inject a more 'literary feel' by hiring Salman Rushdie as 'chief humorist'. The joke's on you...
3. When you get the invoice. Circulation plummets when you employ ugly models. 'This ain't no fag mag,' you say.
4. Cigarette companies withdraw advertising. You are 'redeployed' as Executive Editor-in-chief, *Seattle Correspondent*.

The futile gesture

5. You launch *Mac And Monocle*, 'a promotional magazine for the leisure raincoat wearer.'
6. 'Pure porn for the filthy cinema brigade,' sneers *Arena* editor Dylan Jones. Raincoat sales tumble...
7. As Britain enjoys global warming. You become editor of *Aftershave Almanac* and plug Eau de Kentucky. It's a hit...
8. Until the eczema outbreak. Radio 4 books you as style reporter on a new 'niche' programme.
9. But *Old Folks At Home* only lasts three episodes. You get the job of chief cowboy boot tester for *Cobbler's World*. But get your marching orders...

The killer blow

10. When found testing the boots on staff. You retire to raise horses on the old Kentucky homestead.

The cruel twist

After your death in a rodeo stampede, your novel *Rauncho Notorious* is published. Thousands of copies are sold to men in less than pristine raincoats.

MIKE CONWAY

Goutrage!

The tradition of the splenetic, aged columnist is a long and dyspeptic one. Exclusively male, this doughty breed of fractious Methuselahs earns its keep spraying bilious damnations on the follies of modernity.

The fractious fun is expected to continue with Richard Ingrams's new publication, the *Oldie*. (Although debilitation may have taken a premature hold because the launch has been delayed.) With the prospect of a new clutch of angry old men frothing at the bit, it's perhaps time to consider what qualities distinguish the Goutrage set.

This year saw the publication of John Osborne's *Dejavu*, the belated sequel to *Look Back In Anger*. The new play gives some useful insights into the effect of ageing on its anti-hero, Jimmy Porter. Now living prosperously in a large country house, Porter is as irate as ever but – crucially – he is older, more crabby, and cankered. The nature of his rage has also changed from dynamic to static. Where Young Porter raged at those who hindered his mobility, Old Porter rants at those who disrupt his peace.

The paradigm of the Porter transformation is Sir Kingsley Amis. He has all the elements of a fully paid-up member of Goutrage. Sir Kingsley used to berate suffocating traditional values; now he bemoans the *collapse* of those values. Of course, ideally, such rants are served up in a testy fog of cigar smoke and port fumes, with not a little mischief. For unlike truly miserable people, irate oldies do find happiness. It's just that their idea of happiness is an incandescent fit of rage – or perhaps a quick swoon over one of their fragrant heroines such as Mrs Thatcher.

One of Goutrage's prime exponents was the *Daily Express* columnist George Gale, who died last year. The *Times*'s obituary summed up his style: 'downright rudeness and intolerance combined with refreshing irreverence'. (Gale was especially corrosive on the subjects of left-wing intellectuals, incomprehensible poets and plays with a

'message'.) Rudeness is the easy part, it's the long-suffering air of intolerance that distinguishes the true *Goutrageur*. Oh, the impatience of our hero as he steers a no-nonsense, middle-brow course through the raging storms of long-haired trendiness and half-baked arty pretension.

Perhaps the key factor is the scowling antediluvianism. Change is as welcome as a corked claret. One suspects that Goutrage members have a soft spot for Sir Harry Flashman's great work *Army Reform: The Case Against*. Gale was once expelled from newly-independent Ghana for refusing to stand for its national anthem.

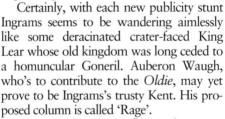

Whether Richard Ingrams's *Oldie* can achieve this level of stubbornness remains to be seen. Ingrams has come a long way since being an anti-establishment rebel in the Sixties, but the signs are not promising. After he appeared in a Sunday newspaper wearing biker's leathers, his old publication *Private Eye* dubbed him an 'ageing Fenian *Observer*bore'. His ex-pal Peter McKay said he looked like a Kings Cross rent boy. Even Nigel Dempster has begun to question his sanity.

Certainly, with each new publicity stunt Ingrams seems to be wandering aimlessly like some deracinated crater-faced King Lear whose old kingdom was long ceded to a homuncular Goneril. Auberon Waugh, who's to contribute to the *Oldie*, may yet prove to be Ingrams's trusty Kent. His proposed column is called 'Rage'.

However, there is one flaw in the rejuvenation plan. Namely, Ingrams's promise that his magazine will be a 'champion for those cast aside'. This doesn't feel sufficiently combative in tone. Perhaps Waugh can tell his old friend that *Goutrageurs* do not clang the bell on the mansion gate pleading the case of the excluded. They already own the mansion. 🐍

(Additional research by Steve Smethurst)

Is a column of spite really a pillar of wisdom? SEAN MACAULAY reports on the spleen-venting elders of the media who form the Goutrage set

Sir Bernard Ingham
Daily Express columnist

His dear friends
'He really did treat the press like shit. There wasn't one he wouldn't have suspected of being a child molester' – John Biffen

His amusing observations
- **Alec Douglas-Home** – 'bomb-happy dangerous political fossil'
- **Edward Heath** – 'revealed his party's stagnant mind in all its revolting crudity'
- **John Biffen** – 'that well-known semi-detached member of the Cabinet'
- **Paddy Ashdown** — 'too blessed pious for my liking'
- **Beggers** – 'a blot on the domestic and tourist landscape'
- 'People who carry firearms might end up under the sod. So be it'
- **The British press** – a 'raddled, disease-racked body'

His outstanding chivalry
'Never have women protested more about hands-on adoration, yet dressed more to encourage it. Life for us lads is one long triumph of restraint over invitation'

His sentimental weak spot
- **Margaret Thatcher**: 'should be president of the EC,' he fumes, saying she enjoys 'world respect'

His senile slip-up
Wrote this simple piece of prose, 'Let me conflate the two incidents, all the lobby journalists foregathered in their afternoon eyrie, all scenting trouble, fuming with synthetic indignation...' before adding, '...and Stevas never used a short word where a long one would do'.

Judge James Pickles
Sun columnist

His dear friends
'Dad isn't worried what people say. If he believes in something he will stick his neck out' – *Carolyn, his daughter*

His amusing observations
- **Lawyers** – 'incapable of bundling papers or numbering photographs'
- **Aids sufferers** – 'perverts who bring about their own misery'
- **Dr Kalim Siddiqui** – 'a rebel-rousing self-publicist...a big-mouth pest'
- **Michael Jackson** – 'a nutter'
- **The monarchy** – 'a pantomime in which no one says anything that matters'
- **Robert Maxwell** – 'a sordid, sleazy slob of lard'

His outstanding chivalry
'Attractive women who do not wear a bra are being hypocritical if they want Page Three girls banned'
- **Mary Archer** – 'arrogant and vain'

His sentimental weak spot
- **Rosie Barnes MP**: the Judge finds her 'sweet and cuddly' and hints that she could have 'a romantic future'
- **Soft drugs**: feels that people should be 'free to take cannabis into their bodies'

His senile slip-up
Shamelessly, he describes **Lord Lane** as an 'ancient dinosaur living in the wrong age'.

Mr Auberon Waugh
Oldie columnist

His dear friends
A woman committed suicide prompted in part, admits Waugh, by the gloom of reading his journalism. '[He is] nastiness personified, very, very unpleasant.' – *Nora Beloff, political columnist*

His amusing observations
- **Public-school education** – 'If boys end up buggered that is a small price to pay'
- **Matthew Parris** – a 'whey-faced poltroon and toady in Mrs Thatcher's accursed *galère*'
- **Sir James Goldsmith** – 'an ambitious grocery merchant...he has a disgustingly ugly face'
- **Sir David English** – 'what a dull dog'
- Has the nerve to call **Anthony Powell** 'a saloon bar pundit, writing abominable English'

His outstanding chivalry
- **Shirley Williams** – has vowed to 'torment and humiliate this loathsome pig-headed woman'
- **Princess Anne** – 'neither very intelligent nor very charming'
- **The 'rape industry'** – 'dominated by ugly women opposed to sex'

His sentimental weak spot
Predictably, he adores the **Princess of Wales**: 'Even if I could think of a single unkind thing to say about her I would refuse'

His senile slip-up
Seems to think there's a Rolling Stone called Ron Spikes. Also makes otiose remarks such as 'I am a snob'.

Has Richard Ingrams finally gone completely ga-ga?

Seasoned media watchers have been much concerned with Richard Ingrams of late. It's been all downhill since he was wrenched from the helm of *Private Eye* by his homuncular protégé Ian Hislop.

Now Ingrams has found a new hobby in his retirement, the *Oldie*, a publication with extra-large print to cater for the antiquated myope. His strenuous efforts to drum up any kind of interest in this product, already nicknamed the *Foldie*, has increasingly resembled a man trying to hammer-throw in a wardrobe.

In one recent interview, the pock-marked organ-player fell apart so drastically, he wound up huddled by the fire barely able to form a coherent sentence. Has it come to this? The great anti-Establishment provocateur of the Sixties now reduced to a gibbering wreck?

Deeply concerned by this news, we dispatched letters to the agony aunts of Fleet Street to seek advice. The letters were written from the point of view of Ingrams's offspring and mentioned obliquely, among other things, Ingrams' secession of *Private Eye*, his 'prank' affair with Pamela Bordes, and his fashion shoot for the *Observer* clad in ludicrous youth garb.

We hope their heartfelt advice is of some use to the grand old man.

Our letter to the agony aunts about Richard Ingrams

> Dear Agony Aunts,
>
> My father has started behaving in the most strange way. For many years he was a successful businessman. He ran his own small business, but then about five or six years ago it all started to go wrong. He had a young man in his twenties working at the company. They got on very well, nothing *homosexual* I don't think, but they did spend a lot of time together. Then my father decided to hand over the company to the young man. None of his office mates agreed and they all left. It got very bitter.
>
> He was at a loose end. I don't know how this affected his relationship with mother, but they are now separated. Dad has gone a bit funny about sex. He even pretended that he was having an affair with a younger woman. It was as if he just wanted to show off, or something.
>
> Now he's taken to dressing up in young people's clothes. He wears denim jackets – with the collar up! – and sunglasses. I do so want to help him before he makes a complete fool of himself. What do you suggest?
>
> Yours sincerely,
>
> E. J. Thribb

What advice do the agony aunts offer the silver-haire

 **Virginia Ironside, wrote:**

'Perhaps your father is having some sort of mid-life crisis...possibly all is not well. I would talk about it to your mum, though of course it would be kinder if you did not mention the business about fancy girlfriends.'

Recommended remedy: He should share his worries with close relatives – and 'my help line is in the *Sunday Mirror* each week.'

 **Anne Lovell, wrote:**

'It seems you feel he's not behaving in the way you think a father should behave. But you have to remember that you have a life of your own to get on with.'

Recommended remedy: He should try for an appointment with Relate ('but there is a long waiting list') or even a local branch of the Catholic Marriage Advisory Council.

Woman's Realm

Gill Cox, wrote:

'It does indeed sound as if your father is having some kind of identity crisis. He's casting around trying to find a way of presenting himself that's different from his past life. However, it doesn't seem he's found a satisfactory answer for himself yet.'

Recommended remedy: He should see a counsellor to 'talk through how he's feeling', or try to contact Relate.

 **Marjorie Proops, wrote:**

'I must admit it does sound as if your father is enjoying a new lease of life and possibly he is even trying to recapture his youth. This sometimes happens to men in middle age, and it is usually only a passing phase. It has probably been caused by his friendship with a younger man.'

Recommended remedy: 'Just keep

We were so worried by the *Oldie* editor's eccentric behaviour, we sent off letters to the agony aunts to ask for their help

Thirty years ago, it was happy Richard Ingrams, the madcap youthful japester

Today, it's miserable Mr Ingrams, grimly fending off the onset of senile depression

x-satirist?

an eye on him, and make sure he does not do anything too silly!'

woman
Sue Frost, wrote:

'Your father may be embarrassing, but is he putting himself at risk? Sometimes the individual wants to shake off constraints…Do you think he is ill?'

Recommended remedy: Try to persuade him to see his doctor and reassure him that you still love him.

The cure: To ease the Ingrams malaise, it's simple. Give him a hug and tell him that you love him. Or could it be the waitresses at the Groucho Club do enough of that already?

OLLIE REED

HE'S NOT QUIET, HE'S NOT MUTED, HE KNOWS HOW TO GET BENEWTED

RAAAAHHHH! When I heard the news I was flabbergasted. My old drinking pal and fellow roisterer Mr Punch to shut up shop?

It was unthinkable. We've supped with the best and swilled with the worst. But we always had a hearty time.

Pipsqueaks

Then the pipsqueaks chimed in with their bleating remarks. What about that heiffer-sized, moon-faced old trout who was moaning on about how it was more fun in her day? Fun? That thunder-thighed old sow wouldn't know fun if it was in a two-

Mr SOFTY

AS YOU know I'm an old softy when it comes to dogs. My dog, The General, was great pals with Toby. What a pair of feisty hounds. Great company too. Those two hellhounds really could lap up a bowl of ale in no time. God help the man who picks on my canine chums. It'll be trouble. Yes? Yes? Good God, man, put 'em up. We'll have it now! Want some? Want some? Eh? Come on, outside!

litre stein with a six-inch head of froth on it.

Fun means flagons of brew, real men clinking their tankards and dropping their kecks for a quick bout of fire-side grappling. I like a togs-off tussle, I do. Especially when I've got a good curry and few meat pies inside me.

You can't beat it for putting a fire in your belly. Not like that pig-breathed old moose.

Piece

If I met her I'd see her right. I'd give her a piece of my mind. Come on, outside! Want some? want some? We'll have it now!

THE QUEEN MUM LIKES the occasional nip and she's respected all over the world. I, too, like the occasional nip and I'm regarded as a hellraiser. It's a funny old world. Yes? Yes? Come on!

THE BIG SCREEN HEAVY WHO LIKES A BEVY

Privacy on parade

If you exploit the media for publicity can you complain when the media start publicising your exploits? **RICHARD LITTLEJOHN** defends press freedom in the wake of the Ashdown affair

t wasn't as if it was someone else's secretary, damn it. I mean, we've all done it, haven't we? Let he who is without sin and all that. Surely a chap is entitled to a little privacy?

It would never have happened in the old days. Lloyd George was a randy old goat. Winston was permanently p*****. But you never saw that splashed all over the *News Chronicle*. Newspapers knew their place then. Edited by gentlemen, not like today's uppity bunch of barrow boys.

Say what you like about Johnny Frog but you don't get any of this nonsense in France. They've got strict privacy laws, you know. Not that they need them, of course. They think it's unusual if a politician doesn't have a mistress. A man's got to relax, for heaven's sake. None of the newspapers' damn business. Oh, don't get me wrong. I'm all in favour of freedom of information. Oh, yes. Free society, after all. Fought two wars. It's just that you have to draw the line somewhere.

A good thrashing, that's what these reptiles need. And a couple of years banged up in solitary. And a fine of several million pounds. That would put a stop to it. It's the only language these ruffians understand.

The Ashdown affair brought out the public school cab-driver tendency in droves. When a politician is caught with his pants down, the great and the good close ranks and squeal like stuck pigs. There but for the grace of God, they think silently to themselves, as they imagine the sound of skeletons sitting down and forming an escape committee at the back of their own long-locked cupboards, and the rustle of raincoats and the rattle of Nikons outside their Kennington love-nests. Something must be done. Pass the humbugs.

Paddy is not the first politician to be caught, as Mr Punch so delicately put it, sh****** his secretary. And he won't be the last. He is, however, to my knowledge, the first to issue a blanket injunction against every single newspaper in England in an attempt to keep his illicit leg-over under wraps.

It was the very same device the chattering classes condemned when it was employed by the Government to prevent the publication of the embarrassing espionage revelations contained in

Peter Wright's MI5 exposé, *Spycatcher*.

And this from a man who claims to be a champion of the need for a British freedom of information act in line with the American model.

Speaking of American models, US-style legislation would not have done Ashdown much good if the American model in question happened to be in his hotel room.

Privacy legislation hasn't protected countless American politicians from so-called 'smoking bimbos'. If a potential presidential candidate – which, in Britain, Paddy effectively is – is discovered to have been indulging in a bit of extra-curricular campaigning with Miss Middle America 1992, it is considered Joe Public's constitutional right to know.

In the land of litigation, a public figure such as Ashdown has no recourse to law to defend his reputation, especially if the allegation is true. Even if it is inaccurate it makes no odds, provided there was absence of malice on the part of the writer or editor.

Whatever the consequences of his adultery, Ashdown would not have been able to gag the press. It would have been political suicide even to attempt to do so.

US politicians can survive sex scandals, as Bill Clinton may yet prove despite his dalliance with Gennifer-with-a-'G'. (It is worth pointing out, however, that they rarely do. Gary Hart, where are you now?)

But an attempted cover-up is a non-starter in a country steeped in conspiracy theories and with a passionate belief in freedom of speech. It wasn't the bungled burglary at the Watergate building that finished Nixon so much as the whitewash at the White House.

There might be a Fifth Amendment, enshrining an accused man's right to silence and affording protection against self-incrimination. But just try using it. Everyone will automatically assume you are guilty. Because you probably are.

Put your trousers on, Paddy. You're bleedin' nicked, as

Regan used to say in *The Sweeney*.

Politicians might be considered fair game but America, like many European countries, has legislation protecting ordinary citizens from invasion of privacy and preventing newspapers publishing irrelevant and intrusive trivia.

Those who argue that self-regulation has failed would like to see something similar here. But where do you draw the line? When is a public figure a private figure? The answer would seem to be when he or she is up to no good and would like to stop the rest of us from finding out.

Politicians and 'personalities' think it is their divine right to inflict their private lives on the general public when it serves their own purposes.

Ashdown's public 'private' image, heavily promoted by the Liberal Democrats' PR machine, is one of happily-married, doting father and husband. In the *Evening Standard* last year, the Ashdowns opened their hearts and their front door. They frankly discussed their perfect marriage.

'It has worked on all planes that marriages have to work on – practical, emotional and physical,' waxed Paddy. If that's the case, why was he poking his secretary for five months?

Paddy Ashdown misrepresented himself to the electorate. If he was a toaster we could take him back under the provisions of the Sale of Goods Act as not being of merchantable quality. If he were a poster, the Advertising Standards Authority might like a word, too. Legal? OK. Decent? Debatable. Honest? Bo*****s.

Let us also consider Cecil Parkinson, while we're on the subject of politicians not being all they pretend to be. In 1981, The *Daily Express* published a glowing profile of a close-knit Parkinson family. Er, no Sara Keays there. No one forced him to pose with Mrs P and his daughter. No one forced him to make speeches or stand for Parliament on a 'party of the family' ticket.

If he had been a builder from Bootle or an estate agent from Esher he would have been entitled to protest that the fact he was rogering his secretary was his own affair. But, as the Americans

acknowledge, those who live by publicity deserve to die by it. They should not be allowed to decide when their behaviour ceases to be public property when the product they are marketing is their own personality and integrity.

No one would ever have heard of Paddy Ashdown or Cecil Parkinson if they hadn't taken a conscious decision to seek high office and manipulate the media to further their ambition.

I'm all in favour of some kind of protection against unwarranted media intrusion. But it's a question of where to draw the line and who you exempt from that protection.

My own view is that no one who has ever employed an agent, public relations consultant or issued a press release should be allowed to scream foul when the attention they have sought becomes unwanted and backfires on them.

It isn't only politicians, either. Television personalities, actors and pop stars are all culpable. They want to decide when the public should be privileged to see them and benefit from the wisdom of their opinions.

The only kind of newspapers most politicians want to see, whatever they say about believing in the freedom of the press, are those which run their speeches in full and publish profiles complete with pictures of a loving family and cuddly Labrador.

In much the same way, if showbiz personalities had their way, Fleet Street would consist of nothing more than a succession of doting *Hello!* magazine clones.

Selina Scott is a woman who once read the news on breakfast television. She now does the same on Sky. She would like the world to understand that she is a very private person. A very private person indeed.

How do we know this? Because she tells us. In *Hello!* over 11 full-colour glossy pages. Here is a woman who clearly likes to put her love of seclusion and privacy on parade.

If she is such a private person, why did she allow *Hello!*☞

into her home? If she wants to remain anonymous, why did she get a job reading the news on television?

Frankly, I couldn't give a monkey's what Selina's kitchen looks like. But I suppose a lot of people could. And that brings us to the difficult question of public interest.

What interests people and what is in the public interest are not necessarily one and the same thing. It does not really further the cause of public interest to pore over the contents of Selina's laundry basket. But the public are interested.

Who decides? The Calcutt committee report, accepted by the press, attempted to set down some guidelines in the wake of an incident in which the *Sunday Sport* gatecrashed a hospital ward to obtain pictures of the actor Gorden Kaye recovering from brain surgery.

This was clearly unacceptable behaviour. But then the *Sunday Sport* is not a proper newspaper and not a yardstick by which to judge the behaviour of the press in general – even the much-derided 'tabloid' press.

There is a feeling in newspaper circles that the dull broadsheets are guilty of serious hypocrisy. They allow the tabloids to do their dirty work for them.

Thus the *Guardian* can tut-tut in its leader columns about the disgraceful behaviour of the 'tabloids' in the Ashdown affair while devoting three pages to it elsewhere in the paper. The *Sunday Times* and others did much the same.

They cover these stories in great depth because they know their readers enjoy them, if only so they can condemn them at the next meeting of the outreach committee. That's why, if you travel regularly on public transport, you will often see the *Sun* tucked away inside the *Independent*. The *Indy* reader, if challenged, will protest that it is his duty to monitor the gutter press.

Newspapers publish what interests the public, not necessarily what is in the public interest.

Calcutt said that papers should not carry pictures of people on private property taken without their permission or with a long-distance lens. Fair enough. But there are circumstances, such as corruption investigations, when the use of such cameras is a legitimate tactic.

One fairly recent complaint about the taking of 'snatched' pictures came from Miss Samantha Fox. She was photographed lying topless by a swimming pool.

Miss Fox is a young woman who has built a career on getting her assets out for the lads – in the right light, with the right kind of make-up and with the right kind of soft-focus lens – and has ruthlessly used the papers to her advantage. Fair game?

Who is a legitimate target? The answer always seems to be: anyone but me. The *Sunday Times* recently homed in on the 'smoking bimbos' who prey on men in the public eye. But, er, no

mention of one of the most famous, Pamela Bordes. I am sure the fact that her conquests included that newspaper's editor was purely coincidental.

Longing for the good old days when the abysmal behaviour of politicians and other public figures went unreported is unrealistic. The media has changed for ever. So has public life. There were no daily press conferences, 24-hour news channels or photo-opportunities when Gladstone was saving fallen women – for himself.

If the royal family attract more attention and criticism than before, it is because Queen Elizabeth voluntarily decided to 'let light in upon magic' in her mother's words. She has encouraged the cameras and grovelling interviewers.

Part of the justification for having the royal family is that it symbolises all that is good and stable about family life in Britain. We pay its members handsomely for the task. So they must expect their marriages and behaviour to be subjected to constant scrutiny. If they don't like it, they can renounce the succession and reject the Civil List. Then they might be entitled to expect the press to leave them alone.

There are breaches of the voluntary code of conduct policed by the Press Complaints Commission. To expect otherwise would be Utopian. But, in general, the newspapers behave much better today than they did even five or six years ago.

We have too many restrictions upon our freedom as it is. Too often the law is used to suppress the truth not to protect the innocent. Ashdown's blanket injunction failed because of a loophole which allowed the *Scotsman* to break the story because English law does not run north of the Border.

There would have been gossip. It might have seeped out at the edges. But if Paddy hadn't blinked, the bulk of the British electorate may never have found out that he was a hypocrite as well as an adulterer.

And just look at how Captain Robert Maxwell, the most blatant self-publicist on earth, used injunctions to prevent exposure of his thieving, evil ways.

The glory-seekers are as much to blame as the public prints which build them up and then delight in ripping them down again. They expect to tell lies and live lies. They cannot grumble when they are found out.

The last attempt to introduce a Privacy Bill in Britain was made by John Browne MP, the worst sort of Brylcreemed Tory. It failed.

Mr Browne-with-an-'e' insisted he was acting from nothing but the purest of motives in the public interest. It had nothing to do with the press interest in his attempts to get his hands on his ex-wife's fortune.

Of course not. 🐍

HONEYSETT

'Right, which one is the boil?'

'For a start you could do with a new burglar alarm'

'Don't worry, the au pair will clean it up'

'And how long have you thought you were a beached
whale, Mr Thompson?'

'It's sweet really, he's taking her out to ram-raid a flower shop'

'It wasn't exactly what I had in mind when I asked the council if
I could donate some money for a seat in the park'

Parlez-vous

Ever wondered what on earth we are talking about? We have. Here, then, is a beginner's guide to understanding Punchspeak

A vid *Punch* reader James Golbey wrote to us to point out a recurring phenomenon in these pages. He said, 'Erm, I have noticed the preponderance of ornate descriptions in your magazine.' Among those which he had espied were Dudley Moore, the 'stature-challenged gagmeister'; Frank Sinatra, the 'besyruped croonster' and the Princess of Wales, the 'highlight-laden would-be thronester'. Eager to demonstrate his understanding of the principles by which such adjectival phrases were constructed, Mr Golbey gamely got into the swing of things by suggesting one of his own, to wit: Oliver Reed, the 'benewted roisterer'.

By now, those readers who are not familiar with the world of Guttersnipe and his fellow *Punch* nibsters – sorry – journalists, not to mention those who are, may be feeling distinctly baffled. What on earth, to put it bluntly, are we talking about? What is a croonster or a gagmeister?

The answer is as follows: much of the content of *Punch* consists of reflections upon, or analysis of, major events of the day, as reported by the popular press. Guttersnipe, for example, reinterprets gos-

Mr Oliver Reed, the 'benewted roisterer'

sip about popular showbusiness or sporting figures for the benefit of readers whose daily newspapers do not lower themselves to such trifling matters.

Now, many of our subscribers have led lives of sheltered gentility and would be shocked if we were to write in the manner favoured by the *soi-disant* popular press. We therefore endeavour to translate their scribblings into a form more acceptable to the sophisticated palate.

Certain rules are always observed, thus...

Titles

Ladies and gentlemen are always referred to by their correct titles. So the celebrated dietician Ms Elizabeth Taylor is often described by her married name, Mrs Laurence Fortensky. On occasion, men will be referred to, plainly, as Bryan Robson or Vincent Jones. This is because they are professional Associationists and therefore

Players, rather than Gentlemen, and do not qualify for the title 'Mr'. Also, the appellation of a person's country of origin is observed, eg, Monsieur Gérard Depardieu, Herr Arnold Schwarzenegger etc.

Names

Many newspapers are composed for the benefit of working people. In order to make the subjects of their stories seem more 'down-to-earth' they give them improbably abbreviated Christian names, such as Vinnie (see 'Jones', above), or Billy. They will even refer to them by such nicknames as 'Wacko Jacko' or 'Big Ron'. Naturally, we at *Punch* do not countenance such overfamiliar soubriquets. It insults so close a friend of our beloved Duchess of York to refer to him as anything other than Mr William Connolly. 'Billy' is simply insufficient for such an admirable court jester. And how distressing it must be for Mr Clifford Richard, the God-fearing tenor, to be referred to so frequently as 'Cliff'.

Professions

It diminishes the talents of gifted individu-

An A to Z of celebrities as described

Miss Debee Ashby, the pulchritudinous Page Three personage;

Ms Priscilla Black, the nasally-amended televisioniste;

Mr Linford Christie, the generously-beloined sprint supremo;

Mr Jason Donovan, the out-and-out all-round entertainer, the red-blooded antipodean songster;

Mr Benjamin Elton, the *faux*-proletarian jokesmith;

Sir Clement Freud, the short-fused

Whitney Houston: 'single songstress'

misery-meister;

Mr Melvyn Gibson, the New World Shakespearian;

Miss Whitney Houston, the defiantly-single tinted songstress;

Mr David Icke, the divine offspring and former custodian of the sticks;

Mr Michael Jackson, the beige chanteur, the Caucasian diva;

The Rt Hon Mr Neil Kinnock MP, the handsomely-befreckled marathon orator, the irascible libelmeister, the tempestuous Taff;

Ms Roulade 'Rula' Lenska, the Polonaise photo-opportunity;

Ms Shirley Maclaine, the famous

fruitcake manufacturer;

Mr Andrew Neil, the triple-wheat-crimped Sabbath publication editor, the cereal-coiffed Caledonian ladies' man;

Ms Sinead O'Connor, the unsolicited opinion, the scantily-coiffured Hibernian chanteuse;

Signor Alastair Pacino, the stature-challenged Latino thespian;

Andrew Neil: 'cereal-coiffed'

Is merely to refer to them as 'the singer' or the comedian'. Signor Francesco Sinatra, for example, does more than merely sing. He croons, hence, 'croonster'. Mr Dudley Moore's many years of experience have elevated him to a higher comic plane. He is, justly, a veritable 'gagmeister'. Similarly, Signor Sylvester Stallone, is not an actor or thespian in the normal sense, being monosyllabic to an extraordinary degree. He is, therefore, simply 'the grunt'.

Descriptions

For those readers unfamiliar with the supposed celebrities about whom we write, we try to give a few brief words of description that will form a handy pen-portrait of the individual in question. In composing these wee cameos one is always conscious of the many demands placed upon one by changing social mores.

For example, many *Punch* readers have elevated themselves, through years of admirable effort, to a higher social plane than that from which they began. Yet they retain a nostalgic yearning for their Cockney roots and the amusing

Mrs Laurence Fortensky, the nuptial aficionado

rhyming slang with which they grew up. For their benefit, a gentleman who favours a toupee or hairpiece may be described as 'besyruped', as 'syrup' equals 'syrup of figs' equals 'wig'.

Then again, many colonial readers will be alive to the new sensitivities of politically correct speech in which the principal aim is to avoid causing offence. They would be shocked to find someone described as 'bald' or 'fat'. Nor would they be appeased by such adjectives as 'depilous' or 'belarded'. For their benefit, then, Mr Paul Daniels, whom vulgarians would deem a slap-headed dwarf magician, might be termed 'follicle-free' or 'tonsorially-challenged', with regard to his lack of hair, whilst his miniscule stature might be described as 'differently heighted'. He is, of course, a 'prestidigitator' by profession.

The pasta-laden lungster Mr Luciano Pavarotti is no calorie-crammed lard-bucket in Mr Punch's eyes. He is either 'fully-sized' or – picking up a theme first established with Mr Daniels – 'nutritionally-challenged', even 'calzone-curved' in a moment of levity. We hope this clears up any confusion.

BOB

K

'Hello Friday – just to let you know I'll be a few seconds late with the tea!'

In Punchspeak

Mr Christopher Quinten, the resting troubadour, who used to give working people his Brian Tilsley in the continuing televisual dramatic serial, *Coronation Street*;

Mr Bertram Reynolds, the lavishly-periwigged colonial entertainer;

Sir James Savile, the-how's-about-that-then-guys-an'-gals;

Mr Christopher Tarrant, the phonographic equestrian of considerable means;

Mr Ruarigh Underwood, the gentleman athlete and flightmeister;

Mr Terence Venables, the erstwhile associationist, sporting executive,

televisual tactical interpreter and mine host, the busy boy;

Miss Fiona Wright, the banana marketing council representative, the erstwhile executive courtesan;

Mr Michael Yarwood, the someone else;

Mr Dweezil and Miss Moon Unit Zappa, the cruelly-benominated celebrity siblings.

Fiona Wright: 'executive courtesan'

TOILET TISSUES

Delsey Andrex CITIZEN'S CHARTER DIXCEL

MCLACHLAN

'Congratulations, David you now go on to meet the West Indies in the final'

'There go Zimbabwe'

'Ah – the traditional sound of lager on wally'

'You're fat and middle-aged – why aren't you captain of England?'

'LET ME KNOW WHEN THE CRICKET'S OVER'

'I'm Jimmy One-day Cricket'

A LOT OF PEOPLE have asked me why I am always so calm. They say, 'Gary, would you still be so unflappable if your house burned down, your team-mates were kidnapped by Abu Nidal terrorists and your wife Michelle were abducted by aliens from the planet Zork?'

Funny you should ask.

I was just cooking Michelle some breakfast when the fire started. I was waiting near the cooker and Michelle passed me the bacon. I'd been hoping that the bacon would come over – I knew all I had to do was put it in the back of the frying pan.

Game

Suddenly the fat caught fire and flames were leaping from the cooker. Within minutes our house and all our possessions were in ruins. As we dashed out, we failed to see the van-load of kidnapped Spurs players careering off the road. It swerved to miss Michelle and ran over both my legs, fracturing every bone in my lower body.

It was as Michelle tried to stem the bleeding that the spaceship landed, and a small green man stepped up to her. 'Gary,' he said to her. 'For years our planet has lingered at the bottom of the Zenith Solar Systems League. But your unique goal-scoring talents could bring back first-class football to Zork in less than three of your earth years. What do you say?' Before she could reply, Michelle had been taken away to begin a new life in the Zork Premier League.

Two halves

It's been tough, but we're not down-hearted. I think you'll be seeing a stronger house in the very near future, there is nowhere better for Michelle to practise her skills and Graham Taylor has promised that having two legs in plaster won't affect my England place.

'STUPID PLONKER'

I am a Spurs player called Gary who scored in the big game against Poland last week. And I was heaped with praise. The boy Mabbutt is also a Spurs player called Gary who scored in the big game against Poland last week. Yet he was called 'a stupid plonker'. At the end of the day, it's a funny old world, isn't it, Jim?

● HAVING spent many years in Europe, I feel I should give John Major some advice as he prepares for the big game against the Dutch at Maastricht. My tactics are always the same. Stay in the centre, wait for a chance to come over from the right-wing, then take it. And steer clear of defence.

He's lean, he's mean, he's Mr Clean

Ballots

It is time. Time for a change. The whole country knows that. We. The people. The *ordinary* people. Of this great country. Have suffered too long from poor government. And short sentences. And yet. Is there an alternative? A real one? Or should we all simply give up?

Millions of you have turned to me for guidance. Some of you have suggested that I should be elected Supreme Ruler. What nonsense. Elected? Piffle. To hell with elected. We've tried elected, and look what we've ended up with. Grey men, low-brows, cheats, lawyers, tricksters, charlatans, underwriters, gyps, flimflam men, racketeers, priapists, thugs, deviates, car salesmen, toadies, cuckolds and windbags. *Balls* to elected. If you want me to be Supreme Ruler, consider it done. It's up to you. Next time some chalk-white swindler with a runny nose and a civil service briefcase writes to tick you off, merely inform him that Bargepole is your master and you answer to none other.

But if, for form's sake, you wish to pursue the discredited forms of democracy, here is my manifesto. If it doesn't make absolute sense to you, you are a fool.

A Bright British Future

That is exactly the sort of horse shit I will eliminate. Only a dick head would think a manifesto needs a title. The future is *not* bright. It is unremittingly dim, and will go on being so until we drop (a) snivelling PR slogans and (b) the word 'British', which has become inextricably synonymous with bad food, cheap dentures, drizzle and chintz.

Therefore, my first act upon assuming power will be to rename this country 'Fat City,' in honour of Dr Thompson, who tried the same trick in Aspen, Colorado. It failed then because the thin, greedy whores and their greedy, bug-eyed ponces wouldn't have it. The whores and ponces are over here, now, *but we still outnumber them*. This is electorally significant. We can screw them. We can render the place uninhabitable for them. And we shall.

The Electoral System

On achieving power, I shall sack the democratically-elected government, the opposition, the giggling white-wristed slickwillies in the middle, and anyone in the House of Lords who got there by political arse-licking, time-serving, bribery or simply sitting there looking like a stuck pig. An immediate second election will be held, at which, to be elected, any Member of Parliament must obtain at least 71 per cent of the vote. Where this does not occur, a Member of Parliament will be selected at random, by a drunken old bag with an electoral roll and a pin. Members elected by vote will be paid £1 per year. Members elected by pin will be paid £500,000 per year.

The first act of this new, reconstituted Parliament will be to confirm me as Supreme Ruler. Its subsequent acts will be of no significance, as the country will be governed by a self-perpetuating oligarchy, itself ruled by me. My Court will consist of Douglas Adams, Little Liz, Nick Mason from Pink Floyd, the bad yellow-eyed woman, Yogi the dealer, my finch Antigone, Hadji from the off-licence, Lovebite, Irma Kurtz and Filthy the Dog. Mr Rory Bremner will impersonate any statesmen that

Voting? A wimp's game. Let **BARGEPOLE** be your Supreme Ruler and you'll never have problems sustaining an election

may be required, for example when hosting banquets for mad, sniggering Japanese businessmen. Mr John Langdon will be Court Speechwriter. The Keeper of the Treasury will be Oofy Prosser, who will also be Court Projectionist. 'Lord' Waddington will be Defender of the People, but, just to make sure, he himself will believe his title to be *Prosecutor* of the People. Lord Lane will be Court Whipping-Boy. Paula from the Academy Club will be Supreme Ruler's Perk, fed on buttermilk and kept gloriously naked, save for Manolo Blahnik shoes, opera gloves and a velvet cord around her wrist.

Expenses of the Court will be met by a special tax, levied on anyone who has ever appeared in the *Financial Times* wearing spectacles and holding either a gold Cross biro or a telephone.

Education

The future of Fat City depends on the education of its citizens. Until now, generations of politicians have sublimated their nasty urges by manipulating our schools to turn out miserable, docile consumers with blighted lives whose only function is either to do as they are told or be sent to prison.

This must change. With immediate effect, all teachers will be sacked and their jobs advertised nationally. To increase competition, all teachers will be paid £250,000 a year plus unlimited expenses, except for primary school teachers in inner city areas. They will be paid £500,000 a year.

The children of Fat City will be educated on strict Socratic principles. There will be no nonsense about relativism. *Pour encourager les autres*, school governors will be forced to do animal noises on television. Failure to know, for example, what the monkey ('Eee, eee') or the gorilla ('Ooh ooh') or the Llama ('Pftui') says will be punished by 50 lashes.

Social Engineering

We will embark upon a wide-ranging programme to improve the quality of life in Fat City. Orbital mirrors and complex geostationary advection systems will be established above the Eastern Atlantic to improve the climate. Mild but effective hallucinogens will be added to the water supply. Quality-controlled Ecstasy will be available from all chemists at a nominal cost. The food 'industry' will be taken under the control of the Court itself and re-staffed with people who are interested in food rather than in money.

We will also address the problems of living in a multicultural society by declaring cultural separatism to be silly, childish and an utter wank. The law of blasphemy will be repealed. Anyone who supports the *fatwah* against Mr Rushdie will be secretly filmed, and the film shown on television, having first been electronically doctored to show the subject apparently reciting the *Credo* in faultless Latin.

to that!

Further measures will include a ruling that men must either shave or grow a proper beard, and that nobody is allowed to call themselves 'black' unless they actually are black. It will also be compulsory to notice what colour people are and where they come from and to do it with *absolute precision*. This will make the whole thing so complicated that everyone will soon realise it's a mug's game and that it's much better to drop the whole thing and get on with having fun.

The Role Of The State

Far too much nonsense has been talked about the role of the state, and all efforts to limit its interference have been doomed. I will solve this problem in the following way: all civil servants will be renamed 'contemptible lackeys' and forced to be addressed, and announce themselves, as such. I anticipate the immediate resignation of 80 per cent of the current Establishment.

As to the rest of them, minor adjustments in communications technology will serve the purpose. Internal mail, network systems and telephone exchanges will be upgraded, providing an internal communications system unmatched anywhere in the world. At the same time, all *external* communications will be removed. The contemptible lackeys will not notice and can be left to communicate happily among themselves without the rest of us even needing to know they are alive.

Broadcasting And The Press

Abuses of press and broadcasting freedom will be curbed. All newspapers and news broadcasts will have to decide how much news there is before they decide how long they will be, rather than, as at present, the other way around. There will be nothing more from Mr Neil Lyndon or indeed any other mid-life wimp suffering from difficulties with girls. There will be no more stuff about rock music in the *Independent*. There will be nothing more from Rees-Mogg. *Any* Rees-Mogg. Nobody will be allowed to take a 'wry', 'sideways' or 'tongue-in-cheek' look at

anything, ever. No more 'funny' stuff about computers. No more whining BBC stuff about exploding instant coffee. The Consumers' Association to be shut down. Playing Kiss FM in supermarkets to be illegal. That sort of thing.

The Arts

To hell with the arts. What do we want with the arts in Fat City? Give a man cheap drink, loose women and a chance to get even with his enemies, and you won't hear any whining about the arts from *him*.

As for architecture, I will, immediately on seizing power, lock all architects up with Prince Charles for a year. Those that come out sane will be shot. Those that go mad will be locked up in the loony bin. It will be good for the people of Fat City – who needs architects? – and good for Prince Charles to have something to do now that he is not going to be King. Did I mention, by the way, that I shall abolish the monarchy? Well, I shall. There's only room for one Supreme Ruler in Fat City.

The Economy

Mostly down to Oofy, this, but a few clear promises won't do any harm. I shall immediately do something about Mr Coleridge. Clean him out, I think. Next: corporations. All McDonald's shops to be nationalised, heavily insured, then torched. Everything owned by the Japanese to be taken away from them, pushy little gamboge buggers that they are. All corporations bigger than they ought to be will have to display 50-foot-high photographs of their directors, naked, outside all their premises. The Confederation of British Industry and the Institute of Directors to be amalgamated, humiliated, and disbanded.

Laws will be passed to abolish retailing. It is a waste of time. Mail order is the thing. All out-of-town malls can therefore be dynamited, while the inner-city shops destroy themselves.

Fiscal Policy

Taxation will be conducted on moral and aesthetic criteria, rather than the current, inequitable system of fiduciary assessment. This means that I, for example, will pay no tax at all, while some sclerotic, hatchet-faced corporate pimp will be taxed into the gutter.

Law And Order

Hell – with these reforms, who needs law and order? We'll be happy. But just in case, I shall immediately pass an edict declaring that, for any new law passed, 100 old laws must be repealed.

So there you have it. On Polling Day, just write 'BARGEPOLE X' on your paper. Alternatively, simply ignore whatever pack of snivelling narks get 'elected' and, instead, just do what I say. You know it makes sense. 🦫

THE FOLLOWING PROGRAM CONTAINS LANGUAGE WHICH MAY BE OFFENSIVE ENOUGH TO KNOCK A BUZZARD OFF A SHIT-WAGON.

Is there life after *Playaway*?

SACHA GIVARSI looked up the children's TV presenters of the Sixties and Seventies to find out if they were still young at heart. Would they undertake some really, *really* exciting, cutting-edge media projects?

That fat kid from the *Double Deckers* who played the tuba and made it look the size of a bag of crisps…what is he up to now? In fact, where *are* they all now? The other *Double Deckers*, the presenters of *Magpie, Blue Peter, Playaway, How, Screentest, Crackerjack* and *Vision On*. And what of Basil Brush and Mr Roy? Certainly Lesley Judd is working. She pops up during a day-time TV maths programme with a handful of chocolate mice and a pair of weighing-scales. But then she was also hosting a radio cookery show on LBC. Cookery? On radio? The only sound effects are the *bing!* of the microwave and Leslie's indefatigable 'Mmm! Mmmm!'

But what of the other icons of children's television. Do they still harbour desires to reprise their old roles? What lengths would they go to do so? How desperate were they for work? Surely it was time to investigate.

We quickly drew up a children's broadcasting legend hitlist. The man at the top, the very embodiment of super-suave tea-time television, was Michael Rodd, the ebony-tressed presenter of *Screentest*. Rodd was the man who brought to Britain's attention the existence of the Children's Film Foundation, a body never heard of before or since. Here was a star who could ask in all earnestness, 'What was the colour of the bearded villain's folder that contained the nuclear secrets which Alan threw down the well before running towards the car park with his sister?' secure in the knowledge that he would receive a suitably excited reply from Manchester Grammar's finest.

Our 'Rory Caversham', an independent producer, rang to find out. Without any warning, and hardly half a ring, the phone was answered. The stern yet mellow voice was unmistakeable, as bright and fresh as if it was 1979 when I was in my school uniform eating beans on toast, stretched out in front of the telly…and boy, did he speak quickly…

MICHAEL RODD: Michael Rodd.
RORY CAVERSHAM: Er, is that Michael Rodd?
  MR: Indeed it is. How can I help?
  RC: Um, Mr Rodd, allow me to introduce myself, I'm Rory Caversham from Briant Caversham, an independent production company. And myself and my partners were wondering really what you were doing…I mean whether

Macho moodster Michael Rodd: was he up for Screentest II?

you might be available.
  MR: Well, that would depend, of course.
  RC: I mean, we've been longtime admirers of yours, well you might even say fans since the days of *Screentest* really.
  MR: It's amazing people still remember, I mean it went off air over eight years ago.
  RC: Is it that long? It seems like yesterday (*much sentimental laughter between the two*). Well, the reason I'm calling is that we're thinking of doing what some would consider an update of the show.
  MR: An update? Go on.
  RC: Well, obviously it would be different. I mean, the thing would need to be adapted for today's youth audience.
  MR: Absolutely, sure.
  RC: What we thought, bearing in mind the current vogue for environmental-style entertainment shows for kids, would be, instead of using clips of films, we'd show clips of vegetables.
  MR: *Vegetables*?
  RC: Yes, fresh farm produce (*MR in stunned silence*). Well, the idea would be really to educate kids about the produce, nutrient values etc, the different types of squash or nutmeg that exist around the world.
  MR: That sounds…interesting…a kind of environmental education style show using the old *Screentest* format…have you got a name yet?
  RC: We thought *Beantest*.
  MR: *Beantest*! I love it. What a superb idea.

RC: And not only that, the contestants would be in costume too...

MR: Costume? What do you mean?

RC: Each show would be themed, but initially at least they'd be dressed as runner beans, large pumpkins, that sort of thing. I mean the point would be to give it that kind of pzazz that the young kids love so much.

MR: (pause) You know something...I think it's absolutely brilliant. It's so *wacky* it could *work*.

What about John Noakes and indeed his trusty helpmate Shep? Sadly John's agent informed me, that 'Noakesy' was living on a houseboat in Spain without a telephone. Such is life. And then it hit me, an overwhelming desire to find the most eccentric performer ever to entertain the youth of Britain – Rick Jones, the long-haired, bearded hero of *Fingerbobs*. A BBC researcher informed us that he was last heard of as the proprietor of an organic health food store in San Juan. Rick's old agent, however, had not heard from him in ten years, and could neither confirm nor deny the rumour. We had wanted to persuade Rick once again to don his mouse disguise for a series of public road safety commercials for the Mongolian government. Alas, his number was disconnected.

Then we struck gold. Our man 'Ben Stacey' tracked down Roy North, the gravel-voiced sidekick to surely the most charming hand puppet ever to walk God's earth, Basil Brush.

ROY NORTH: Hello?

BEN STACEY: Is that Roy North?

RN: Yes it is.

BS: This is Ben Stacey. I work for a record company called Geffen Records.

RN: Gettin?

BS: Geffen Records. The reason I'm calling is that one of our biggest artists is a band called Van Halen. Have you heard of them?

RN: Van who?

BS: Van Halen, they're one of the biggest heavy metal bands in the world.

RN: Right.

Rug-laden Roy North: keen to bring back Basil Brush?

BS: The reason I'm calling is that the lead guitarist Eddie Van Halen has a daughter, Katie, who's eight, and somehow they've managed to get hold of some of the videos of your shows with Basil.

RN: Really? He's lucky, I've only got one!

BS: Basically I got a fax from him in LA yesterday, and apparently his daughter is a great fan of yours and Basil's...and he too has become quite a fan. Anyway, the upshot of it is that he's written a song, for his daughter, based on the Basil Brush thing. It's a kind of metal anthem called 'Basil Goes Boom'.

RN: What?

BS: Yes, he's recorded the song, and he's asked us over here to make contact with you to see whether you and Basil...

RN: Ivan (Basil's creator is Ivan Owen).

BS: Sorry, Ivan. To see whether you'd be prepared to do a little rap over the track, the two of you, some kind of scripted chat.

RN: 'Cos you know we're hoping to make a comeback next year. We're going to make a pilot and we hope to go out on the network next year...on Central. So how did this all come about?

BS: Actually it was an English friend of the Van Halen's who passed on the tapes to them. What can I say, you made a big hit with their daughter. I mean, I've actually heard the song, it's quite, er, metallic, quite heavy, kind of a little like early Slayer, the first album, do you know it?

RN: Can't say I do.

BS: Anyway, thus far all they've done is sampled the boom boom. It sounds terrific. What they'd like to do is script it really, I mean whether the Basil Brush angle is going to click with the American public is irrelevant, the song's really commercial.

RN: I get you.

BS: I just wanted to run it past you and see what you thought really.

RN: Yeah, it sounds fun...I mean is it like how they've done various singles in the past. Cliff Richard and 'Summer Holiday', you know putting a little voice on top, a little snippet.

BS: I suppose so. I mean, Van Halen are massive Stateside. They usually play to 100,000 or so at a time, so it should be fun.

RN: Would there be a fee involved, I mean I ask not only for me but for Ivan as well since he lives in Devon. Anyway, can I write all this down? So that's Gessin Records is it?

BS: Geffen...Geffen Records...And the daughter would very much like to meet you when they come to tour here, as would Eddie.

RN: No problem – you must understand that I've aged a little, I mean I still look roughly the same.

BS: Good.

RN: Of course, Basil's still the same, because you know puppets don't age. Did you know we were originally a record plugging show? I mean we were the first show to put Demis Roussos on. Did you know that?

BS: No. Er, well, that's great. If you could get on to Basil, then we can get the ball rolling.

RN: Wonderful, well I'm sure Ivan should be pretty keen...great, super, I'll get back to you certainly by the end of the week. It's the same number is it?

BS: Yes (It was the phone at the Pizza Hut, Tottenham Court Road).

But sadly, after all this drollery, our next target was untouchable. Protected by four, yes *four*, agents, the ex-presenter of *Play School*, Chloe Ashcroft was not to be ours. We had originally intended to pose as representatives of Mattel Toys USA, a company who wished to take advantage of the fact that *Play School* had become a cult hit among children in the Midwest. Would Chloe be prepared to pose with our new toys in glossy American mags? But these were not just facsimiles of Big Ted and Little Ted, no: this time Hamble was dressed head to toe in leather astride a miniature Harley Davidson. Hamble from Hades the line was to be called. Never mind, perhaps next time. But what of Chloe's *Playaway* cohort, Brian Cant? The man who had brought *Chigley* and *Camberwick Green* to us. And, of course, *Trumpton*. We left a message and didn't have to wait too long. ☞

🐍 Go with hoax

Playaway beefcake Brian Cant: who does he play with now?

BRIAN CANT: Is Ben Stacey there please?
BEN STACEY: Speaking. Is that Brian Cant?
BC: Yes it is.
BS: Great, I've been trying to get hold of you. Basically my father who I believe you knew in the Sixties...he organised lots of the roadhouse shows?
BC: Oh yes.
BS: Well, I'm working for him now, and he's still in theatre, working in the US, actually. He does quite a lot on Broadway in fact. Anyway, my father and his theatrical consortium have always been great fans of *Trumpton*.
BC: Oh yes.
BS: And always looked at it as perhaps a format with great theatrical potential particularly with the kids audience in mind. I mean what they're considering at the moment is making *Trumpton* into a live-action, full-blown Broadway show, with perhaps a major star playing the train driver. They're looking at Pacino right now. I mean this doesn't exclude you because they'd like to keep the British angle. With you as narrator perhaps on a plinth to stage left or something.
BC: Really (*lots of laughter*).
BS: So what do you think?
BC: Yes, it sounds really fun. About three years ago, I was called to a bread commercial: Windmill Bread. I didn't know what it was all about till I got there and one of them said 'You may recognise this,' and it was all in the style of *Camberwick Green*. They were two guys who had come up through *Play School* and *Trumpton* as well, I mean the commercials were fairly far out, Windy Miller's head falls off when he eats the wrong bread or something like that. Fairly wacky. Again, they were worried they wouldn't get the same voice, after all these years. Well, it all sounds great, very interesting indeed. I'm just going off to do a play in Wales for five weeks...

Sadly, Cant's Broadway dream remained unfulfilled. But what of the fabulous *Magpie* team? All was about to be revealed as we tracked down madcap Jenny Hanley, the woman at the heart of a million schoolboy fantasies.

DAVID PALMER: Hello.
JENNY HANLEY: Mr David Palmer please.
DP: Yes, you're talking to him.
JH: Am I? This is good then, this is Jenny Hanley speaking.
DP: Jenny! Super. I want to talk to you...
JH: Fire away.
DP: I'm working with a company, in fact we manufacture Strepsils.
JH: Strepsils?
DP: You know, the lozenges. Basically we're sponsoring a new event which is starting this summer. It's a kind of sports/entertainment event. It's actually the annual aquasports and rollerskating world championships. In Bucharest, this summer.
JH: Wow, that sounds *super*.
DP: Basically, we're putting together this package of presenters. So far we've got an American, Dwight Buchanan, an Italian called Gianfranco Roselli and a guy called Benito Pepys. We thought of you really because we all remember the good old days, you know *Magpie*. Just out of interest, when did it finish?
JH: This is going to shock you David...but it was 12 years ago.
DP: 12 years ago! My!
JH: Funnily enough, I just saw Mick (*Robinson, the Brian May lookalike*) the other day, and he hasn't changed at all.
DP: How is Mick?
JH: Very well, he's got his own company *Six for Gold*.
DP: What?
JH: (*sings Magpie song*)'...five for silver, *six for gold...*'
DP: Oh from the theme tune. Great. Who elso used to do it?
JH: Thomasino Boyd, who joined us for the last couple of years, and before that (*in Scots accent*) Doogie Rae.
DP: Oh what happened to him.
JH: Oh, he had the bobble hat concession in the Cairngorms.
DP: He had the *what*?
JH: He had the bobble hat concession in the Cairngorms.
DP: Are you *serious*?
JH: Absolutely true. (*At this point La Hanley's sprog begins whining in the background*)...yes, be with you shortly, poppet. David, have you ever played football in moonshoes?
DP: No, I haven't.
JH: Do you know what moonshoes are?
DP: Are they those huge inflatable snow boots?
JH: They're the bouncy things, they're not snow boots, they've got bungee ropes in the base. The problem is you never know which way you might wobble.
DP: Can you swim?
JH: Yes, why?
DP: Well, we may need some 'in pool' commentary. And you'll be wearing a swimming hat.
JH: I think it's terrific, the only proviso I would make is that I'm not prepared to do a parachute jump.
DP: Fine, no problem. You know the Dougie Rae thing, it's still bothering me, how exactly did he get the bobble hat concession?
JH: Well, he found them the best ski runs in the Cairngorms when they started and they couldn't afford to give him anything very spectacular, so he said, 'Can I have the ski shop and the bobble hat concession?' And you know what? The stupid prat got it.

Philip Schofield, eat your heart out. 🐍

Tea-time temptress Jenny Hanley: is a comeback overdue?

206

the cartoons: